Evolutionary Political Economy in Action

The world is in turmoil, the dynamics of political economy seem to have entered a phase where a 'return to normal' cannot be expected. Since the financial crisis, conventional economic theory has proven itself to be rather helpless and political decision makers have become suspicious about this type of economic consultancy. This book offers a different approach. It promises to describe political and economic dynamics as interwoven as they are in real life and it adds to that an evolutionary perspective. The latter allows for a long-run view, which makes it possible to discuss the emergence and exit of social institutions.

Evolutionary Political Economy in Action consists of two parts. Part I provides a broad range of issues that show how flexible evolutionary political economy can handle acute policy problems in Europe: should Europe support the revived build-up of NATO forces on its Eastern border, or should it rather aim at economic cooperation with Russia? How can democracy for a whole continent be reasonably further developed; what is the role of economies of scope? Do the new protest movements against inequality provide alternatives? What could a vision for a unified, socioecological Europe look like? Part II takes a closer look at Cyprus and Greece, where the problems of the financial crisis have been exacerbated by the 'solutions' imposed on them by the troika. In all of these essays, the authors demonstrate the unique insights which can be garnered from adopting an evolutionary political economy approach and consider the real solutions that such an approach points towards.

This volume is extremely useful for social scientists in the fields of economics, politics and sociology who are interested to learn what evolutionary political economy is, how it proceeds and what it can provide.

Hardy Hanappi is a researcher at the University of Technology in Vienna, Austria, a Jean Monnet Chair for political economy of the European integration, and president of the Vienna Institute for Political Economy Research (VIPER). His expertise is in economic modelling, simulation and game theory. More recently he has focused on the political economy of European unification.

Savvas Katsikides is University Professor and Jean Monnet Chair at the University of Cyprus.

Manuel Scholz-Wäckerle is Senior Lecturer at the Department of Socioeconomics, Vienna University of Economics and Business, Austria.

Routledge Advances in Heterodox Economics

Edited by Mark Setterfield
Trinity College, USA
and
Peter Kriesler
University of New South Wales

Over the past two decades, the intellectual agendas of heterodox economists have taken a decidedly pluralist turn. Leading thinkers have begun to move beyond the established paradigms of Austrian, feminist, Institutional-evolutionary, Marxian, Post Keynesian, radical, social and Sraffian economics, opening up new lines of analysis, criticism and dialogue among dissenting schools of thought. This cross-fertilisation of ideas is creating a new generation of scholarship in which novel combinations of heterodox ideas are being brought to bear on important contemporary and historical problems.

Routledge Advances in Heterodox Economics aims to promote this new scholarship by publishing innovative books in heterodox economic theory, policy, philosophy, intellectual history, institutional history and pedagogy. Syntheses or critical engagement of two or more heterodox traditions are especially encouraged.

For a full list of titles in this series, please visit www.routledge.com/series/RAHE

28. A New Economic Theory of Public Support for the Arts
Evolution, Veblen and the predatory arts
Arnaldo Barone

29. Varieties of Economic Inequality
Edited by Sebastiano Fadda and Pasquale Tridico

30. Reclaiming Pluralism in Economics
Edited by Jerry Courvisanos, Jamie Doughney and Alex Millmow

31. Policy Implications of Evolutionary and Institutional Economics
Edited by Claudius Gräbner, Torsten Heinrich and Henning Schwardt

32. The Financialization of GDP
Implications for economic theory and policy
Jacob Assa

33. Evolutionary Political Economy in Action
A Cyprus Symposium
Edited by Hardy Hanappi, Savvas Katsikides and Manuel Scholz-Wäckerle

Evolutionary Political Economy in Action

A Cyprus Symposium

Edited by
Hardy Hanappi, Savvas Katsikides and Manuel Scholz-Wäckerle

Routledge
Taylor & Francis Group
LONDON AND NEW YORK

First published 2017
by Routledge
2 Park Square, Milton Park, Abingdon, Oxon OX14 4RN

and by Routledge
605 Third Avenue, New York, NY 10017

Routledge is an imprint of the Taylor & Francis Group, an informa business

British Library Cataloguing in Publication Data
A catalogue record for this book is available from the British Library

Library of Congress Cataloging in Publication Data
Names: Hanappi, Gerhard, 1951- editor. | Katsikides, Savvas, editor. | Scholz-Wäckerle, Manuel, 1981- editor.
Title: Evolutionary political economy in action : a Cyprus symposium / edited by Hardy Hanappi, Savvas Katsikides and Manuel Scholz-Wäckerle.
Description: Abingdon, Oxon ; New York, NY : Routledge, 2017. | Includes index.
Identifiers: LCCN 2016034470| ISBN 9781138204119 (hardback) | ISBN 9781315470139 (ebook)
Subjects: LCSH: Economic history—21st century. | Global Financial Crisis, 2008-2009. | Evolutionary economics. | Europe—Economic policy—21st century.
Classification: LCC HC59.3 .E96 2017 | DDC 330.1—dc23
LC record available at https://lccn.loc.gov/2016034470

ISBN: 978-1-138-20411-9 (hbk)
ISBN: 978-1-315-47013-9 (ebk)

Typeset in Times New Roman
by Swales & Willis Ltd, Exeter, Devon, UK

Contents

Figures

Tables

Contributors

Andreas Assiotis is Chief Economist of the Hellenic Bank, Cyprus. He holds a BSc in Management, an MSc in Economics and a PhD in Economics from Southern Illinois University (2011). Currently, he is employed in the Department of Economics at the University of Cyprus. His research interests are macroeconomics, economic growth and development and financial economics.

Charlie Dannreuther is Lecturer in European political economy at the School of Politics and International Studies at the University of Leeds, UK. His research interest is in exploring international modes of social regulation and their role in the renegotiation of the subject – a topic building on the French School of regulation.

Svenja Flechtner is a researcher at the Europa Universität Flensburg, where she teaches international and institutional economics with special emphasis on economic inequality. Her recent particular interest is in the institutional change that might be induced by new forms of social protest.

Hardy Hanappi is a researcher at the University of Technology in Vienna, Austria, a Jean Monnet Chair for political economy of the European integration, and president of the Vienna Institute for Political Economy Research (VIPER). His expertise is in economic modelling, simulation and game theory. More recently he has focused on the political economy of European unification.

Christis Hassapis is Associate Professor at the Department of Economics, University of Cyprus. He has a Bachelor's degree in Mechanical Engineering from The George Washington University and a Master's and a PhD in Economics from Boston College, USA. He is Vice Dean, Graduate School, University of Cyprus (2015–), Group Chairman, Bank of Cyprus Group (2013–2014) and a board member of the University of Cyprus Council.

Ioanna Kastelli is Senior Researcher at the Laboratory of Industrial and Energy Economics of the National Technical University of Athens, Greece and Adjunct Professor at the Hellenic Open University. Her academic and professional interests focus on economics of technology, industrial economics, industrial policy and entrepreneurship. She is currently teaching microeconomics, economic analysis of industrial decisions, innovation and entrepreneurship and business administration.

Savvas Katsikides is Professor at the University of Cyprus and Jean Monnet Chair for European Economic Integration. He is the Dean of the Faculty of Social Sciences and Education. His expertise is in social and economic Europe and society/technology.

Pavlos Koktsidis is Adjunct Lecturer, Political Scientist at the Department of Social and Political Sciences, University of Cyprus. He received his BA(Hons) in Politics with International Relations from Lancaster University; MA in Comparative Ethnic Conflict from Queen's University of Belfast; Certificate in Political Research from the University of Edinburgh; and PhD from Queen's University of Belfast. He holds a doctorate in Security and Conflict Analysis from Queen's University of Belfast, Northern Ireland.

Bernhard Leubolt is a university assistant in the Department of Socioeconomics at Vienna University of Economics and Business, Austria. This department has a strong theoretical focus on socio-ecological transformation of contemporary economies; the exploration of such possibilities thus constitutes a central topic of his investigations.

Makiko Narita is University Professor teaching Economic Cooperation and International Communication at the faculty of economics at Nagasaki University, Japan. A special focus of recent research is on European Economy and World Economy.

Klaus Nielsen is Professor of Institutional Economics at the Department of Management at Birkbeck, University of London. He is an expert in studies on Eastern European countries and China and has contributed substantially to the understanding of transformation processes in these countries.

Malcolm Sawyer is Emeritus Professor at Leeds University in the UK. He has published numerous books and articles and also has led large European research projects. His contributions to economic policy – in theory and practice – have been internationally recognized; his work has produced a wide and generally very positive response.

Annika R. Scharbert is a university assistant in the Department of Socioeconomics at Vienna University of Economics and Business, Austria. This department has a strong theoretical focus on socio-ecological transformation of contemporary economies; the exploration of such possibilities thus constitutes a central topic of his investigations.

Manuel Scholz-Wäckerle holds a position as Senior Lecturer at the Department of Socioeconomics at Vienna University of Economics and Business, Austria. Manuel is trained in economics and computer science and has received a doctorate in the social and economic science at the Vienna University of Technology in 2010. His research interests involve evolutionary political economy, institutional economics, agent-based modelling (micro-meso-macro) as well as the social ecological transformation.

Nikolaos Skourias is Chief Investment Strategist at Iniochos Investment Advisory. He is also a university professor at the University of Cyprus.

Lia-Paschalia Spyridou is Lecturer in Journalism and Media at the Department of Social and Political Sciences at the University of Cyprus. Currently she coordinates the BA in Journalism. Her research interests lie in the fields of new(er) and alternative media, journalism and internet politics.

Stavros Tombazos is Associate Professor at the University of Cyprus, Department of Social and Political Sciences. He published *Time in Marx: The Categories of Time in Marx's Capital* (Historical Materialism Book, 2015).

Pasquale Tridico is University Professor at University Roma Tre, Italy as well as Jean Monnet Chair of the European Union. His recent research focus is on inequality in Europe and evolutionary political economy. He also is a very active organiser and consultant in economic and political practice, e.g. in his function as secretary general of the European Association of Evolutionary Political Economy (EAEPE).

Panos Xidonas is a university professor at the University of Cyprus and associate professor of Finance at ESSCA Grande École, Angers, France.

Georgia Yiangou is a researcher at the University of Cyprus. She received her PhD and BA from the University of Cyprus and her MSc from Aberystwyth, Wales. Her expertise is on strategic issues, energy security and political economy.

Stavros Zografakis is Associate Professor at the Department of Agricultural Economics and Rural Development at the Agricultural University of Athens, Greece. His academic and professional interests are in the areas of general equilibrium models, social account matrices, income distribution, inequality and poverty, migration, consumer prices and international competitiveness. He has worked as an adviser at the Economic Office of the Prime Minister, of the Minister of Employment and Social Security (on employment and social exclusion issues) and of the Assistant Minister of External Affairs. He is currently teaching Theory and Policies of International Trade, Macroeconomic Theory and Political Economy.

Introduction

Cyprus is a very special place. It has been a hotbed of cultural development for more than 3,000 years and its – not only geographical – position at the crossroad of different empires and their traditions still is a fundamental advantage for the conquest of new territory. To mix different perspectives, to soften worn-out attitudes and get rid of obsolete prejudices, to merge core issues of seemingly unrelated scientific disciplines, all these practices are particularly well embedded in a place like Cyprus.

A *symposium*, as it was understood in ancient Greece, was a drinking party. The underlying motive for supporting a social gathering of philosophers and their friends with substances – mainly alcohol – that seduce to more uncontrolled expression of opinions and more extroverted behaviour in general is very interesting: in spelling out more daring hypotheses, in expressing wild emotional feelings of love and hate with respect to the views of other participants of the symposium, in showing deep despair in one moment and unfounded excessive joy in the next, in being hard to understand and slowly falling into speechless meditation, in all these exceptional developments well-respected authorities tacitly escaped authority in the course of an ongoing symposium. Giving up on exerting one's authority makes it easier to pay deference to other participants' authority, or more precisely, to pay attention to the content of what they are saying.

Nowadays a scientific symposium is just a kind of workshop meeting of scientists; the ancient spirit has been replaced by the vague intention of behaving cooperatively and following a mutually constructive style of exchanging knowledge. When we planned to organize a conference of the European Association for Evolutionary Political Economy (EAEPE) in Cyprus and to call it the *Cyprus Symposium*, we had this type of modern scientific event in mind. But in the course of this EAEPE conference, the ancient meaning of a symposium did strike back. The exceptional landscape in which the wonderful conference location was embedded as well as the many side attractions – including a wine-drinking party – opened up an atmosphere of general friendship among all participants. Contrary to the standard of eager self-marketing of competitors in a world of A-journal publication that prevails at so many international conferences, the Cyprus Symposium became a kind of friendly discussion club; an event where starting points for interventions into the real political process were discussed – mostly replacing the usual sequence of displays of individual greatness in conference sessions. The distinctions between the different streams of thought and preferred objects of investigations within EAEPE – a fact that has haunted this organization since its foundation – these distinctions started to become realized as fruitful interfaces rather than as probable lines of breakage of the organization. Scholars from agent-based simulation modelling discussed with economic historians, debates between hard-core post-Keynesians, Schumpetereans and Marxists mixed with those of pragmatic political activists, seemingly detached topics like the formalization of dialectic reasoning coalesced with mundane views about the design of EU institutions.

After this experience the three editors of the two books covering the most important contributions to this Cyprus Symposium really had a hard time structuring all this wealth of ideas. The sheer amount of work presented lead to the conclusion that two volumes were needed to transmit the manifold content and thus the spirit of this conference. We finally came up with the decision to have four parts, two in volume 1 and two in volume 2. The first volume would focus more on the special focus of the event while the second volume would be more in line with event-independent usual distinction between theory and method.

Volume 1 therefore has the title *Evolutionary Political Economy in Action* – this is what we did and discussed in Cyprus. Scholars in political economy necessarily are themselves part of the political process; in times of radical transformation of Europe this is becoming more evident every day. While in the long period after World War II it often seemed to be sufficient to point at important topics (e.g. the importance of an economic meso-level), to criticize wrong methodologies (e.g. the preferred enemy of neo-classical economics) or to interpret what a great economist of the past *really* intended to say (e.g. Darwin, Marx, Keynes, Schumpeter), in the process of European metamorphosis we are now forced to propose quick and not-too-dirty action plans on what to do next. The strange scientific tribe of academic economists traditionally is not very good at that. Today academic careers in the field are made of mathematical versatility and membership of the club of politically untouchables. Political passion hurts. The experiences at the Cyprus Symposium, the hotly debated policy issues that were of immediate importance for European citizens in the next few years, these motives for our scientific work, they pointed in the opposite direction: passion is needed, it is at the core of the intrinsic motivation of a scientist, our theory building has to return to address the grand problems of practice in Europe's political economy. This is what the chapters in volume 1 aim for.

The first part covers a broad range of topics concerning selected problems and how to change them for the better. This ranges from the danger of military conflicts at Europe's eastern border via several aspects of welfare decline and vanishing growth prospects to questions on how to form resistance against obviously destructive political forces. The second part of volume 1 provides spotlights on the very special situation of the crisis in Greece and Cyprus. This part of Europe had often been accused of being the origin of the problems of European unification; even today several scholars in political economy refuse to consider Greece as just another member state of the EU; for them it is an exceptional type of state with an extraordinarily corrupt bureaucracy and population, which just has to be forced to correct its behaviour. This is the background of the set of so-called austerity measures that are prescribed by certain EU politicians and supported by economists treating Greece as a singular problem of a population with a general tendency towards unethical and economically unsustainable behaviour.

The contributions in the second part of volume 1 do not share this perspective but instead propose to take a much more detailed look at the processes that took place in Greece and Cyprus in the last ten years. Replacing the mono-causal and highly ignorant view just described by insightful analysis of what really happened in certain policy areas often enables the authors to come up with much more useful proposals for improvements. As a common feature of emphasis, they consider the crisis in these states not simply as a local failure based on national misbehaviour but dig deeper into the relationship between European partner countries. Despite the evident need to reconsider local political and bureaucratic structures, there certainly is the need to modify Europe's economic policy, in particular its banking system and financial architecture too. As in the first part of volume 1, the emphasis is on using theory to solve practical problems, a maxim too often missing in the neo-classical paradigm but pivotal for evolutionary political economy.

The second volume, with the title *Theory and Method of Evolutionary Political Economy*, is structured more conventionally into a part on recent theoretical achievements in the area of evolutionary political economy and a part on the new set of methods which this approach has acquired and produced. Theory building in evolutionary political economy, by the very nature of its aspirations, is a very wide field. Not only in biological systems, the emergence of a large variety out of which new forms, new combinations, emerge, a similar drive towards a diverse set of evolutionary theory fragments occurs in theoretical contributions of our discipline. In the selected chapters topics like the role of creative industries, conceptual boundaries between biology and political economy, a reappraisal of classical forerunners of evolutionary political economy (Polanyi, Goodwin, Marx), the role of unions, a study of a country-specific emergence of evolutionary thought (Russia), and finally an evolutionary investigation into the market of corporate control are dealt with. Each of these chapters follows a unique line of research under the common umbrella of evolutionary political economy. The purpose of part 1 of the second volume is to stimulate researchers in specific lines of research in evolutionary political economy to take a look at other scientists' findings – across the wide and rich area that we cover. It appears to be a most innovative strategy to learn with conclusions by analogy,[1] a forbidden theoretical territory for most neo-classical economic theory, which works by making deductions from axioms. For evolutionary political economy conclusion by analogy is a major tool for innovative theoretical breakthroughs.

The last part in volume 2 is devoted to the particular attention that evolutionary political economy has to pay to its methodological toolbox. Contrary to neo-classical economic theory, which more or less just adopted the standard mathematical apparatus of classical mechanics of the early nineteenth century, our discipline still is struggling to develop its own take on methodological issues. What can be said so far is that computer simulation techniques certainly will play a major role. Of course, the historical fact that the same mathematical genius who developed the computer, John von Neumann, also was the one who set out to develop a new formal language for the social sciences, i.e. game theory, is remarkable.[2] For many decades now a radical change in the methods to be used in the social sciences seems to be in the air. For evolutionary political economy one of the major kick-offs came in 1982 when Richard Nelson and Sidney Winter published their book on evolutionary economics; their central method was the use of computer programs for firm behaviour.

The papers selected for this part of the book are meant to provide examples for the simulation approach in evolutionary political economy; they also should throw a light on some meta-issues to enable the reader to explore advantages and limits of the newly emerging essential methods of our research field. Macroeconomic policy is largely influenced by economic models; traditionally these models were this has depended on the use of dynamic stochastic general equilibrium (DSGE) models. However, during the Great Recession, critique has grown concerning DSGE models from several directions. In the second part of the second volume, the methodological pitfalls of DSGE are discussed (Chapter 9) and contrasted with the potential and promise made by agent-based modelling (ABM). ABM has become an alternative on macroeconomic scale (Chapter 10) today and computational simulation allows the implementation of complex models with, for instance, endogenous credit-driven business cycles (Chapter 11). Otherwise ABM allows multi-country economies (e.g. artificial monetary unions) to be simulated and different fiscal policy settings to be tested (Chapter 12). This bottom-up computational method works particularly well for testing policy experiments, even in very specific regional environments. It is shown how the method can be used to study the socioeconomic impact of natural disasters and potential policy responses to them (Chapter 13). Thereby we highlight the versatile application area of ABM for different economic policy settings and the strong interdependences between micro-, meso- as well as and macro-level dynamics. We have indicated that evolutionary political economy places the scientist at the centre of the political process. To this extent it is necessary to discuss the implications of this for formal modelling (Chapter 14). This important scientific effort is often neglected in the economic mainstream, as shown in the example of the Transatlantic Trade and Investment Partnership (TTIP).

In sum, these two volumes contain an extremely rich and widespread collection of innovative ideas. In doing so they provide an example of an evolutionary process, more precisely, of the stage of this process when material is organized as a wide variety from which the following selection process will then select and recombine the most promising ones. No other stage of theory evolution is as challenging – but also as intellectually rewarding – as this stage. We are glad to invite the readers of these two volumes to share with us this exciting experience.

Hardy Hanappi, Savvas Katsikides and Manuel Scholz-Wäckerle
Vienna 2016

Notes

1 See Ribeiro (2014).
2 Compare Hanappi (2013, pp. 3–26).

References

Hanappi H. (ed.) (2013) *Game Theory Relaunched.* New York: Intech Publishers.

Nelson R. and Winter S. (1982) *An Evolutionary Theory of Economic Change.* Cambridge, MA: Belknap Press.

Ribeiro H.J. (ed.) (2014) *Systematic Approaches to Argument by Analogy.* Heidelberg: Springer Publishers.

Part I

Political economy in action

In this part the authors show how evolutionary political economy can be applied as a tool to understand *and to intervene* in political practice.

1 NATO expansion versus consolidation of the EU

Intra- and interclass dynamics in the context of the next Cold War

Hardy Hanappi

Introduction

After 8 years of recession following the financial collapse in September 2008, and with no return to pre-crisis conditions in sight, the global political economy now has taken a turn characterized by substantially stronger state interventions, including not just economic but also military actions. The expansion of NATO towards Eastern Europe had started decades ago, but even after the implosion of the Warsaw Pact on 1 July 1991, there still remained a north–south band of nation states providing some distance between NATO forces and Russian troops. Only now, when – after the Eastern Enlargement of the EU in 2004 – more and more Eastern states became NATO members, a more explosive situation emerged.

The crisis of 2008 itself coincided with a change in US leadership; the Obama administration immediately started to shift the military focus from the Near East to the Pacific coast of China. This not only produced new turmoil in the eastern Mediterranean (see Hanappi, 2014), it showed in a very general and dramatic way that military and political intervention is no substitute for deep economic change.

Of course, the special situation of the EU has to be taken into account. After many years of disastrous austerity policy (see Hanappi, 2013, 2015a), even the most sanguine top decision makers in the EU recognized that they would soon be only one step away from a total collapse of the European project. This prospect lead to a twofold reaction: (1) internally EU institutions (Commission, Parliament, and European Central Bank (ECB)) tried to invoke a shift in decision power away from the heads of state of EU members and towards central EU bodies; and (2) externally a combined action with NATO was initiated, which was meant to diverge the attention of EU citizens towards extra-EU goals, i.e. first to start association agreements with new eastern states, which then could end as NATO membership. In 2015 both action lines ran into severe problems.

The parliamentary elections in May 2014 not only proved that discontent with EU policy had already grown dramatically; the aftermath of the fight for the position of the president of the Commission made clear that the conflict between Brussels and the club of heads of state was not decided yet. The preliminary solution that crystallized in 2015 was to accept Angela Merkel as the informal leader of the EU – at least as long as she supported the European unification project. Only in autumn 2015 the dramatic immigration waves from Africa and the Middle East surprised European policy makers, Merkel's open-doors policy produced resistance in Germany as well as in several other European countries. Nevertheless, the ideological flexibility of Merkel led to her support for a more restrictive immigration policy in 2016, since this appeared to be necessary to secure her dominant role.

With respect to the external strategy the case of Ukraine is telling. The dynamics typically are dominated by military strategies (NATO and Russian forces), and the temporary parallel between the EU's economic welfare goals and NATO's strategic objectives has rapidly vanished. Today the Ukraine is an economic disaster. Nevertheless, the same external EU strategy is still on the agenda in Georgia, Moldavia, and soon in Belarus. To win a new NATO member with a border to Russia, a certain degree of externally provoked instability and provocation seems to be unavoidable. And instability in this case always runs the risk of interventions from the Russian side. The economic and democratic goals of a European Union evidently cannot be assumed to be identical to the expansionary military strategy of NATO. As all economic data of the last 25 years shows, cooperation and trade between Europe and Russia has been a welfare-increasing component for Europeans. From an economic point of view there was no reason to stop this process; indeed, economic practices on both sides had developed a *modus vivendi* that in the long run promised to lead to a peaceful co-existence of both social systems.[1]

The contradiction between the military goal of establishing NATO as the only global military force, i.e. eliminating the role of the Red Army, and the peace project of a welfare-enhancing European unification can hardly be hidden by smooth diplomatic rhetoric any more. In the meantime, the military interventions of the strong global powers in the Middle East during the last 50 years have produced civil wars with high-tech weaponry, collapsed states and a flood of refugees to Europe that demonstrate the severe economic impact which interventions based mainly on military strategies can produce.

Being confronted with these consequences – masses of immigrants, collapse of eastern trade, a new Cold War climate in diplomatic relations – the European population rather abruptly is forced to realize how directly its living conditions are linked to non-European geo-political strategies and global inequalities between continents. The latter manifest themselves as the other swelling stream of migration from North Africa that also can be traced back to a misguided development policy, at least since the end of World War II.

In what follows this chapter will concentrate on the roots and the immediate consequences, which the mentioned global processes have in – and on – Europe. Why and how did cooperation between Europe and Russia become successful? What is the logic of military expansionism? Which economic goals and groups are linked to it? What is the relative strength of Europe's contradictory class dynamic forces? Which coalitions can be formed that can prevent a return to a cold war, or even to a civil war? The wake-up call for European citizens could hardly have been more drastic: permanent high unemployment rates, flattening or decreasing income levels with surging inequality in income and wealth – and now a return to several police-state measures and strong nationalist-state policy in the name of managing the refugee crisis. On top of it, an increasing part of the population of several EU countries in a confused protest against their dwindling economic prosperity is supporting the right-wing parties engineering the latter trend. The original tenets of the European project are in severe danger.

Record of empirically observed events

The first step towards an understanding of the complicated network of interdependent class forces that are involved in recent European dynamics is to take a look at the historical record it produced. As a starting point, the end of World War II is an appropriate choice. The history of the latent military conflict between the USA and the USSR (between NATO forces and the Warsaw Pact, later reduced to Russia's army) on Europe's territory is shown in Figure 1.1. It is evident that there is a continuous expansion of the NATO controlled area. The largest gain clearly was possible when EU enlargement coincided with the military goals of NATO after 1990.

Note also that this eastern expansion threatened the access of Russia to the Mediterranean Sea, which explains Russia's military intervention on the Crimean Peninsula as well as its involvement in the battles at the Syrian coast shore. These two points for Russia are the two remaining access points to the Black Sea and the Mediterranean Sea, if the Ukraine becomes a NATO member state – a most likely future event.

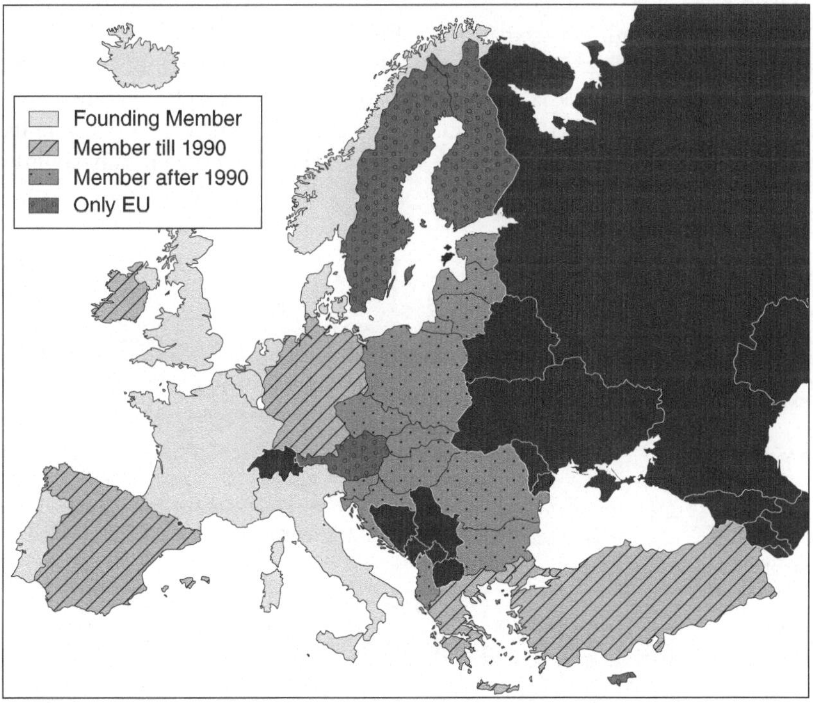

Figure 1.1 NATO expansion

Moreover, a glance at this militarily organized geographical landscape reveals why the fight to influence any solution in Syria is so important for Russia: with the strong NATO member Turkey in its west, the fate of the states still under Russian influence, namely Azerbaijan and Georgia, is more likely to follow the route of former Eastern European satellite states if Russia's influence in the Middle East evaporates completely.

After having lost its grip on Afghanistan and with the uncontrollable Islamic neighbour Iran, Russia's influence around the Caspian Sea would be the next logical target for NATO. From an economic point of view these considerations of military strategy are also of vital importance for Europe, since the area holds major sources of energy that European countries may need in the future. It therefore is important to understand global military dynamics to assess the role it plays in European policy. Taking into consideration that the military force of the USA is estimated to be several times bigger than that of the five next strongest nations taken together, it is necessary to understand the driving forces of US politics.

Taking a look at this development from the point of view of the USA shows that the internal evolution of US policy is closely linked to the country's military expenditure policy. Evidently Republican circles, if they win the presidency, use their political power to increase military expenditure – not least due to their closer links to the US weapons industry. As shown in Figure 1.2a, the two large pushes in military expenditure of the USA are attributable to the policy stances of Ronald Reagan and George Bush.[2] Total NATO military expenditure follows the dynamics of US military expansion. The diagram also shows how dominant NATO actually is. After a brief surge just before the breakdown of the USSR, military expenditure of Russia and its allies now has fallen to a level comparable to that of 1975 and is about one-tenth of the expenditure of NATO. Despite its tremendous economic upswing, China's military expenditure also is only slightly higher than that of Russia, both being dwarfed by the US numbers.

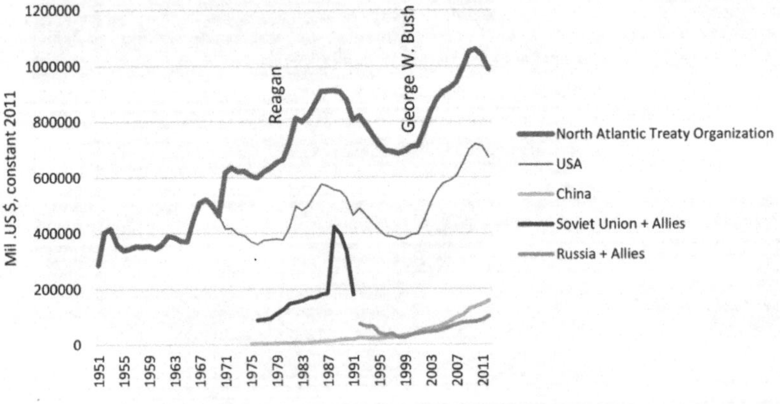

Figure 1.2a Military expenditure in selected countries – the period after World War II

Zooming in to see a more detailed picture of the time just before the breakdown of the USSR (Figure 1.2b) shows that it was the turn away from expansion to reduction of military expenditure in the USA (since 1987) and the USSR (since 1989) that was the most significant element. Europe and the Near East stayed on the track of a slight increase. In the first 2 years of his presidency (1981–1989), Reagan increased military expenditure by 32%; at the end of his term he had reached an increase of 53%.

After the end of the USSR the Clinton presidency (1993–2001) led the military budget of the USA back to the levels of the mid-1970s (Figure 1.2c). But then George Bush Junior again initiated a tremendous boost of 83% increase during his presidency (2001–2009). The military potential in Europe as well as in the Near East and Russia was left far behind.

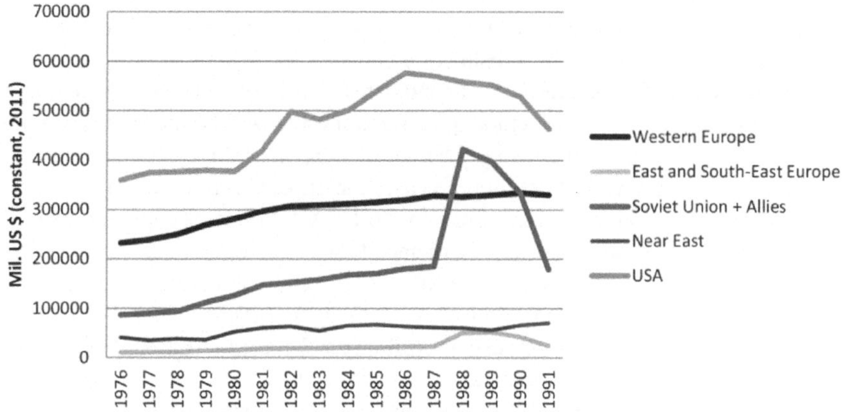

Figure 1.2b Military expenditure in selected countries – the Reagan era

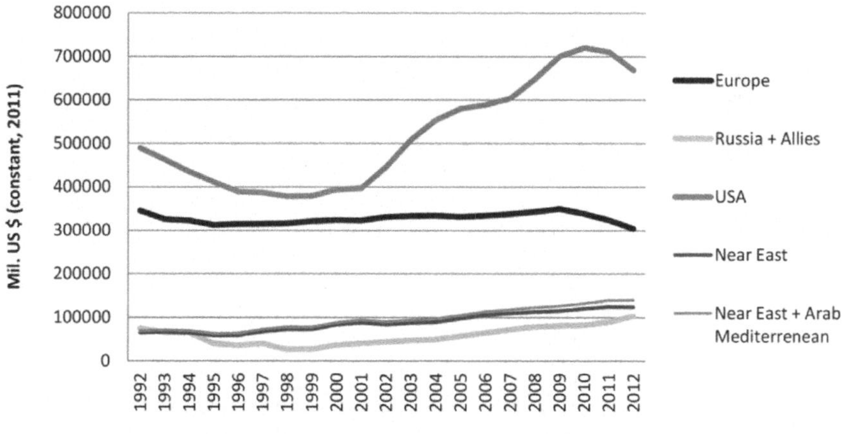

Figure 1.2c Military expenditure in selected countries – the Bush era

Then came Barack Obama and the focus on military intervention in the Near East was loosened. Attention was shifted to the Pacific Basin, in particular to China.

As a matter of fact, an increase in military spending always implies a demand pull for certain domestic industries, which the additional government expenditure causes. In a first step this can only be done by curbing government expenditure in other areas, in most cases by reducing social transfers. With the crisis years starting in 2008, the Obama administration stopped the strong increase in military expenditure and thus the shift within US industries. Nevertheless, the economic drift towards rapidly growing inequality in the USA remained; social tensions were continuously increasing. This indicates that in recent decades the opposition between the leading elites of Democrats and Republicans in the USA became less and less important while the power of the small elite of super-rich families that governs the large transnational companies (TNCs), *vis-à-vis* the majority of US citizens, explodes. This is the background in front of which the race for the next presidency in the USA takes place. The role of the president as representing a political party therefore becomes less important; it rather will be a distinction between two groups of TNCs that will be the background for the presidential candidates. It currently can be expected that the next president – whether Democrat or Republican – will be inclined to follow the path of big industry, either along the lines of weapons industry and its network, or along the lines of Wall Street. In both cases the impact on Europe probably will be the effort to implement tighter links to the USA – in one case predominantly military links, in the other case mainly financial links.

As a consequence, it is likely that after 2016 relations between Europe and Russia will be called into question even more aggressively by the USA. This might take place in the form of stronger military US forces in Europe[3] as well as a stronger dominance of US finance.[4]

In contrast to this upcoming threat the positive development of economic interdependences and growth between Europe and Russia in recent years has been remarkable (Figure 1.3). It is significant that the most recent interruption of further

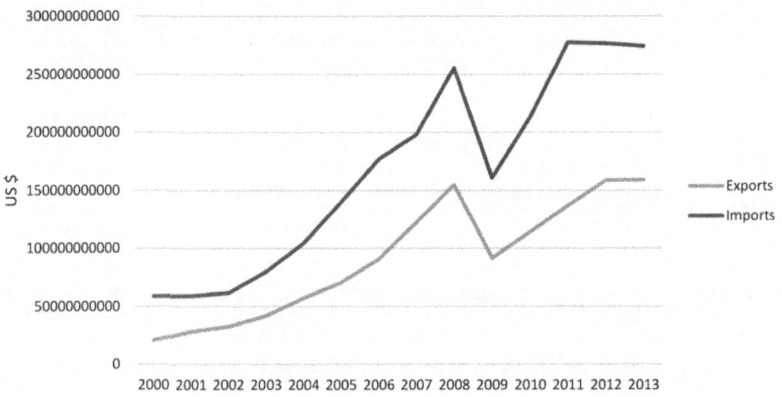

Figure 1.3 Trade between EU28 and Russia

cooperative evolution, the crisis in the Ukraine, was characterized by a quick interplay between economic and military actions. Economic insurrection can and will lead to military reactions (upheavals of paramilitary groups, civil war), which in turn will produce economically significant effects. Rather sooner than later such an outbreak of internal violence caused by this spiral of economic decline and loss of democratic political institutions will invite foreign states to intervene. Indeed, expecting such a development has always been a good reason for foreign powers to help to stir unrest in a country.[5]

This could be a more general pattern for several other states at the eastern border of NATO. And it is exactly this type of disadvantageous scenario of local civil war that is in direct conflict with the development of a prosperous and unified Europe. While military strategy would point towards a stepwise conquest of more and more territories of the former USSR that then eventually will force Russia to surrender, i.e. to subordinate its army to the command of NATO, a strategy of further increase of European economic welfare would try to establish more and more stable trade relations to exploit the fruits of enhanced division of labour. At this point it has to be noted that NATO strategy is not just the result of NATO's top military command structure. This top command of the military is closely bound to the *economic goals of the most influential power group* in the country that contributes most to the finance of NATO, namely the USA.[6] In the 1960s left-leaning economists called this power group the *military–industrial complex of the USA*.[7]

It still plays an extremely important role, not only for an understanding of the evolution of the class structure in the ruling class of the USA, but also for the dynamics of global political economy. Despite a decline in global arms sales in 2010 due to recessionary pressures, the USA increased its market share, accounting for a whopping 53% of trade that year.

Once goals are set, the just-mentioned military strategy is straightforward and, as is usual in command-oriented hierarchical organizations, just needs a consequent personnel for the operative performance. In contrast, the route to prosperous economic cooperation of a future Europe is a much more complicated task. It can only be implemented by a loosely connected network of actors situated at different levels of Europe's distributed political economy.[8]

Prelude to a stylized model of the sequence of events

Like any other model the one presented here first has to lay bare what is to be considered as essential, and what is thought to be ignorable. One of the most decisive events always is the presidential election in the USA. As displayed in Figure 1.2a, there is a rather close relationship between military expenditure push and the victory of a conservative candidate. Seen from the other side of the coin one could argue that the economic interests of a certain part of industry (related to weapons production[9]) puts forward a presidential candidate in the hope of being favoured by a subsequent policy. So voting success depends on financial election support and election support depends on expected additional gains once the candidate is successful.On the other side of the Atlantic, in Europe, the most essential feature is the success of further unification and under which general economic policy regime it takes place. The great divide in Europe that currently is approaching thus concerns that either one out of a set of accelerated unification scenarios takes place, or one of the possible nationalist implosion scenarios will turn out as a future trajectory. Which of the two ways will be followed will be the result of the current European metamorphosis process,[10] a phase transition of the European power structure.

The rapid dynamics of a metamorphosis are characterized by the necessity that political agents, e.g. formalized as the players in a game theoretic setting, have to find satisficing solutions to a set of burning – *interdependent* – social and economic problems. When metamorphosis starts there already exists a power structure, usually multi-layered and with well-established alliances that guarantee a certain capacity to stabilize minor irritations.[11] But then the simultaneous occurrence of multiple, not conventionally solvable contradictions signals that a profound metamorphosis cannot be avoided.[12] In the language of game theory this means a change of the rules of the game, including the set of players and their payoffs. The question therefore is how to determine the dynamics that lead from the existing power structure game at the beginning of metamorphosis to a possible new game structure, given that some existing players lose their importance and new players can quickly emerge. Moreover, the confusing situation produced by urgency on the one hand and limited information-processing capacity (perceiving plus interpreting and synthesizing variables and models) on the other hand gives additional momentum to the role of information and communication technology (ICT) as well as to the excessive emergence of pre-scientific metaphors – from the fallback to religious beliefs to praise of the purity of ancient forms of social biotopes, e.g. older governance regimes[13] or imagined Aryan-race societies. Along the lines of the set of problems the major old players formulate their answers to each question using their internal model that was derived from the mechanics of the outgoing crystal growth phase. Their recipes do not work any more, e.g. austerity policy fails, old alliances start to crumble and eventually some players disappear from the bigger stage.[14] At the same time new players are trying to jump on this bigger stage, and to do so they often have to form new alliances and coalitions. The respective plans to form a coalition then lead to bargaining and temporary joining of forces until a relatively stable new political power structure is reached.

It is this type of stepwise procedure that for both sets of scenarios, more Europe and 'no Europe', has to be represented by a model. Figure 1.4 presents a sketch of the structure of such a model.

The European development is embedded in the evolution of the world economy and *in the mid run* the most important influence from outside Europe will come from the most powerful country in the world: the USA. As described above, the presidential elections in 2016 are driven by specific parts of US industry supporting their respective political frontrunner. Depending on the outcome of this election the efforts to dominate Europe will either focus mainly on financial dominance (Democratic Party, Hillary Clinton, Wall Street), or on military dominance

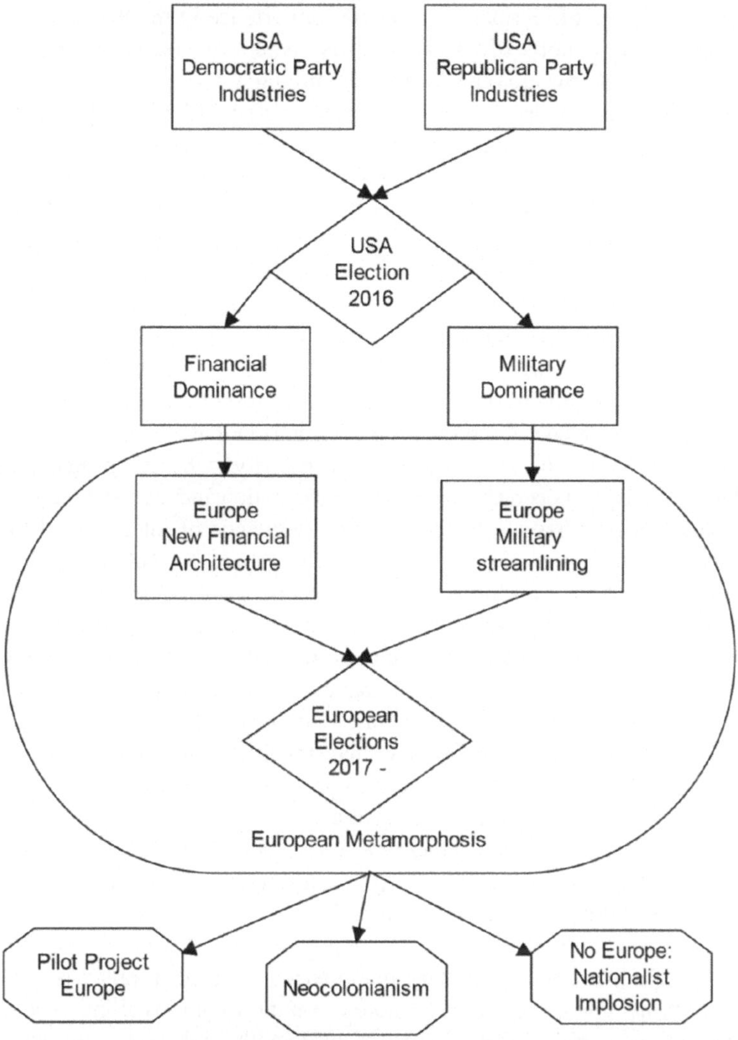

Figure 1.4 A model of mid-run evolution of Europe

(Republican Party, Donald Trump, military–industrial complex). This will have an important influence on Europe's metamorphosis, i.e. the fundamental restructuring of the network of European political power relations.

A first compressed expression of this impact will be seen at European elections in some major EU member states, in 2017 in Germany and France and in 2018 in Italy.[15] The economic consequences of different types of dominance for certain European countries are somewhat difficult to disentangle. France and the UK do have important military-oriented sectors, Germany – in particular if the UK suffers a drawback with Brexit – can point at its central role in finance. On the other hand, a major basis of Germany's financial importance in the material production sphere is the exports of its car industry. And with decreasing imports of China and Brazil in this area this basis is dwindling away.

In the European election year 2017 a pivotal role will be played by nationalist parties on the extreme right. It can be expected that their support from across the Atlantic will be higher if military dominance is the name of the new game. In that case these elections may turn out to be the trigger event for the death blow of European unification. This mid-run result is shown on the far right in Figure 1.4. It implies that a US-governed NATO rules the split set of European nation states, a type of global neocolonialism with the USA as neocolonial superpower.[16] Local nationalist heads of state will be materially and financially supported to keep their populations in clean hierarchical order. There are designs of mechanisms of indirect democracy that – complemented with manipulative use of information technology – can avoid too much coercive power and can conform to democratic-looking constitutional law. A mid-run consequence for the majority of the European population would most likely be a decrease in political participation and thus real income.[17]

But this does not have to happen. For a dominance of international finance groups with home-based Wall Street military expansion of NATO need not be the preferred road to invest in profitable projects. Even if they concentrate on the short run, these groups are keener to promise their investors that in the mid run there will be a smooth stream of returns. In economic terms, they are forced to pretend that they optimize mean-variance utility functions. As far as can be seen at the moment, they would 'cooperate' with a British or a German financial ally to guarantee returns from European investments.[18] The question then is how the profit rates from which these interest rates are deducted can be made. Two answers to this question appear to be feasible.

One possibility is an arrangement with the globally powerful international finance group that allows a future EU governance to install its own little neocolonial network south-east of Europe. With such an arrangement for the Middle East and North Africa there would also be the opportunity to integrate NATO-oriented groups that are interested in military dominance. After all, Frontex is a NATO organization that could play an even more essential role in installing neocolonial viceroys in the colonies.[19] The problem of sufficiently high profit rates would be solved by keeping crude oil and gas prices extremely low, supported also by cheap wages of labour immigrants from Central Africa and India. This would take the heat out of NATO expansion towards Russia – though at least the thread potential from the Middle East would rise – and European finance institutions even as subsidiaries of US banks could perhaps participate a bit. The current development (May 2016) seems to hint at this type of mid-run perspective of the EU. Europe's big business as well as several heads of state of EU countries, who follow its wishes, are assuming to be able to continue business as usual if this solution is envisaged.

The other possibility would be an emancipatory jump forward towards a newly structured European unification project. This project has been labelled Pilot Project Europe (compare Hanappi, 2013). The main point to avoid neocolonialism would be a substantially improved integration policy of a Europe with open borders, combined with a restructuring of labour organization (labour time reduction, coordinated incomes policy, etc.) and close cooperation at eye level with developing countries. This type of policy will probably induce a few TNCs to transfer their headquarters to North America, but for many small and medium-sized enterprises, which provide the overwhelming majority of European employment, this scenario means a better chance of survival. If trade ties are not monopolized by TNCs – an issue to be solved politically – then a different type of growth phase, namely growth of a different kind of welfare, can be envisaged. And this is exactly the point where productivity-increasing investment could set in, which in turn might enable a modest rate of interest for European investment banks too. This scenario is called a *pilot* project because it entails features that never existed before in any large modern society; it is exploring new ground. To be implemented it will need very skilled coalition building (national, international, global) cutting across the traditional lines of any 19th-century class codex.[20]

Of course, this sketch of a model should be implemented as a computer simulation with estimated quantities, and relations between the essential endogenous variables. Unfortunately, simulation models of social metamorphosis processes are rare. The major obstacles are how to model: (1) emergence and disappearance of agents, variables and relations; (2) internal models of agents that also regard the fact that the same agent often maintains different models (sometimes of the same process) and switches by conclusions of analogy; and (3) the fitting process that allows only a limited amount of possible combinations of the different (internal model-guided) actions of the involved agents.[21] But these are only the difficulties of translating ideas into a formal algorithmic language.

A problem that is at least as challenging as this simulation language difficulty is to uncover the dynamics of class structures of the European – and global – societies, which in the end govern the motions of agents in day-by-day political life. This will be dealt with in the next section.

Coalition options and class dynamics

Start with what is immediately perceived. What can easily be observed is an immensely grown influence of processes in the information sphere, which can to a large extent be explained by the omnipresence of advanced ICT and a worldwide surge of alienation, which in turn is fuelled by an exploding global division of labour and global value chains. All these elements have to be duly considered; their immediate impact on metamorphosis dynamics cannot be doubted. Nevertheless, there still exists a deeper level of explanation, namely the level at which the dynamics of social classes is studied – their emergence, their interaction and eventually their disappearance. This level is *deeper* since it assumes that the actions based on internal models of physical individuals are not just given, innate properties; they are assumed to be substantially framed by class-specific socialization. Class dynamics have been a central topic of classic political economy in Britain in the 19th century.[22] Only with the advent of marginalist economic theory towards the end of the century was the concept of class dynamics lost from sight and substituted by the less useful focus on physical human individuals. Almost 150 years later it can safely be stated that the project of methodological individualism – the tenet of the marginalist approach – failed. Returning to what Karl Marx analysed as the evolution of class struggle in his time shows how precarious these issues are. Marx's conclusion was that in the history of class struggles a purification process had finally reduced the number of classes, so that in the 19th century only two classes, the capitalist class and the proletariat, would stand in direct opposition. The victory of the proletariat, which he fought for, would finally end all class struggles. This forecast of the second half of the 19th century turned out to be – at least – premature.

If today the classical procedure to define classes according to their role in the social production process is applied, then this is still possible (compare Hanappi and Hanappi-Egger, 2012a, b). But with globally distributed production processes and the diverse cultural conditions they are embedded in, it is better to start with the assumption that there are more than just two social strata to be considered. A first warning already came in the 20th century when the phenomenon of a mass movement of Fascists was hard to understand from the perspective of an over-simplified two-class perspective. The same can be said about the class of finance capitalists that Rudolf Hilferding had characterized at the beginning of the 20th century (Hilferding, 1910). For the 21st century a profound theory of the prevailing class structures and their dynamics does not exist yet.

What are the classes, the social strata,[23] to be distinguished in the 21st century? The minimum set of distinctions to be made is: (1) distinctions at a global level (continents, regions); (2) distinctions at a continental level (country groups); (3) distinctions between public and private agents (state institutions and private firms); (4) sectors of private firms and finance firms; (5) firm owners, firm managers, workers, unemployed, children/pupils/students (CPS), retired; and (6) male, female. Since a minimum of class consciousness is a necessary condition for class action, a common language and territorial closeness play an important role: classes first appear at the national level. It is at this level that the role in the production process becomes the distinctive characteristic for further class membership. Firm owners constitute the capitalist faction of the national ruling class, the leaders of state institutions form the state faction of the national ruling class, money owners (banks) are the third faction of the ruling class, low-level management and workers constitute two factions of the national working class. The remaining social strata (CPS, unemployed, retired, etc.) are not directly involved in the production process, but today nevertheless are sufficiently organized to maintain their respective *surrogate class consciousness*. The same holds for *women*, whose surrogate class consciousness due to reasons of a common type of socialization (and biological reconnaissance) has expanded to the global level. In general membership in one of the social strata or classes more or less overlaps with membership in a different one. With respect to race, membership in a non-white race of the USA to a large extent overlaps with membership of the working class.

These overlaps therefore also produce a more or less split surrogate class consciousness. More important even is the loss of a one-to-one relationship between class status and class consciousness if the enormously increased influence of modern information technologies is taken into account (compare Dicken, 2015, pp. 83–98). In several historical episodes this has led to an inversion of the traditional direction of causation: it was not the economic base that determined the superstructure of class consciousness, but it was an – eventually manipulated – group consciousness that shook up the economic base. The most drastic example, of course, is the temporary success of a stipulated Aryan race that in World War II destroyed large parts of the world economy. The ever more important influence of alienation in global production systems adds to such dangers and leads to a highly fragile system of classes and social strata. In short, the current process of metamorphosis will need very skilled 'political entrepreneurs' to arrive at a relatively stable set of more durable coalitions.

To provide a simple example of the difficulties of coalition building: in Europe the three factions of the ruling class (firm owners, bankers and state executives) exist at both levels, continental as well as within each nation. For some national factions, usually firm-owner factions, unconstrained economic interaction with Russia is favourable, whereas for another faction, e.g. the state executives that are closely cooperating with certain US departments,[24] trade sanctions against Russia are the preferred strategy. Things are getting even more complicated if not only the conflicts within the same class are considered but also factions of the working class are added. In other words, a rich playground for strategic coalition building with respect to the three mid-term scenarios mentioned in the previous section becomes visible.

The fact that in a metamorphosis phase decisions usually have to be taken rather fast implies an additional feature: There is no time for extended analysis and profound information processing[25]; therefore, bluffing and pretending start to become a general habit. The opponent will not have the time to discover the trick anyway. This then is the type of dynamics that leads to suddenly escalating bubbles, first in the communication sphere but often also emanating into the material world. In the current situation of a rather long and profound metamorphosis phase – since 2009 the world is tumbling through repeated disasters along different dimensions – these bubbles don't have the time to become too large. They are exploded by *ad hoc* measures, but their origin is not really understood and the basic contradictions are only transferred into another dimension. Instead of learning, only short-sighted crisis management becomes general practice.

For a complete understanding of the dynamics of the complicated network that determines the final choice between NATO expansion and consolidation of the EU a simulation device would be extremely helpful. But this clearly goes beyond the scope of this chapter. Here only the rough guidelines for such a device can be explained, and the necessity to base it on a careful analysis of a larger set of classes (as well as social strata not covered by the traditional class definition) and their respective (surrogate) class consciousness has been emphasized.

Conclusion

The process of a unification of Europe – politically, economically and culturally – has been on its way since the end of World War II. As a response to the successful relaunch of US dominance in the early 1980s and its negative impact on Europe, unification gained momentum in the mid-1980s. The end of the bipolar world at the beginning of the next decade inspired European politicians as well as military leaders of NATO to reach out for Eastern European countries. For more than two decades their goals more or less coincided; the economic integration envisaged by European economic leaders mostly ran parallel to military expansion plans.[26]

Then the global crisis pushed the world economy into a metamorphosis phase. While economic policy in the USA reacted astonishingly fast and to some extent successfully, the European policy process reacted slowly and disintegration set in. NATO, being dominated by the USA, also quickly saw a window of opportunity to advance further towards Russia. Cautiously, of course: by coupling the deteriorating economic situation in some countries and the possible remedy by closer ties to the EU with the offer to join NATO, the plan was to use the crisis as a vehicle for further expansion. By and large such a plan had worked since 1990 (Figure 1.1). But in the case of the Ukraine NATO aspirations – in the eyes of Russia at least – had crossed a red line. To lose the major military stronghold in the Black Sea was not an acceptable option for Putin. Neither was the loss of access to the Mediterranean Sea via Syria's ports easy to swallow, hence Russia's support for Assad early on.

From a European perspective these global war games look dangerous and are economically very undesirable.[27] EU member Cyprus is just some 250 km from the warzone in Syria and EU member Greece is flooded by refugees, while Moscow is 2,300 km away and Washington at 9,500 km is just on the other end of the world. For Europe the danger of bearing the direct and indirect cost of this conflict is extremely high due to the pure facts of geography alone. What makes the NATO expansion scenario even worse is that increased economic welfare in the EU member states was based on economic integration and advances in internal division of labour, and this integration included former USSR satellite states as well as Russia itself. Economic sanctions that are part of a cold war strategy hit Europe's further development substantially. To avoid the scenario on the far right at the bottom of Figure 1.4 therefore clearly is in the interest of the vast majority of Europe's population.

Taking a look at Figure 1.4 with the eyes of a game theorist and considering it as an extensive form game it is straightforward to apply backward induction, i.e. to start with the most desired outcome, the best future scenario, and work upwards to find the necessary switch points to arrive there. As already argued, the NATO expansion scenario should be avoided. For the remaining two scenarios in Figure 1.4 the pilot project Europe would be preferable since it promises a much greater long-run stability of modestly increasing welfare of a larger number of people; welfare includes countries neighbouring Europe. But, despite this advantage, the scenario of European neocolonialism currently seems to have a higher probability of becoming reality. The reason for this puzzling result can be found in the strange class dynamics that characterize European countries since the early 1990s. In western and central EU countries the prevailing class compromises between the two large camps of local conservatives and local social democrats have eroded any kind of class consciousness – amplified by the general trends underlined in the last paragraphs of the previous section. When the global crisis hit these societies in 2009 most suddenly, impoverished households blamed a diffuse 'political elite' and could easily be agitated by neonationalist right-wing parties. The goals of national elites (consisting of conservative and social democratic leaders) were *split* into *local country-specific tasks*; the necessary financial centre of gravity in Brussels still only commands 1% of the financial power of the EU. The ECB, due to its control of the euro, turned out to be the only institution with enough power to interfere in European politics at all. It thus is no surprise that local national leaders jump on every train of US superpower, be it financial cooperation, be it military aid, to achieve national advantages and to withstand local right-wing challengers. There is turmoil in the marketplace of political survival with rapidly changing alliances and surprising turns of policy. In such a situation the strongest player with the most all-embracing attitude, i.e. openness towards financial US dominance *plus* explicit support of NATO goals, has the pole position. This player today has a name: Angela Merkel. And it is exactly this twofold strategy of the strongest player that makes a neocolonial scenario the best guess for the near future.

Fortunately, the near future will not necessarily prevail in the mid run. Moving up the game tree in Figure 1.4, the random draw of nature at the root – the outcome of presidential elections in the USA from a European perspective is an exogenous event – can improve the chances of a more finance-dominated regime. In that case the possibilities for coalitions in Europe pushing a pilot project Europe at least in the mid run could improve. As the history of Europe's political economy shows, the best guess for a catalyst of such a development can only be a newly emergent player, an alliance of European intellectual workers; another social stratum with a sophisticated surrogate class consciousness. In a sense this would be the final arrival of Antonio Gramsci's (aggregate) 'organic intellectual' (Gramsci, 1930), a global new social entity overcoming the fallback into right-wing nationalism and possibly a third world war. This is what can be hoped and worked for.

Notes

1 The difference between the two systems does not fit into the traditional theoretical framework of *capitalism versus socialism*. It goes beyond the scope of this text to explain the essential differences between the ways in which surplus exploitation works in these two types of society.

2 Previous expansion reflects the Vietnam war, initiated by the Democrat J.F. Kennedy, showing that more aggressive foreign policy is not necessarily the sole domain of Republicans.

3 This process already is running ahead of the US election. In early 2015 meetings of NATO ministers decided that a new Multi-National Division Southeast would be established in Romania. Six NATO Force Integration Units would also be established to coordinate preparations for defence of new eastern members of NATO.

4 European financial intermediaries had developed a different style of banking that with the growing dominance of US banks will rapidly vanish. The stronger involvement in overarching questions of welfare policy will be substituted by stricter rule sets and agenda setting dictated from a main US hub.

5 More recent examples include former Yugoslavia, Afghanistan, Iraq and the Ukraine.

6 Given the strictly hierarchical organization of an army it is easy to identify the dominance of the USA in NATO: from 1951 up until the present day the Supreme Allied Commander Europe has always been a general (or admiral) of the US Army.

7 The term was introduced by US President Eisenhower in 1961, when in a speech he warned to 'guard against the potential influence of the *military–industrial complex*'. During the Reagan presidency this concept gained importance again.

8 This difficulty has been discussed extensively (see e.g. Gramme and Hobolt, 2015; Rose,2015).

9 Ignoring all further repercussions, the direct suppliers of weapons include Lockheed Martin, Boeing, Raytheon, Northrop Grumman, General Dynamics, United Technologies Corporation, and L-3 Communications. In 2013 each of these firms sold arms for more than US$10 billion.

10 Compare Hanappi and Scholz-Wäckerle (2015) for a detailed discussion of alternation between crystal growth phases and metamorphosis phases in societies.

11 The vast literature on the stability of economic equilibrium growth paths is the theoretical mirror image of an outgoing crystal growth phase.

12 See Hanappi (2016a) for a possible list of Europe's set of most burning problems and their interdependence.

13 The classic text for this idea stems from Karl Marx: 'At the very time when men appear engaged in revolutionizing things and themselves, in bringing about what never was before, at such very epochs of revolutionary crises do they anxiously conjure up into their service the spirits of the past, assume their names, their battle cries, their costumes to enact a new historic scene in such time-honoured disguise and with such borrowed language' (Marx, 1852).

14 Examples are PASOK in Greece, Andreotti's Democrazia Cristiana in Italy and the labour union organizations in the UK.

15 The year 2016 (most probably) will lead to new elections in Spain and the impact of the Brexit referendum in the UK. If Spain turns left and thus joins Greece and Portugal, then this certainly influences internal politics in France and Italy. If additionally, Brexit becomes reality – which has a low probability – then in 2017 from the five main countries of the EU only three (France, Germany and Italy) remain as the core.

16 Donald Trump's slogan 'Make the USA big again!' plays directly with this vision.

17 Additionally, the nationalist split would reverse the income-increasing effects of division of labour between EU member states.

18 At the moment the most important transmitter of the goals of international finance to European governance is ECB president Mario Draghi, a former Goldman Sachs director. It can be assumed that his intervention in 2012 saved Greece from Grexit (see Hanappi, 2015b), which fits pretty well in the argument given above.

19 Colonialism managed to make profits from world trade by using different, pre-existing economic and cultural properties of countries, and uniting them with a global hegemony of military strength of a dominant state. Neocolonialism achieves an analogous result, but now with the dominance of a TNC using its global value chains. Two new types of resistance emerge too: global migration movements and a global rise of consumption aspiration levels transported by new ICTs.

20 It often is forgotten that even Lenin's success in 1918 was based on a successful coalition-building process between proletariat, farmers and farm workers. Despite the terrible deterioration of the USSR that followed, this surprising takeover of power in a highly militarized feudal regime shows the strength of vision building if it is combined with skilled pragmatism.

21 This, of course, can be understood as a hint to the analogous problem in theoretical physics when it deals with phase transitions (see Hanappi, 2016b). To describe social-phase transitions much more sophisticated modelling is needed, since molecules don't use internal model building to choose their actions.

22 Compare Wright (2005) for the history of the class concept from a sociological perspective.

23 'Social strata' is a wider concept than class structure in the sense that it allows for a group consciousness that is not directly linked to the immediate position in the production process. If the firm-owner faction of the ruling class with its profits finances a group of high-income managers for the direct control of the work process, then this group can be added to this faction of the ruling class. But if a group of retired elderly people or a group of children/pupils/students is considered, then they are elements of the system of social strata.

24 As the WikiLeaks Files show: 'Behind closed doors, State Department personnel use both carrots and the threat of sticks . . . to ensure that their European allies come to heel. The expectation is unmistakable – whenever powerful groups or individuals on the continent challenge Washington's authority . . . European governments are to make the problems go away or suffer serious damages in their bilateral relationships with the United States. For the most part, as a long parade of cables suggests, they fall in line' (Busch, 2015, p. 210).

25 This is the reason why the well-developed game-theoretic perspective on coalition formation (compare Ray 2007), can barely be applied by the players in this game.

26 A first divergence can be seen in the EU accession of Bulgaria and Romania in 2007. This clearly was rather in the military interest to reach the shores of the Black Sea, while the accession of economically more advanced countries, like Croatia, would have been a priority from the point of view of economic integration.

27 Some EU countries will vividly remember the costs of war in Iraq that were not balanced by any political or economic benefit.

References

Busch M., (2015), *The WikiLeaks Files. The World According to US Empire*, Verso, London.

Dicken P., (2015), *Global Shift. Mapping the Changing Contours of the World Economy*, Sage, London.

Gramme O. and Hobolt S., (2015), *Democratic Politics in a European Union under Stress*, Oxford University Press, Oxford.

Gramsci A., (1930), Prison Notebooks, in: *Further Selections from the Prison Notebooks*, Electric Book Company, London, 1999.

Hanappi H., (2013), Can Europe Survive? Ten Commandments for Europe's Next Ten Years, in: A. Balcerzak (ed.) *Growth Perspectives in Europe*, Polish Economic Society, Torun, pp. 27–92.

Hanappi H., (ed.), (2014), *South-East Europe in Evolution*, Routledge, London.

Hanappi H., (2015a), Unemployment in Mediterranean EU Countries. Fighting Youth Unemployment, in S. Katsikides and P. I. Koktsidis (eds) *Societies in Transition. The Social Implications of Economic, Political and Security Transformations*, Springer, Cham.

Hanappi H., (2015b), *From Political Crisis to Europe's Second Renaissance?*, Policy brief published as MPRA 67922, Munich Personal RePEc Archive, Munich.

Hanappi H., (2016a), Shangri-La Governance,A Sketch of an Integral Solution for European Economic Policy Based on a Synthesis of Europe's Problems, in: S. Katsikides and H. Hanappi H. (eds.) *Society and Economics in Europe,* Springer International, Switzerland, pp. 1–18.

Hanappi H., (2016b), Evolutionary Political Economy Goes Quantum Theory. A Preview, forthcoming in *Papers in Evolutionary Political Economy* (PEPE).

Hanappi H. and Hanappi-Egger E., (2012a), *Social Identity and Class Consciousness*, published as MPRA 60491, Munich Personal RePEc Archive, Munich.

Hanappi H. and Hanappi-Egger E., (2012b), *Middle Class or in the Middle of a Class?* Paper contributed to the Joint AHE/FAPE/IIPPE Conference in Paris, 5–8 July 2012. Available at: http://www.econ.tuwien.ac.at/hanappi/Papers/Hanappi_Hanappi-Egger_2012b.pdf (accessed 11 September 2016).

Hanappi H. and Scholz-Wäckerle M., (2015), Evolutionary Political Economy: Content and Method, forthcoming in *Forum for Social Economics*, Routledge, New York.

Hilferding R., (1910), *Das Finanzkapital*, Europäische Verlagsanstalt, Frankfurt am Main.

Marx K., (1852), *The Eighteenth Brumaire of Louis Bonaparte*, translated by Saul K. Padover from the German edition of 1869, Karl Marx Library, McGraw-Hill Books, New York.

Ray D., (2007), *A Game-Theoretic Perspective on Coalition Formation*, Oxford University Press, Oxford.

Rose R., (2015), *Representing Europeans. A Pragmatic Approach*, Oxford University Press, Oxford.

Wright E. O., (2005), *Approaches to Class Analysis*, Cambridge University Press, Cambridge.

2 Spanish regions under the euro crisis

Did the crisis escalate interregional tensions?

Makiko Narita

Introduction

The Spanish economy has been emerging from the recession that started in the late 2000s. However, there are still regional differences or disparities within Spain, which cause interregional tension. In particular, the Catalan independence movement has been discontented with the redistribution system of the central government: Catalonia is one of the richest regions and pays a large amount of taxes, but receives a lower share in tax payments.[1] Catalonia is the only case in Europe. The Scottish independence campaign has given rise to separatism in some European regions, such as Flanders in Belgium or northern Italy. In Spain, the Basque country also has called for independence.[2] In the past, these regional tensions derived mainly from ethnic or religious differences but the economic crises in the 2000s have led to conflict between more prosperous regions and poorer regions. In particular, in Europe, wealthier regions would like to separate from the country to which they belong.

Spain has attained convergence with the European Union (EU) since the late 1980s, but during this time, regional disparities have increased rather than narrowed within the country (Narita, 2003). Then, the question arises about how much the crises impact on regional disparities. What kind of measure is necessary to decrease regional disparities? This chapter aims to analyse these questions and provide implications for our findings.

The first section analyses the euro crisis in the 2000s and the Spanish economy, followed by an examination of the effects of the crisis on Spanish regions and a discussion of regional policy and foreign direct investment, both of which are expected to decrease regional disparities.

Spain under the crisis

After economic prosperity for several years in the 2000s, which proved to be the bubble economy, Spain fell into recession. The main reason was that the bubble burst in the construction and real-estate sector. The Greek sovereign debt crisis that started in 2009 has worsened Spain's situation.[3] Spain experienced severe economic decline since 2007 with negative growth in 2009 and 2010 (Figure 2.1). The unemployment rate has been increasing and is the highest in the EU, reaching 26.1% in 2013 (Figure 2.2). The public balance has been negative since 2008 and was 10.6% of gross domestic product (GDP) in 2012 (Figure 2.3).

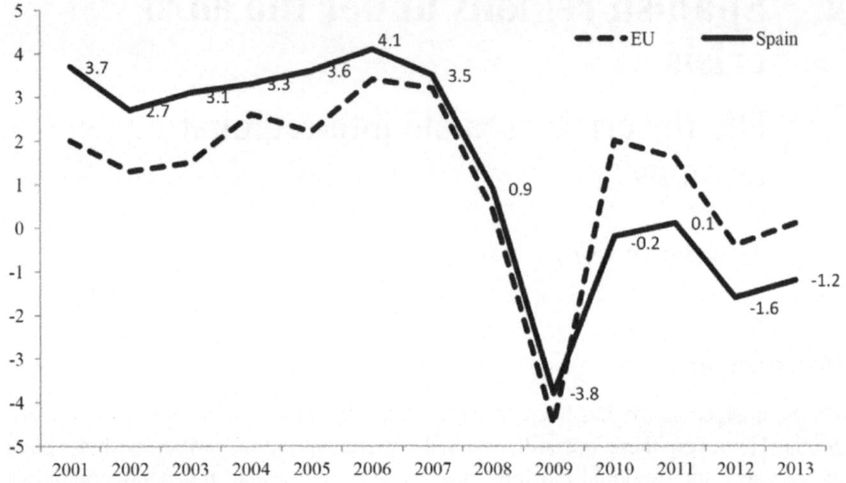

Figure 2.1 Growth rate, EU and Spain (%)

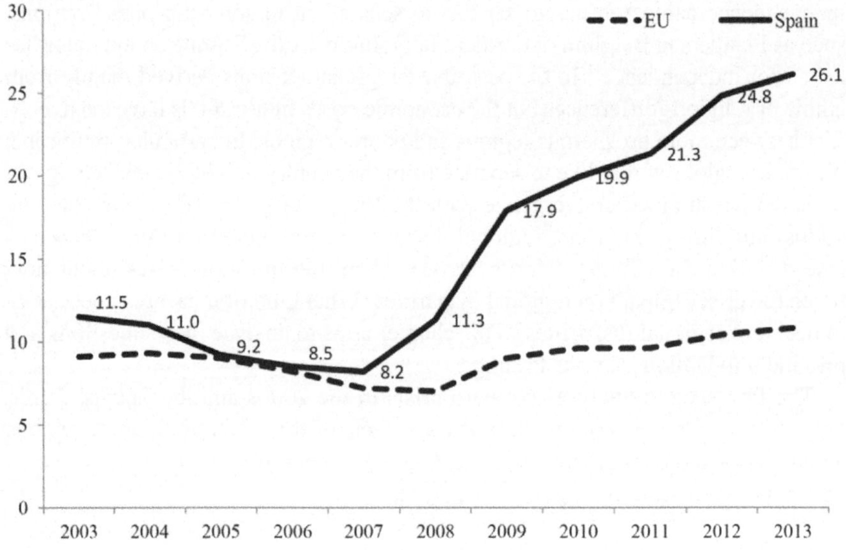

Figure 2.2 Unemployment rate, EU and Spain (%)

Chislett (2013) points out several impacts of the crisis: soaring unemployment, banking crisis, a ballooning deficit, an increase in emigration, loss of confidence in politicians and institutions, and declining living standards.

Facing a difficult economic condition, Spain has to tackle five tasks: first, cut the fiscal deficit; second, implement labour market reform to decrease high unemployment; third, clear the housing and construction bubble; fourth, improve

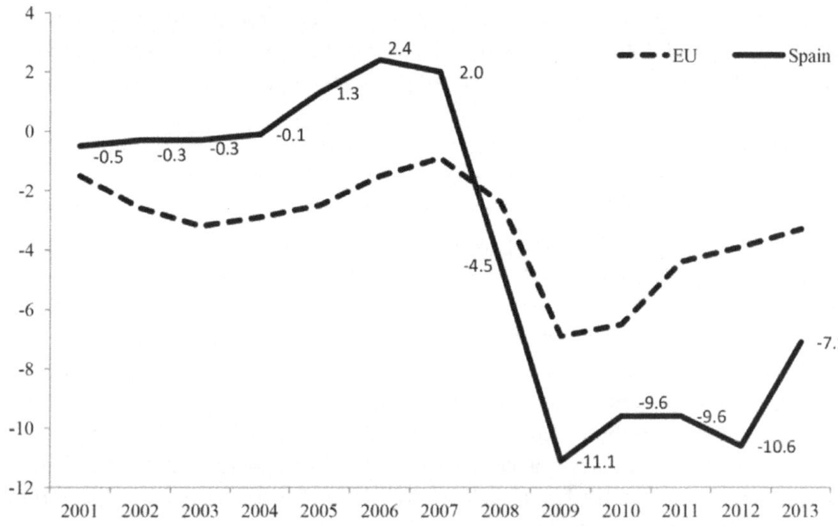

Figure 2.3 Public balance (surplus+ and deficit–, percentage of GDP), EU and Spain

productivity; and fifth, reform financial markets for the recovery of the fragile banking sector (IMF, 2010).

First, Spain carried out an austerity programme, including cutting or freezing public salaries, reducing health and education expenditure and increasing value-added tax and income tax.[4] Spain had to reduce its excessive deficit to the EU threshold by 2013 but the 3% target by 2013 proved to be unrealistic, and eventually, Spain was rescued by the EU and given until 2016 to meet the reference.

In addition, regional governments are responsible for Spain's large fiscal deficit. Spain's 17 autonomous communities account for about a third of public spending.[5] Not all communities require the regional deficit target, and some communities are discontented with the central government austerity plan. For example, a Catalonia independence campaign has taken place.

Second, the rigid Spanish labour market is the most critical problem. The government has carried out labour market reform aiming at a more flexible labour market. The Labour Reform Law in September 2010 included removing the dual structure between full-time and temporary employment, decreasing labour time and increasing the chance for especially young workers to obtain jobs.[6] A further labour market reform was carried out in 2012 by which, for example, the maximum severance pay that employees can receive was cut from 45 days to 33 days of salary per year with a cap of 24 months' pay.

To cope with the third and fourth tasks, the government has promoted development mainly in the high-technology and environment industries.[7] In the construction and real-estate sector, it is necessary for Spain to clear its housing and construction bubble with 700,000 unsold houses, to absorb unemployed people previously employed in the construction sector[8] and to deal with house prices that have declined by more than 35% since the first quarter of 2008.[9] The General Industrial Policy was adopted in December 2010, which included promoting international competitiveness, research and development (R&D) and exports, and strengthening important industrial sectors such as biotechnology, information technology and renewable energy. In addition, strengthening small and medium firms, the sales of important sectors would increase to 44% of total sales by 2020. This law is aimed at ensuring sustainable growth in the medium and long term.[10]

Lastly, in spite of restructuring involving the saving of banks by El Fondo de Reestructuración Ordenada Bancaria (Fund for Orderly Bank Restructuring),[11] the government eventually called for a financing package of €100 billion from the European Commission, the European Central Bank and the International Monetary Fund (IMF) (the troika) in June 2012. This was different from the bailouts received by Greece, Ireland and Portugal because it was restricted to recapitalizing Spain's banks.[12]

The economy has been recovering since 2013. As the amount of exports is growing, the Spanish current account was in surplus in 2013. The budget deficit was reduced from 10.6% of GDP in 2012 to 7.1% in 2013. Financial support from the troika ended in January 2014.

Nevertheless, economic recovery has been slower. The Spanish growth rate is lower than the EU average (Figure 2.1), and the unemployment rate remains high (Figure 2.2). In particular, the unemployment rate of young workers (aged below 25 years) is more than 55%, and close to 60% of those unemployed had not worked for more than a year.[13]

Spanish regions under the crisis

Spain has 17 autonomous communities and two autonomous cities. They account for one-third of the country's public spending, and have not cut their deficits enough. In a period of crisis, regional crises tend to be less prioritized, since the most urgent issues to tackle are those of a macroeconomic nature. However, the effects of the crisis will spread equally to the regions, and economic and social disparities will expand. The Gini coefficient has been increasing (Figure 2.4), and dispersion of regional GDP shows increasing differences between regions (Figure 2.5). This means that Spain has become less equal.

Several studies have been undertaken on the effects of the crisis on Spanish regions. Bandrés and Gadea (2013) classified autonomous communities into three groups according to the characteristics of industry type, human capital, unemploymentrate and openness. The regions least affected by the crisis are the Basque country, Navarre, and Madrid, which have high shares of industry, sufficient human capital and lower unemployment and are open to foreign countries. The authors point out that intermediately affected regions are Aragon, Catalonia, La Rioja and Balearic Islands, and the most affected regions are Valencia, Castile-La Mancha and Andalusia. Mas Ivars and Pérez García (2013) focused on capital stock, and regions with high productivity of capital were less affected by the crisis. Madrid, Catalonia, Basque country and Navarre have produced better economic performances. Whereas these studies were carried out for the period 2011 or 2012, this study extends the analysis to 2013.

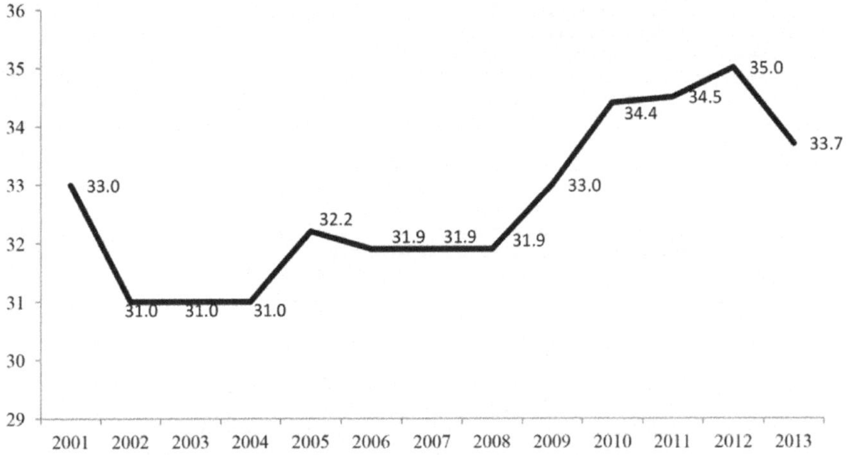

Figure 2.4 Gini coefficient of Spain

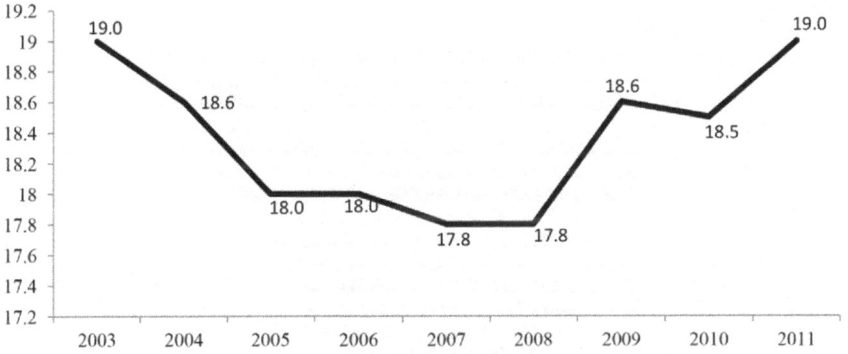

Figure 2.5 Dispersion of regional GDP in Spain (%)

Source: Eurostat

During the crisis, the gap between the regions did not narrow. Madrid, Catalonia, Basque country and Navarre faced less economic decline than the Spanish average (−1.38%) (Figure 2.6), and enjoyed high GDP per capita (Figure 2.7).

These four regions were less affected by labour market deterioration. Unemployment rates were lower than the national average. In particular, the unemployment rates of Navarre (16.45%) and Basque country (16.66%) were the lowest in Spain in the last quarter of 2013 (Figure 2.8).

With regard to industrial structure, regions with higher income levels have comparative advantages for high-technology industries. According to the Instituto Nacional de Estadística, Catalonia and the Basque country accounted for 51% of Spanish production in the machinery and equipment industry, and 41% in the information technology, electronic, optical and electrical products industries in 2013.

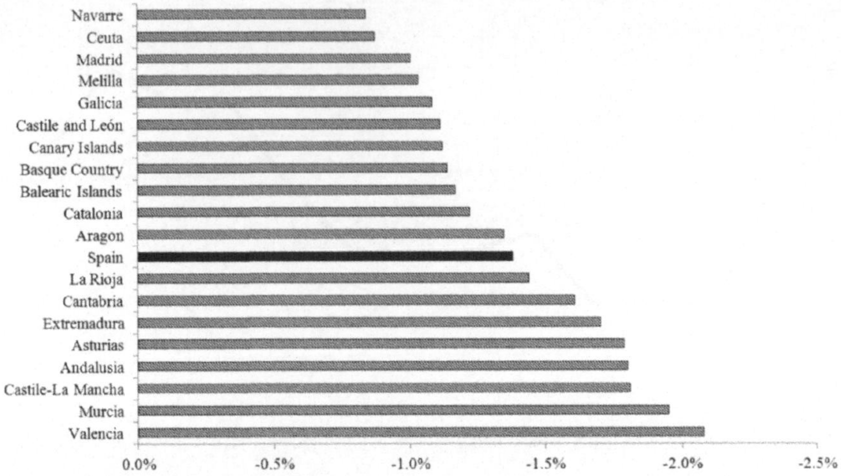

Figure 2.6 Growth rate of Spanish regions (2008–2013, average)

Source: Instituto Nacional de Estadística

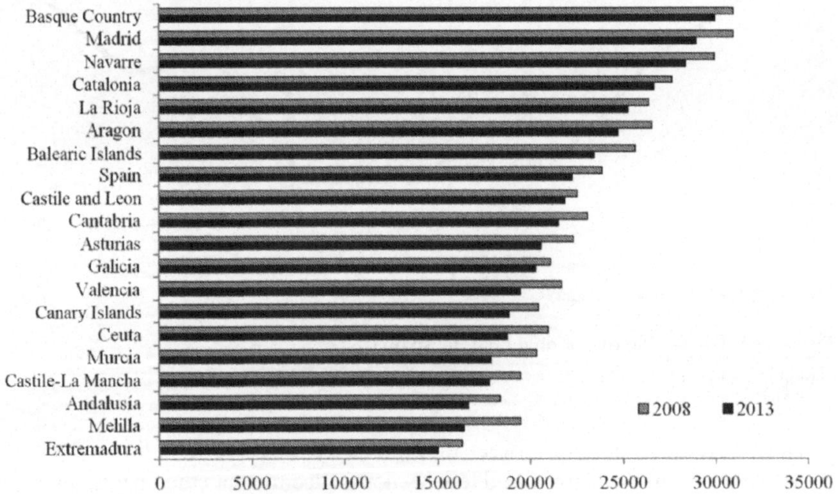

Figure 2.7 GDP per capita of Spanish regions (2008–2013, euro)

Source: Instituto Nacional de Estadística

Regional policy for Spanish regions

The EU carries out regional policy to promote economic, social and regional cohesion, that is, to decrease regional disparities. Leaving these disparities in place would undermine European integration itself. The main part of the EU's regional policy is financial assistance to improve the economic well-being of regions.

During the period 2007–2013, Spanish regions received about €26 billion for convergence.[14] Since some regions are not eligible because they are less

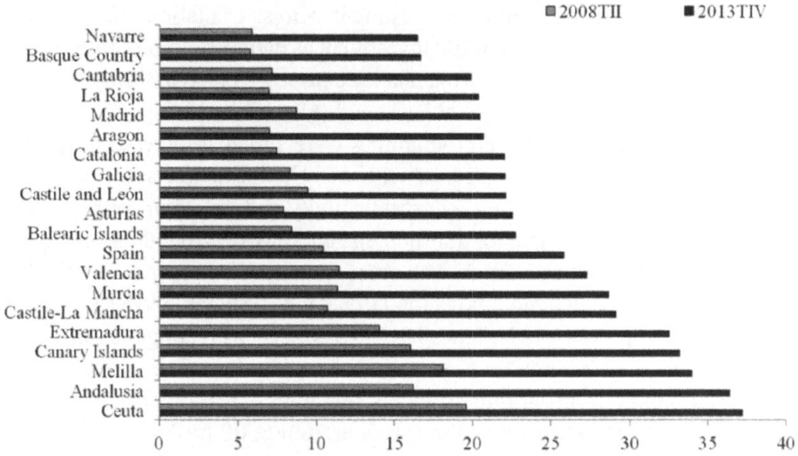

Figure 2.8 Unemployment rate of Spanish regions (2008–2013, %). 2008 TII, second quarter of 2008; 2013 TIV, last quarter of 2013

Source: Instituto Nacional de Estadística

Table 2.1 Breakdown of finance for regional development (millions of euros)

Region	*EU investment*	*National public contribution*	*Total public contribution*
Castile-la Mancha	1,439	635	2,074
Canary Islands	1,019	656	1,675
Castile and Leon	818	357	1,175
Extremadura	1,580	683	2,263
Murcia	524	220	744
Asturias	395	159	554
Ceuta	45	20	65
Melilla	44	20	64
La Rioja	33	33	65
Andalusia	6,531	2,037	8,568
Valencia	1,326	913	2,240
Galicia	2,192	981	3,172
Basque country	241	260	500
Catalonia	679	719	1,398
Cantabria	89	89	178
Navarre	47	47	94
Aragon	163	163	326
Balearic Islands	107	119	226
Madrid	337	357	694
Total	17,609	8,468	26,075

Source: Inforegio (http://ec.europa.eu/regional_policy)

developed regions whose GDP per capita is less than 75% of the EU average, they received financial assistance for other purposes such as regional competitiveness and employment.

Table 2.1 shows that Catalonia, Balearic Islands and Madrid received more national public contribution than EU investment. Rioja, Cantabria, Navarre and Aragon received the same amount of EU investment as national public contribution. The objectives of all these regions are to enhance competitiveness and employment.

Andalusia received the most financial assistance (€8.6 billion) in Spain. Under the convergence objective, the regional programmes were aimed at increasing regional per capita GDP to achieve convergence with the European average, increasing regional productivity and increasing industrial activity and employment rates. The funds went towards a programme for transport and energy (31% of total investment), the environment, natural surroundings, water resources and risk prevention (29.7%), entrepreneurial development and innovation (19%) and sustainable local and urban development (10.1%).[15] Even if the funds have had effects on creating jobs and stimulating innovation, the convergence within Spanish regions has not been realized.

For Basque country, programmes under the regional competitiveness and employment objectives were carried out with around €500 million. The greater part of the budget was allocated to enhancing the knowledge economy, innovation, and business development (about 71.5% of the total investment).[16] The main purpose of the programme is to increase the rate of investment in R&D as a proportion of GDP and to improve businesses' productivity and competitiveness. As mentioned in the previous section, the Basque country attained a higher percentage of investment in R&D to GDP and retained higher GDP per capita.

Regional policy would be effective for improving the business climate because it enhances investment in infrastructure and R&D. Nevertheless, regional disparities were not reduced during the period 2007–2013.

Since 2000, 13 counties have become new members of the EU. Most are Central and Eastern European countries and are less developed than Spain. The total allocation to Spain during the period 2014–2020 will be €29 billion, and only Extremadura is eligible as a 'less developed region'. Hence, Spanish regions will not be able to depend so heavily on financial assistance through the EU's regional policy, and are required to allocate more finance to enhance regional competitiveness.

Foreign direct investment

Foreign direct investment is regarded as an engine for developing an economy because it stimulates employment and production in the recipient country. Moreover, it is not a mere capital flow from foreign countries; technology and knowledge are also transferred to the recipient country. For firms, foreign direct investment offers an opportunity to reorganize or extend their business. Hence, whether Spain attracts foreign direct investment depends on whether the country would be an appropriate location for doing business.

Figure 2.9 shows the amount of foreign direct investment Spain attracted. The global financial crisis caused the amount of inward investment to decrease from €39 billion in 2008 to €18 billion in 2012.[17]

The EU countries are main investors by country in Spain. They accounted for more than 80% of total investment during the period, except 2009 and 2012. The United States also has made substantial investment in Spain, and emerging countries

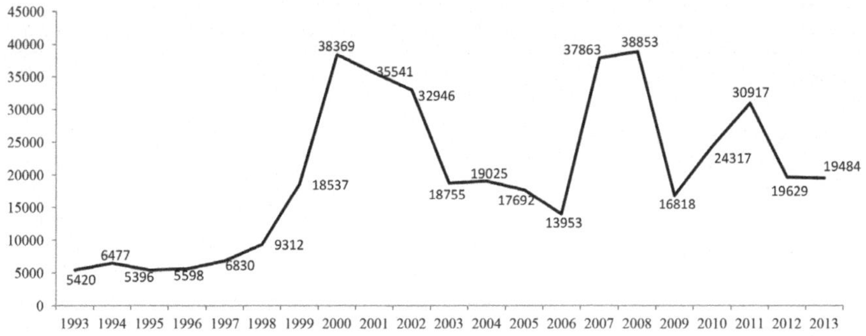

Figure 2.9 Foreign direct investment in Spain (gross, millions of euro)

Source: Información Comercial Española (2014)

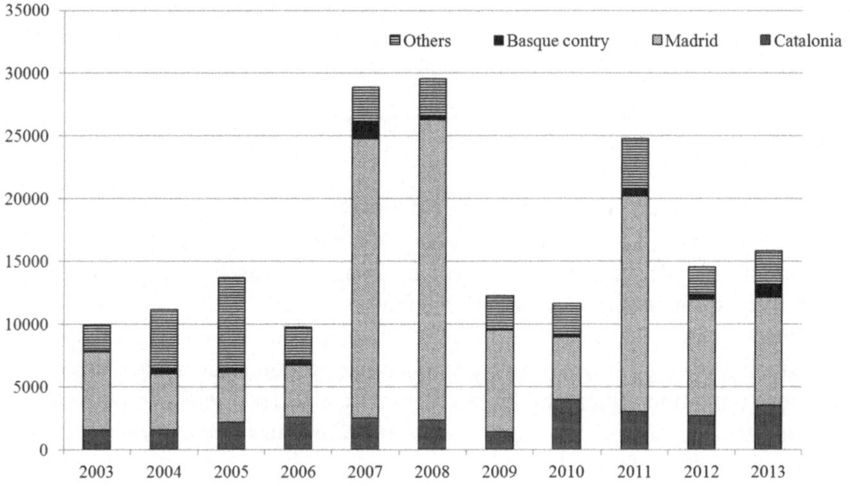

Figure 2.10 Foreign direct investment in Spanish regions (millions of euro)

Source: Información Comercial Española (various years)

have increased their investment in Spain recently. Measured by sector, the most foreign investment was directed to real-estate, services and commerce sectors until the mid-2000s, while manufacturing and renewable-energy industries have received much direct investment recently.[18] Several big investment projects have been carried out, even in the crisis era. Since the increase of capital and merger and acquisitions were apparent from the investment pattern, firms face the need to restructure.

Measured by region, Madrid and Catalonia have attracted the most investment in Spain. These two autonomous communities have received around 80% of inward investment (Figure 2.10). Even as the other 15 communities in Spain have attracted only a little investment, Basque country received relatively high foreign investment during the crisis. Table 2.2 compares foreign direct investment in 2009 when it started to fall with that in 2012. It shows that investment in Basque country, Navarre, Asturias

Table 2.2 Foreign direct investment in Spanish regions in 2009 and 2012 (millions of euros)

Region	*2009*	*2012*	*2012–2009*
Madrid	7,637	8,728	14.30%
Catalonia	1,365	2,603	9.10%
Basque Country	98	434	342.90%
Balearic Islands	410	247	–39.80%
Andulusia	306	231	–24.50%
Galicia	159	174	9.40%
Navarre	26	161	519.20%
Aragon	132	150	13.60%
Valencia	447	91	–79.60%
Canary Islands	77	68	–11.70%
Asturias	6	63	950%
Castile-La Mancha	170	51	–70%
Extremadura	27	32	18.50%
Cantabria	11	22	100%
Muricia	12	18	50%
Castile and León	72	15	–79.20%
La Rioja	4	10	150%
Ceuta and Melilla	1	1	0

Source: Información Comercial Española (2013)

and La Rioja increased during the crisis. On the other hand, foreign direct investment in Valencia, Castile-La Mancha and Castile and Leon decreased significantly.

Dunning (1993) pointed out that three advantages are essential for foreign direct investment in the eclectic paradigm, namely, ownership-specific, internalization and location-specific advantages. The location-specific advantage is important in attracting foreign direct investment, because location advantages consist of political, economic and natural factors that firms consider when deciding to locate abroad. Among them, cheap labour costs, skilled labour force and easy access to foreign markets are focused on.

First, Figure 2.11 shows that regions which attracted much direct investment have higher labour costs. Labour costs in Madrid, Catalonia, Navarre and Basque country are much higher than those of other regions. This means that labour costs could not be a decisive factor for foreign direct investment.

Second, the more important factor is quality of labour. These four regions of Madrid, Catalonia, Navarre and Basque country have labour forces with high education attainment (Figures 2.12 and Figure 2.13). In particular, Spain outweighs even the EU at tertiary level. As for expenditure on R&D, these regions attained higher levels (Figure 2.14).

Third, regarding access to the European market, Basque country, Navarre and Catalonia have geographic advantages. They are located next to France, providing access to the European market. Madrid, situated in the centre of Spain, retains an advantage in accessing Iberian markets, as well as those of Europe and Latin America, with its highly advanced infrastructure.[19]

Moreover, regional governments are eager to attract foreign investment and do so through their own investment-promoting offices. For example, the Catalan

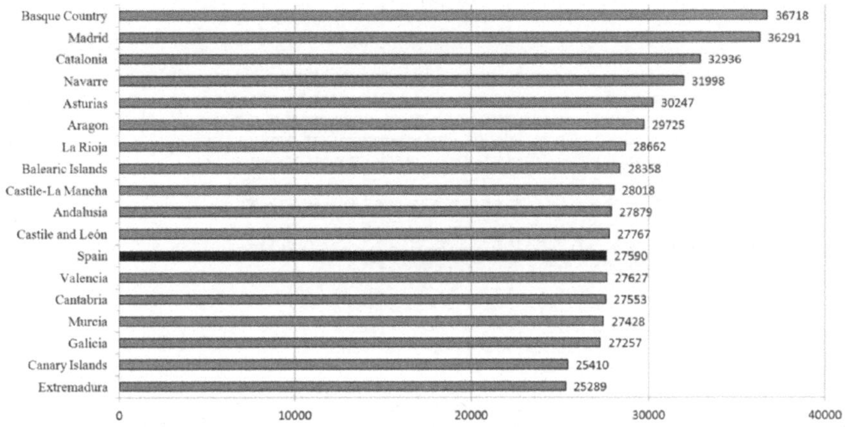

Figure 2.11 Labour costs in 2013 in Spanish regions (euro)

Source: Instituto Nacional de Estadística

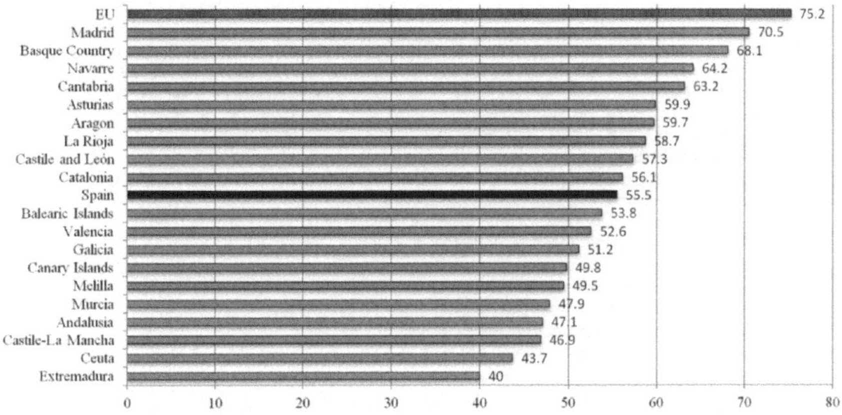

Figure 2.12 Spanish population aged 25–64 with upper secondary education attainment, 2013 (%)

Source: Eurostat

government has an investment agency named ACCIÓ, which has an international network, including an office in Tokyo to promote Japanese investment in Catalonia.[20] In addition, regional offices in Madrid (Invest in Madrid) and Basque country (SPRI) offer assistance for regional and foreign investment in those regions.

Within Spain, two cities, Barcelona, the capital city of the autonomous community of Catalonia, and Madrid, were ranked among the top ten leading cities in which to do business (sixth and seventh places respectively) in the European Cities Monitor 2011. This ranking is decided by various factors, such as costs, availability of qualified labour force and infrastructure.[21] Among them, Madrid and Barcelona ranked in the highest positions in terms of availability of qualified staff

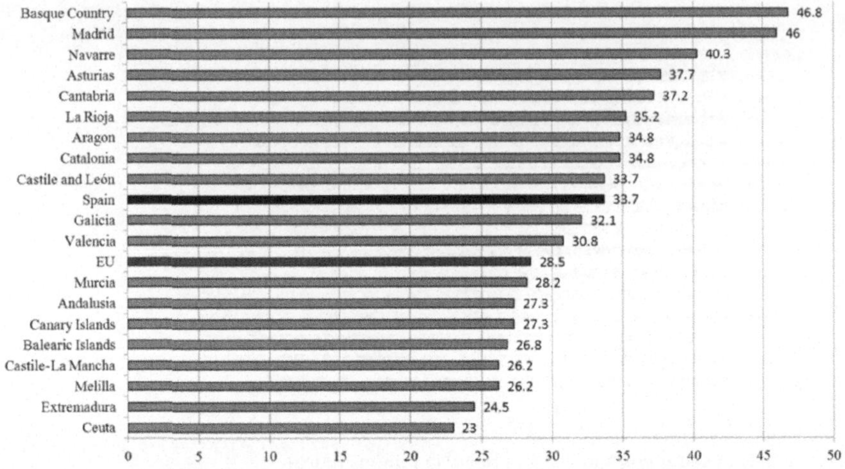

Figure 2.13 Spanish population aged 25–64 with tertiary education attainment, 2013 (%)

Source: Eurostat

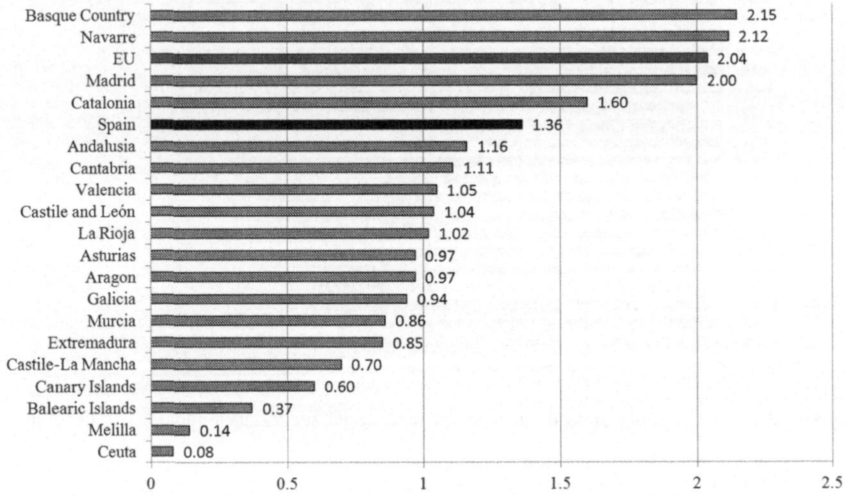

Figure 2.14 R&D expenditure in 2013 by Spanish region (% of GDP)

Source: Eurostat

(fifth and 12th places, respectively), cost of staff (ninth and 11th places, respectively) and quality of life for employees (fifth and top places, respectively).

Conclusion

This chapter studied the impacts of the financial crisis and euro crisis on Spanish regions, and examined regional policy and foreign direct investment as measures for decreasing regional disparities. The results are as follows.

First, Spain experienced recession after 2008 due to the financial crisis and euro crisis. Even though the Spanish economy has been recovering since 2013, the speed of recovery differs at regional level. Hence, regional disparities have increased rather than decreased. Less developed regions, such as Valencia, Castile-la Mancha, and Andalusia, have suffered as a result of the crisis and economic decline more than advanced regions, such as Madrid, Catalonia and Basque country. The latter group of regions has similar characteristics of lower unemployment, higher educational levels, larger spending on R&D and greater comparative advantages for high-technology industries.

Second, even if EU regional policy has effects on reducing regional imbalances to some extent, the use of funds is more important. Investments for enhancing R&D and regional competitiveness are more effective for revitalizing regions. Advanced regions tend to prioritize the knowledge-based economy and innovation.

Third, foreign direct investment remains important for regional development. To attract foreign investment, factors such as high quality of labour force or support from regional institutions are important. With regard to location of foreign firms, there is a kind of agglomeration effect.

The Catalan referendum was judged unconstitutional by Spain's constitutional court. Nevertheless, once intraregional tension escalates, similar campaigns will occur. The nationalism or independence campaigns of such regions will not cease without economic recovery.

This study did not consider in detail each region's measures for reconstructing their economies. This task is for future research.

Notes

1 More than 80% of the votes cast in a Catalan government independence referendum on 9 November 2014 were in favour of independence.

2 In the Basque country, there is a nationalist organization named ETA, which promotes gaining independence for the Basque country through armed activity. In 2011, ETA announced a definitive cessation of its armed activity.

3 The Greek government asked the EU and the IMF for a bailout in April 23, 2010. Ireland and Portugal also called for a bailout in November 2010 and May 2011, respectively.

4 The government has carried out measures in response to the recession since 2008, but the deficit has deteriorated. Spain was regarded as having 'an excessive fiscal deficit' in 2009.

5 'A great burden for Zapatero to bear: The Spanish prime minister has become a reluctant convert to reform – but maybe too little, too late' (*The Economist*, January 20, 2011).

6 See 'El PSOE salva en el Congreso su reforma laboral', El País, September 9, 2010. For the contents of the revision, see *Boletín Oficial del Estado*, Gobierno de España, June 17, 2010.

7 For details, see *Boletín Oficial del Estado*, Gobierno de España, March 5, 2011.

8 The construction sector absorbed 13% of jobs at its height. See 'A great burden for Zapatero to bear: The Spanish prime minister has become a reluctant convert to reform – but maybe too little, too late', *The Economist*, January 20, 2011.

9 See 'Location, location, location', *The Economist*, January 2, 2014.

10 For details, see Ministerio de Industria, Turismo y Comercio (2010).

11 Since saving banks (*Cajas*) involved bad loans for housing or construction firms, 45 saving banks have been restructured to fewer than 20 banks.

12 Spanish Prime Minister Mariano Rajoy refused to describe this financing package as a 'bailout'. See 'Going to extra time', *The Economist*, January 16, 2012.

13 See Chislett (2013).

14 Other than the objective for regional development, Spain received cohesion funds and some Spanish regions received funds for cross-border, transnational and interregional cooperation.
15 See Inforegio (2007a).
16 See Inforegio (2007b).
17 In addition, Spain is the ninth largest investor, and reduced outward investment during the crisis. In particular, inward direct investment plays an important role in the recovery of the Spanish economy. Thus, we provide a detailed description of inward direct investment in Spain below.
18 For details, see Información Comercial Española (2013).
19 Madrid is the centre of the rail and road system that connects the entire Iberian peninsula to the rest of Europe. The city's airport is the largest in terms of cargo and passengers, and is Europe's hub for Latin America.
20 A lot of Japanese firms were supported by the ACCIÓ when they started operating in Spain.
21 For companies, important factors in deciding where to locate are 'easy access to markets, customers or clients', 'availability of qualified staff' and 'transport links with other cities and internationally'.

References

Bandrés, E. and Gadea, M. D. (2013) 'Crisis económica y ciclos regionales en España,' *Papeles de Economía Española,* 138, pp. 2–29.

Chislett, W. (2013) *Emerging Spain?* Working Paper 14/2013, Real Instituto Elcano. Available at http://www.realinstitutoelcano.com [Accessed on July 7, 2015].

Dunning, J. H. (1993) Trade, Location of Economic Activity and the Multinational Enterprises: A Search for an Eclectic Approach, in: Dunning, J. H. (Ed.) *United Nations Library on Transnational Corporations*, Vol. I, London, Routledge.

El País. (2010, September 9) 'El PSOE salva en el Congreso su reforma laboral,' Available at http://elpais.com [Accessed on January 15, 2016].

Eurostat. Available at: http://ec.europa.eu/eurostat [Accessed on July 5, 2015].

Gobierno de España. (2015) *Boletín Oficial del Estado.* Available at http://www.boe.es [Accessed on July 7, 2015].

IMF. (2010) 'Spain: 2010 Article IV Consultation,' *IMF Country Report* No. 10/254. Available at http://www.imf.org [Accessed on July 6, 2015].

Inforegio. Available at http://ec.europa.eu/regional_policy [Accessed on July 7, 2015].

Inforegio. (2007a) 'Operational Programme "Andalusia"'. Available at http://ec.europa.eu/regional_policy/en [Accessed on July 7, 2015].

Inforegio. (2007b) 'Operational Programme "Basque country"'. Available at http://ec.europa.eu/regional_policy/en [Accessed on July 7, 2015].

Información Comercial Española. (2005, 2007, 2011, 2013, and 2014) *El Sector Exterior.* Available at http://www.revistasice.com [Accessed on July 6, 2015].

Instituto Nacional de Estadística. (various years) *Anuario Estadístico de España*. Available at http://www.ine.es [Accessed on July 7, 2015].

Mas Ivars, M. and Pérez García, F. (2013) 'La acumulación de capital en España y sus regiones; Las consecuencias de la crisis,' *Papeles de Economía Española,* 138, pp. 31–45.

Ministerio de Industria, Turismo y Comercio. (2010) *Plan Integral de Política Industrial 2020 (PIN2020)*. Available at htpp://www.minetur.gov.es [Accessed on July 10, 2015].

Narita, M. (2003, in Japanese) 'Regional Development in Spain: Lessons from Madrid and Cataluña,' *Journal of Business and Economics,* 82–4, pp.141–162.

The Economist. Available at http://www.economist.com [Accessed on December 29, 2015].

3 Some simple macroeconomic remarks on slower economic growth

Malcolm Sawyer

Introduction

The macroeconomic analysis of slower growth (of gross domestic product (GDP) or similar) takes on high relevance for two rather different reasons. The first reason is motivated by the prospects and recent experiences of growth in industrialized economies which were slower than that experienced earlier in the post-war period, and the projection of slower growth into the future. There has been some tendency for the rate of growth to be lower over the past 30 years or so. Bergeaud et al. (2015) review per capita GDP for 17 industrialized countries over the period 1890 to 2013. They note that 'almost all countries have suffered from a significant decline in GDP per capita growth during the last decades of the period'. Syverson (2016) considers specifically the slowdown in US productivity growth and explanations. He notes though that 'several studies have noted recent productivity slowdowns in other economically advanced countries . . . Furthermore, Cette et al. (2015) document that, as in the U.S., these slowdowns began before the 2008–2009 financial crisis and recession'. How far the financial crisis has reinforced these tendencies remains to be seen, though growth over the past decade has been remarkably slow in many countries. The theme of secular stagnation has been raised; this can be viewed as a combination of the prospect of slower growth and a tendency for investment requirements to fall short of savings.[1]

The second (and more important) reason comes from ecological and environmental concerns which question the sustainability of the pace of economic growth (even at the somewhat lower rates seen in many industrialized countries before the global financial crisis) through the impacts on the ecological footprint, carbon use and climate change, and the need for slower growth (and many other measures) to address those environmental concerns. Antal (2014), for example, notes that:

> on a global level, past economic growth has been accompanied by increasingly serious environmental problems including climate change, various types of pollution, and the loss of biodiversity and ecosystems . . . If economic growth continues, these are calls for fast and sustained decoupling between GDP and environmental projects. Whether sufficient fast decoupling is feasible is central for sustainability: if not, then output growth is unsustainable.

We do not enter into debates here on whether the growth patterns can be reconfigured to be compatible with environmental sustainability nor with question of how slow growth would need to be to be environmentally sustainable. Instead we focus on the macroeconomic analysis of slow growth (though there are some remarks on the zero-growth case). Further, we do not enquire into how a lower growth rate could be achieved nor how investment would be brought into line with that required for lower and sustainable growth, but rather focus on the macroeconomic consequences of slower growth and lower investment.

The paper considers some rather simple macroeconomic relationships, with a view to indicating the direction of economic policies if slower growth is to be compatible with high levels of gainful employment. The objective of full employment is viewed as a, if not the major, one for macroeconomic policies, recognizing that some attention has to be paid to the definition of full employment and the social conditioning of that notion, which is undertaken below. Hence a key concern here is whether slower growth is potentially compatible with full employment.

One of the key starting points is that when the (trend) rate of growth of output is lower, then the (trend) rate of growth of the capital stock would be similarly lower, and hence the rate of investment (relative to output) would also be lower. A lower rate of investment has implications for the level of output (relative to capacity), distribution of income, rate of profits and consumer expenditure. It then readily follows that macroeconomic policies have to be considered. It is argued that the prospects of lower growth would lead to firms undertaking lower rates of investment which, in the absence of government actions, would lead to unemployment. It is also argued that lower rates of profit and of interest accompany slower growth. Monetary policy would need to be deployed to achieve lower interest rate. The thrust of the argument here is that slower growth and lower investment rate require the opposite of austerity programmes with the expansion of budget deficits and of public services (and more generally of social services provided by a range of non-profit organizations). The role of state policies is examined in terms of a greater role for public expenditure and budget deficit to underpin full employment, and the redirection of investment in ways which are consistent with environmental concerns and with the restoration of full employment.

In this paper the term output is viewed in terms of a modified GDP. There should be no inference drawn that GDP as currently measured is a good indicator of economic welfare. Output uses resources and depletes natural resources and the environment and whether it is socially useful is not considered here. GDP is generally limited to what may be termed market activities, and to activities which are undertaken outside the household. Here output should be viewed in terms of the addition of a range of non-market activities, and employment corresponding, though including non-market labour employment.

The relationship between output and (un)employment is often summarized in terms of 'Okun's Law' with notions that a 1 percentage point change in unemployment would be associated with the order of 2 to 3 percentage changes in output in the original formulation (Okun, 1962), with rather smaller effects found in the meta-study of Perman et al. (2015). Those authors review two types of study: those which 'use first difference (with output and unemployment variables expressed in first differences)' and 'gap model (with output and unemployment variables expressed in terms of the cyclical components or deviations from long-term trends)'. Okun's Law, as currently interpreted, is located within a particular theoretical framework with long-term trends unaffected by short-term events, and generally assumes an unchanging relationship between unemployment rate and employment rate. Although Okun's Law is often invoked to suggest that growth is required to sustain low unemployment, that is a misreading of Okun's Law which relates to levels of output and unemployment, as nothing can be inferred from Okun's Law on growth and unemployment. As Antal (2014) notes, the textbook version of Okun's Law 'says that every 2% deviation of economic growth from its average value (approximately 3%) corresponds to –1% change in the rate of unemployment'. This illustrates that Okun's Law is a cyclical relationship, and not a long-term one, and in terms of the quote from Antal would tell us nothing if the average rate of economic growth were lower (or higher).

The relationships between investment and unemployment can point in different directions. One line of argument is that investment adding to the capital stock is a substitution of capital for labour, thereby raising unemployment. In our approach the possibilities of substitution are viewed as limited, and the emphasis placed on investment as a component of aggregate demand, and thereby having a positive effect on employment. Smith and Zoega (2009) remark that 'the investment–unemployment relationship does not hold a prominent place in most of the explanations and models put forward for persistently high unemployment'. But 'the macroeconomic data show a strong medium- to long-term relationship between investment and unemployment', and then continue to indicate some of the nature of the evidence. They also indicate that this type of evidence 'has led Blanchard (2000) to label the medium-run relationship between investment and unemployment, which is very obvious in the data as the 'Modigliani Puzzle' (see also Modigliani, 2000)'. The relationship is such that higher investment goes alongside lower unemployment, and this also runs counter to notions that capital acts as a substitute for labour such that higher capital stock involves lower employment and higher unemployment.

In the macroeconomic analysis which follows, and specifically with regard to the links between unemployment rate and the rate of investment, we use a post-Keynesian/Kaleckian perspective with the focus on conditions of demand. A lower rate of investment involving a lower level of demand is associated with a high rate of unemployment: in other words, the level of economic activity would adjust to bring savings and investment into line. The other side of that coin is the rejection of neo-classical ideas that adjustment in prices, whether that of real wages or interest rate, could ensure equality between desired savings and investment compatible with full employment.

The simple macroeconomics of slower growth

The macroeconomic analysis is set in a monetary production economy. Investment plans and other expenditure plans can be brought to fruition through the availability of money created by central bank and by the banking system. Here we do not set out the determinants of investment expenditures (though see Fontana and Sawyer, 2016, for such); rather the focus is on investment and its relationship with output.

Capacity utilization

The national income accounts identity provides:

$$S = I + BD + NX \tag{1}$$

Gross investment is labelled I, private gross savings S, and budget deficit BD (equal government expenditure minus tax revenue) and NX net exports including net income. Investment requirements are taken to be related with the growth of capacity output and depreciation, i.e.:

$$I = (v\Delta Y^* + dK) \tag{2}$$

where v is capital–capacity output ratio, Δ used to signify a difference in following variable, Y^* capacity output, K a measure of the capital stock and d the rate of depreciation. The capital–capacity output ratio is treated as constant for the purposes of analysis with a set of fixed coefficient production functions assumed, and hence no substitutability between the factors of production. Specifically it is assumed that the factor proportions would not respond to changes in relative prices. The average capital–capacity output could though be expected to shift over time depending on sectoral shifts of production and on the nature of technical change. But the direction of such shifts does not depend on relative prices, and may well depend on research and development policies on the nature of technical change. In so far as the sectoral shifts are in the direction of services, there may be a tendency for the capital–output ratio to decline, which would further lower investment requirements.

This equation for investment is the trend level of investment, and over the long haul the highest sustainable rate of investment in that a faster rate of investment than that indicated by equation (2) would involve a falling capacity utilization, a rising capital–actual output ratio and a tendency to a falling rate of profit and hence unsustainable. The level of actual investment fluctuates over time, and is dependent on perceived incentives, state of confidence and 'animal spirits', and banks' willingness to provide loans. The level of investment indicated by equation (2) may not be achieved through a lack of banks' willingness to provide loans to finance investment and/or through low 'animal spirits'.

Gross savings is the sum of net savings taken to be a proportion s of income plus depreciation, and hence gross savings = $sY + dK$, with an autonomous component of consumer expenditure and budget deficit taken as proportional to income, i.e. $b.Y$, and net exports also proportional to income, $x.Y$. Then equation (1) becomes:

$$sY + d.v.Y^* = vDY^* + d.v.Y^* + b.Y + x.Y, \tag{3}$$

and then

$$(s - b - x).u = v.g \tag{4}$$

where u is capacity utilization and g is the growth of capacity output.

Equation (4) can be rearranged to give $g = (s - b - x).u/v$, which in the absence of a budget deficit and net exports and capacity utilization of 1 would give the result $g = s/v$: a well-known formula corresponding to Harrod's warranted rate of growth (and the same formula comes from the Solow neo-classical growth model, albeit with the growth rate equal to the 'natural' rate of growth and v being a variable which adjusts). This is an algebraic relationship relating to the conditions for steady growth: it does not tell us whether such a growth rate will be achieved, or whether actual investment behaviour, for example, would be consistent with this growth rate. It is also known from the Harrod-based literature that this type of warranted growth rate may be somewhat unstable.

The first clear implication coming from equation (4) is that a lower rate of growth (whether coming from slower growth of population, of productivity or the need to adjust to ecological constraints) would tend to translate into a lower rate of capacity utilization. A lower trend growth rate and the associated lower rate of investment then imply, *ceteris paribus*, a lower rate of capacity utilization (which together with a constant capital–capacity output ratio gives a higher capital to achieved output ratio).

The tendency to lower capacity utilization (and higher unemployment) from lower growth can potentially be offset in various ways. In the framework adopted here four possibilities stand out. The first is that net exports increase, but that clearly is not an option available to all countries, and is not further discussed. The second is the use of budget deficits, the third the adjustment of the savings propensity and fourth the capital–output ratio, and we now discuss those in turn.

The implications for budget deficits are straightforward. In the face of slower growth and investment requirements, higher budget deficits would be needed as part of seeking to maintain high levels of capacity utilization; and it means the rejection of fiscal policies which seek the lock-in of balanced budgets. The budget deficit is the overall budget position, i.e. primary budget position and interest payments on the government debt as this is the one relevant for the demand side of the economy. It is well known that such a deficit position (relative to GDP) will lead the outstanding debt converging on a ratio to GDP of $b/(g + p)$ where b is the budget deficit ratio to GDP, g (real) growth rate and p rate of inflation. The budget deficit is, of course, the difference between government expenditure and tax revenues. It could be anticipated that slower growth would lead to lower requirements for public investment, and in so far as higher budget deficit involves higher expenditure rather than lower tax revenues, this would involve a rise in consumption expenditure, albeit undertaken by the government.

The rate of capacity utilization could be maintained under conditions of slower growth with an appropriate downward adjustment to the savings ratio, as can be seen from equation (4). In effect, lower investment rate could be matched by a lower savings propensity to maintain high rate of capacity utilization. There are though no straightforward mechanisms, such as a change in the rate of interest, which would diminish the tendency to save. Savings (and dissavings) could be viewed as driven by two rather different forces. The first is household saving particularly related to pension provision, and as such depends on demographics and on the extent of unfunded state provision. The second is corporate savings and in so far as internal funding requirements for investment are diminished, corporations may reduce their retained earnings and hence distribute a higher level of dividends. What is though apparent is that slower growth would need to go alongside the discouragement of savings rather than encouragement. But that should be done in a way which does not create unsustainable debt, as one way through which household savings is reduced is when some households to go into debt.

There is a more benign way to reduce the propensity to save, and that is through the redistribution of income from profits and rents to wages, and the reduction of income inequality in general. It is generally the case that the overall propensity to save out of profits (combining savings in the form of retained earnings by corporations and savings out of dividends) is greater than the propensity to save out of wages. Similarly, the propensity to save by the rich is higher than that of the poor. Hence, the mentioned shifts in the distribution of income would tend to reduce the propensity to save.[2]

It should be then noted that lower growth would be associated with a lower national savings ratio, whether through lower private savings (s in the equations) or through public dissavings (budget deficit). Expenditure on consumption of goods and services, whether private or public, would be higher. Further useful consumption could be higher as resources whose use is not recorded as investment but whose deployment is related with growth, notably advertising, marketing and other forms of consumption promotion, would be released for other uses.

This discussion has overtones of that of Kalecki (1944) on 'three ways to full employment', where he promoted budget deficits and income redistribution as suitable ways, and indicated the limitations of promoting investment.

The fourth adjustment factor to be considered relates to the capital–(capacity) output ratio. Equation (4) indicates that a higher capital–output ratio would involve higher capacity utilization (for a given rate of growth). It would seem unlikely that there will be adjustment processes by which capital–output ratio would rise in the face of slower growth.

There is little reason to think that the changes in savings rate and the capital–output ratio which would be required to maintain capacity utilization would come about through market processes (we come to the employment issue shortly). It is being assumed here that the capital–(capacity) output is largely technically determined and is not significantly influenced by relative prices (of capital equipment and labour). Obviously the capital–(capacity) output ratio varies between sectors and as technology and the composition of output change, the capital–output ratio would be affected.

Unemployment

The rates of unemployment and of employment are of more direct social concern than the rate of capacity utilization, and our interest lies in the possibilities for the achievement of full employment. The move from discussion in terms of the rate of capacity utilization to (un)employment rates can be readily set out. The relationship between employment, measured in terms of person hours, E and output Q is expressed as $E = A(t)Q$ where $A(t)$ is a technically determined ratio at time t (and for convenience a constant employment–output ratio with respect to relative prices is assumed).

The employment rate is then given by:

$$E/Ef = A(t)\ (Q/Q^*).(Q^*/E^*).(E^*/Ef) = (Q/Q^*).(E^*/Ef) = u.(E^*/Ef) \quad (5)$$

where Ef is the socially accepted view of full employment, capacity utilization, and E/Ef could be thought of as the employment rate, $u = Q/Q^*$ (Q^* capacity output), Q^*/E^* is labour productivity ($=A(t)$), assuming labour productivity is not dependent on the rate of capacity utilization) and E^*/Ef is ratio of 'capacity employment' to 'full employment'. Unemployment rate is then given by $1 - (E/Ef)$. The achievement of what may be regarded as full employment depends on an appropriate level of demand which would be reflected in the capacity utilization term in the above equation, and on 'capacity employment' which reflects the productive capacity of the economy. Clearly, reaching anything approaching full employment requires the appropriate level of demand (reflected in u) and of capacity (reflected in E^*). The employment rate is then dependent on rate of capacity utilization, which, as discussed above, would be lower under slower growth unless compensated by changes in budget position and/or savings ratio. The other factor which comes in depends on the size of productive capacity, as reflected in the ratio of capacity employment to full employment.

It has been argued above that in the face of slower growth and lower investment, fiscal policy (in the form of budget deficit) should be a major instrument for securing a high rate of capacity utilization, and that argument carries over to securing full employment. The budget deficit is, of course, the difference between government expenditure and tax revenues. From the perspective of aggregate demand, it is the scale of the budget deficit which is relevant, and we would argue that the overall scale of public expenditure and of tax revenues is a matter of political choice relating to the role of the state and its size. However, the focus of attention has generally been on the role of public expenditure in the creation of jobs. In the context of slower growth and of the need for environmental protection, there can be plenty of suggestions for the ways in which public expenditure can provide socially useful services as well as employment opportunities. Alcott (2013), for example, examines the role of 'job guarantee' under a situation of degrowth through the provision of employment by government. The argument deployed here is that the achievement of full employment in the context of slower growth would require the development of sufficient capacity (reflected in E^*) and the achievement of high levels of demand (reflected in u). A slower rate of growth would yield through lower investment requirements a higher rate of unemployment unless offset by fiscal policy and/or adjustments to savings behaviour. But the other side of that argument is that fiscal policy, whether through increased public expenditure on socially useful projects or through reduced taxation, is able to overcome any tendencies to unemployment. The budget deficit so required to enable full employment would be sustainable over time, as indicated above (provided there is positive nominal growth).

Defining full employment

The employment rate (and thereby what may be regarded as the unemployment rate) could be addressed by changing the notion of what constitutes a fully employed labour force.

What would constitute a fully employed labour force is never a straightforward matter.[3]

It can be readily agreed that 'everyone has the right to work, to free choice of employment, to just and favourable conditions of work and to protection against unemployment' (UN, 1948), though who is included in 'everyone' is not specified, e.g. from what age. The other side of this is, though. who does society deem to have to work in order to have an income? That is, to whom would society provide support, noting that support here includes inheritance of wealth, family members, charity as well as social security?

First, the notion of employment should not be limited to paid employment but also include unpaid work. Notable here would be the inclusion of care work of the young, the elderly and the infirm. There are inevitably 'boundary issues' – would, for example, food preparation within the home be included as unpaid work on the basis that similar tasks carried out in a restaurant would be included as employment? However, with the inclusion of unpaid work as part of employment, it would also be necessary to include non-market activities as part of output.

On the other side, seeking to define how many persons and how many hours worked would constitute full employment is problematic as it comes from an interaction of social and legal norms and pressures and individual choices. The neo-classical approach is to derive labour supply decisions from individual utility maximization (subject to budget constraint) with little regard to social norms.

A reduction in working time is often advocated in response to slower growth and to environmental concerns as a means of alleviating unemployment. This assumes that people treat a reduction in working time as more leisure and not as enforced underemployment. Consider now proposals to reduce working time, whether through shorter week or working lifetime. It is only possible here to give a broad-brush approach. In doing so it is assumed that there remains a given relationship between output and employment hours, and hence shorter working time would be broadly matched by reduction of output of the same proportion. It is also assumed that shorter working time does not change the relationship between capital stock and capacity output.[4] Shorter working time is equivalent to a reduction in Ef. In the simple equation above, whether a reduction in Ef leads to an increase in the employment rate depends on the balance between E^* and Ef. This can be thought of in the following way: a reduction in Ef reduces the scale of the economy (in terms of labour supply), but does not change the equivalent of equation (4). The reduction in working time could lead to a higher employment if either there was a rise in the E^*/Ef ratio or if there was a consequent change in one of the parameters in equation (4), and specifically if the savings ratio fell and hence the consumption ratio rose.

The focus here is on the growth of output with its effects on investment and employment, and the division of that growth between growth of employment (measured in person hours) and the growth of (labour) productivity left to one side. There can be interplay between the growth rate of output and the growth of labour productivity as, for example, postulated in Verdoorn's Law, whereby higher demand fosters labour productivity growth. The ways in which the benefits of productivity growth are shared between growth of output and growth (generally negative) of person hours worked are viewed as a broad societal choice on which we do not comment further here.

The obvious proposition which flows from this is that slower growth and lower investment (relative to GDP) would lead to a lower employment and higher unemployment rate unless it is offset by appropriate government policies. The use of fiscal policy in the shape of a budget deficit would be needed to sustain the level of employment. In demand terms the appropriate measure of budget deficit is the total deficit including interest payments, and as such the debt ratio to GDP would converge to deficit divided by nominal growth rate. Growth of output of less than the growth of labour productivity would lead to rising unemployment unless there are variations in the working lifetime which are socially acceptable. A person's working lifetime which is shortened by involuntary unemployment is not socially acceptable.

In a zero-growth case (assuming no population growth and no inflation), then net national savings would fall to zero along with net investment, which further implies that the budget deficit would be zero (leaving aside the foreign sector). There would still be a need for some form of financial sector which in effect recycles depreciation allowances since, although net investment would be zero, there would still be gross investment to maintain the capital stock. Similarly, although overall savings would be zero, there would be some groups saving (e.g. those of working age) and some dissaving (e.g. those of retirement age), though clearly there are alternative mechanisms for pension provision such as those provided by a pay-as-you-go pension scheme.

Full employment is seen as the general idea that the number without meaningful work is equal to the number of vacancies (and there is no significant long-term unemployment). Further, individuals are working the hours they wish to work (in light of wages and social norms) and there is not underemployment and disguised unemployment. The decisions to seek employment and how many hours to work are often represented as coming from individual utility maximization. This is not an approach to be followed and it has to be recognized that decisions and choices are socially conditioned. Employment and work should be interpreted to include work outside the labour market as well as paid work in the labour market. The concepts of what constitutes employment and what unemployment need much greater attention than we can give here. Nevertheless the essential point is that the reorganization of the economy alongside appropriate macroeconomic policies is required to ensure that sustainable growth at a slower rate does not lead to substantial unemployment and degradation of individuals. Further, the hours worked (in terms of annual hours and length of working life) would be adjusted so that in effect higher labour productivity is taken in terms of working time reduction rather than higher output. This would help with work/life balance and also enable work to be spread more evenly rather than many working long hours and others having no work at all.

The simple relationships outlined in this section are used to express one simple idea. There are conditions which would need to be satisfied if slower growth is to be combined with full employment (which is treated as socially determined). Those conditions will not be fulfilled through the operation of market mechanisms. Savings and lower investment will not be aligned at high-capacity utilization through some interest rate adjustments, and require the intervention of budget deficits. Sufficient capacity to cater for full employment will not be provided by 'leaving it to the market' (and the capacity has to be in the 'right places'). The adjustment of the size of the workforce such that full employment can be maintained does not come through wage adjustments but rather through changes in working time and length of working life, for which there has to be collective action and changes in social norms of behaviour.

Rate of profit, rate of interest and the rate of growth

The effects of a slower rate of growth extend beyond those on capacity utilization and employment, and in this section we consider effects and interrelationships with rate of profit and rate of interest.

Rate of profit

Post-Keynesian and Kaleckian macroeconomic analysis has emphasized the role of the distribution of income between wages and profits for aggregate demand and the significance of profits for investment and developed links between the rate of growth and the rate of profit. Savings are treated in terms of differential savings out of wages and out of profits. This reflects the view that wages and profits have different functions. Wages are a payment for labour, and through various social norms the vast bulk of wages are spent on consumption. At the individual level, there will be savings out of wages for life-cycle reasons, but that turns into pensions which are largely spent, and for individual workers over their lifetime wages are largely spent. At the aggregate level, the dissaving by retired workers largely offset saving by active workers, leaving overall savings out of wages close to zero. Profits accrue to corporations, a high proportion of which are saved (retained earnings). Thus consider the savings out of profits to be substantially greater than savings out of wages. Some rather simple but powerful conclusions can be derived from a model based on these propositions.

In a closed private-sector economy, from the savings–investment equation, with differential savings out of wages (*W*) and out of profits (*P*):

$$NI = s_p P + s_w W \tag{6}$$

where *NI* is net investment (and hence savings treated in net terms), with investment treated as the driving force. The rate of profit is then given by:

$$P/K = [g_K - (s_w u/v)]/[s_p - s_w] \tag{7}$$

where g_K is growth of capital stock equal to *I/K*, *u* is capacity utilization and *v* capital–output ratio (hence $u/v = Y/K$). With the 'classical savings function' of no savings out of wages, this equation reduces to the 'Cambridge equation' of gK = s_p.rate of profit. The particular significance of this type of equation is that a lower growth rate (of output and of the capital stock) would be associated with a lower rate of profit.

As the terms in the equations above are net of depreciation, there would still be gross profits equal to depreciation, assumed then to be used to fund replacement investment. There is the possibility that there will be response of savings behaviour to a lower rate of growth, and in particular as corporate savings may be undertaken in order to internal fund investment, the propensity to save out of profits would fall. The rate of profit could then be maintained in the face of lower growth through lower corporate savings: higher dividend payments feed through into higher consumption.

A particularly interesting case arises in the case of zero growth, and hence zero net investment requirements. In the 'Cambridge equation' case, the rate of profit would fall to zero. When there is savings out of wages, the implications of equation (6) would be for the rate of profit to become negative: however, it would have to be recognized that under zero growth, savings out of wages could well fall to zero.

Now introducing the public sector and modifying equations (5) and (6) for budget deficit (expressed relative to the capital stock as $b.u/v$) would yield:

$$P/K = [g_K + b.u/v - (s_w u/v)]/[s_p - s_w] \tag{8}$$

and a similar adjustment could be used to incorporate foreign trade. This equation replicates a well-known proposition that budget deficit (and net exports) has a similar impact on the rate of profit as investment. Equation (7) in effect presents a menu of choices by which the rate of profit could be maintained in circumstances of lower growth. The two obvious ones are the use of budget deficits as a means of absorbing the savings out of profits and a decline in savings out of profits.

In the case of zero growth, equation (7) implies that a budget deficit would be required for there to be a positive rate of profit (even if savings out of wages were zero). However under conditions of zero growth a budget deficit would lead to continually rising debt relative to output (whereas under positive growth the debt–output ratio would converge on deficit–output ratio divided by nominal growth rate).

Rate of interest

A slower rate of growth would have implications also for the (real) rate of interest. In general, by the rate of interest here is meant what is deemed to be rate of interest on what is regarded as a risk-free financial asset such as government bonds; other rates of interest would be higher.

The work of Piketty (2014) focused on one significant issue arising from the relationship between the rate of growth and the rate of interest (though he refers more generally to the rate of return on wealth).[5] Piketty (2014) placed central importance on the implications of the excess of the rate of return on wealth over the rate of growth for the evolution of inequality of wealth and the wealth–income ratio. Wealth can increase at the pace of the rate of return on wealth if the propensity to save out of rentier income is unity; and more generally, wealth can increase faster than income if $s.r > g$ where r is the rate of return on wealth and s is propensity to save out of rentier income based on wealth. A substantial gap between growth rate and of return on wealth will lead to rising wealth–income ratio and rising inequality of wealth. This has overtones of the argument examined above with regard to the rate of profit.

There are a range of arguments coming from different theoretical positions which suggest that the rate of interest and the rate of growth either should be, or generally are, closely aligned. It can be first noted that Taylor's (1993) original rule for monetary policy for setting the central bank policy interest rate was that 'the 2-percent "equilibrium" real rate is close to the assumed steady-state growth rate of 2.2 percent' (p. 202).

The 'golden rule of capital accumulation' in the framework of a neo-classical model with the marginal productivity of capital equal to the interest rate generates the equality of the rate of interest and the rate of growth (for the achievement of optimality in that framework) (Phelps, 1967).

Pasinetti (1981) speaks of a 'fair rate of interest', which leaves 'unchanged the distribution of income between interest and non-interest income groups, regardless of lending and borrowing activities' (Lavoie and Seccareccia, 1999, p. 543).

> Under these conditions, an amount of money equivalent to one hour of labor time, if lent at that normal [fair] rate of interest, will still be worth one hour of labor time when recovered with its interest payments. The purchasing power of the rentier will increase if the productivity of the overall economy has increased. The relative situation of the rentiers in the social hierarchy stays the same, whatever the economic conditions.
>
> (Lavoie, 1996, p. 537)

The 'fair rate of interest' is a normative rule which some have advocated as a guide for the central bank interest rate-setting procedures.[6] It takes on further significance when pension arrangements are considered and when the rentiers are workers and former workers with accumulated financial assets relating to pension provision. The 'fair rate' of interest (or more generally, rate of return) would be one which in effect preserves (in relative terms) pension contributions. A set of funded pension arrangements (and more generally intergenerational transfers) in which a pensioner cohort would receive in relative (to GDP) terms equal to what had been saved into the funds would involve a rate of return on savings equal to the rate of growth. This is in effect a rate of interest which in Pasinetti's terms is a 'fair rate' of interest (Pasinetti, 1981).

These and other arguments point in the direction of a slower growth rate alongside lower rates of interest, with something approaching equality between the growth rate and the risk-free interest rate (as, for example, on government bonds). What is missing are the mechanisms by which a lower set of interest rates would be achieved, though, as discussed in Rochon and Setterfield (2007), the central bank would have a key role in the setting of a low policy interest rate.

The setting of the interest rate has some clear and obvious implications for fiscal policy. The sustainability of a budget deficit depends on the level of interest rates (and specifically the post-tax interest rate on government bonds, rt). If that rate is less than the growth rate, then any primary budget deficit of d (relative to GDP) would lead to an eventual debt ratio (to GDP) of $b = d/(g - rt)$ (where g and rt are either both in real terms or both in nominal terms). If $rt > g$ then a primary budget deficit would lead to a growing debt ratio. In a similar vein, a continuing total budget deficit of d (including interest payments) leads to the debt–GDP ratio stabilizing at d'/g, where here g is in nominal terms. This implies that $b + rd = gd$, i.e., $b = (g - r)d$, and hence if g is less than r the primary budget deficit is negative (i.e. the primary budget is in surplus). The case where $g = r$ is of particular interest. Pasinetti (1998, p. 163) remarks that this case represents the 'golden rule' of capital accumulation. In this case, the public budget can be permanently in deficit and the public debt can thereby increase indefinitely, but national income increases at the same rate (g) so that the D/Y ratio remains constant. Another way of looking at this case is to say that the government budget has a deficit, which is wholly due to interest payments.

Concluding remarks

There are two basic arguments in this paper. The first is that slower economic growth and the associated lower levels of investment do not necessarily involve unemployment. In contrast, it is relatively easy to write down the conditions under which higher unemployment would not be involved. It is much more difficult to ensure that those conditions are met. There is an absence of what could be termed market adjustment processes which would yield full employment. This has pointed to roles for fiscal policy and for a redistribution policy. The second is that slower growth will likely involve a lower rate of profit and a lower rate of interest, and policies (here monetary policies) should be geared towards securing a lower rate of interest.

Notes

1 This is reflected in our approach below. However, the mainstream perspective is that the investment schedule and the savings schedule do not interest at a positive rate of interest. For a range of discussions on secular stagnation, see Teulings and Baldwin (2014).
2 The wage-led vs. profit-led literature has emphasized the role of the distribution of income (as between wages and profits) on the level of demand and thereby the level of economic activity. Within that literature there has generally been support for the view that a shift from wages to profits lowers economic activity (see, for example, Lavoie and Stockhammer (2013). In Sawyer (2011), I used that notion to argue that a progressive way to reduce budget deficit is to reduce inequality and shift the distribution of income away from profits towards wages.
3 We use here the term fully employed labour force. What constitutes full employment is not necessarily the employment of the fully employed labour force, for it is recognized that there is some turnover within employment, and full employment would be more akin to a situation where the number seeking work is equal to the number of job vacancies (elsewhere I added also that no one seeking work should be unemployed for more than say 6 months).
4 A reduction in working time which meant that capital equipment was employed for less time per week could imply a rise in the capital–capacity output ratio.
5 See, amongst many others, Sawyer (2015) for a critique of Piketty (2014).
6 For extensive discussion, see Rochon and Setterfield (2007).

References

Alcott, B. (2013), 'Should degrowth embrace the job guarantee?', *Journal of Cleaner Production*, 38, pp. 56–60.

Antal, M. (2014), 'Green goals and full employment: are they compatible?', *Ecological Economics*, 107, pp. 276–286.

Bergeaud, A., Cette, G. and Lecat, R. (2015), *GDP Per Capita in Advanced Countries over the 20th Century*, Working Paper, 549, Paris, Banque de France.

Blanchard, O. (2000), *The Economics of Unemployment: Shocks, Institutions, and Interactions*, Lionel Robbins Lectures, Cambridge, MA: MIT Press.

Cette, G., Fernald, J., and Mojon, B. (2015), *The Pre-global Financial-crisis Slowdown in Productivity'*, Working Paper, Paris, Banque de France.

Fontana, G., and Sawyer, M. (2016), 'Towards post-Keynesian ecological macroeconomics', *Ecological Economics*, 121, pp. 186–195, http://dx.doi.org/10.1016/j.ecolecon.2015.03.017.

Kalecki, M. (1944), 'Three ways to full employment' in *Oxford University Institute of Statistics, The Economics of Full Employment*, Oxford: Blackwell.

Lavoie, M. (1996), 'Monetary policy in an economy with endogenous credit money' in E. Nell and G. Deleplace (eds), *Money in Motion*, London: Macmillan, pp. 532–545.

Lavoie, M. and Seccareccia, M. (1999), 'Interest rate: fair' in P. O'Hara (ed.), *Encyclopedia of Political Economy*, vol. 1, London: Routledge, pp. 543–545.

Lavoie, M. and Stockhammer, E. (eds) (2013), *Wage-led Growth: an Equitable Strategy for Economic Recovery*, Houndmills: Palgrave Macmillan.

Modigliani, F. (2000), Europe's economic problems. Prepared for testimony before the Monetary Committee of the European Central Bank.

Okun, A. (1962), 'Potential GNP: its measurement and significance', *Proceedings of the Business and Economic Statistics Section of the American Statistical Association*, pp. 98–104.

Pasinetti, L. (1981), *Structural Change and Economic Growth: A Theoretical Essay on the Dynamics of the Wealth of Nations*, Cambridge: Cambridge University Press.

Pasinetti, L. (1998), 'The myth (or folly) of the 3% deficit-GDP Maastricht "parameter"', *Cambridge Journal of Economics*, 22, pp. 103–116.

Perman, R., Stephan, G. and Tavéra, C. (2015), 'Okun's Law—a meta-analysis', *The Manchester School*, 83(1), pp. 101–126.

Phelps, E. (1967),*Golden Rules of Economic Growth*, New York: Norton.

Piketty, T. (2014), *Capital in the 21st Century*, translated by A. Goldhammer, Cambridge, MA: Harvard University Press.

Rochon, L.-P. and Setterfield, M. (2007), 'Interest rate, income distribution, and monetary policy dominance: post Keynesians and the "fair rate" of interest', *Journal of Post Keynesian Economics*, 30(1), pp. 13–42.

Sawyer, M. (2011), 'Progressive approaches to budget deficits', in O. Onaran, T. Niechoj, E. Stockhammer, A. Truger, and T. van Treeck (eds), *Stabilising an Unequal Economy? Public Debt, Financial Regulation, and Income Distribution*, Marburg: Metropolis Verlag, pp. 143–159.

Sawyer, M. (2015), 'Confronting inequality: review article on Thomas Piketty on 'Capital in the 21st century',' *International Review of Applied Economics*, 29(6), pp. 878–889.

Smith, R. and Zoega, G. (2009), 'Keynes, investment, unemployment and expectations', *International Review of Applied Economics*, 23(4), pp. 427–444, doi:10.1080/02692170902954767

Syverson, C. (2016), 'Challenges to mismeasurement explanations for the U.S. productivity slow-down', NBER Working Paper w21974, Cambridge, MA, National Bureau of Economic Research.

Taylor, J. (1993), 'Discretion vs. policy rules in practice', *Carnegie-Rochester Conference Series on Public Policy*, 39, pp. 195–214.

Teulings, C. and Baldwin, R. (eds) (2014), *Secular Stagnation: Facts, Causes, and Cures*, VoxEu.org eBook, London: CEPR Press.

UN. (1948), Universal Declaration of Human Rights. Available at: http://www.un.org/en/documents/udhr (accessed 10 September 2016).

4 Welfare capitalism versus financial capitalism during globalisation[1]

Pasquale Tridico

Financial capitalism

In the last two decades, in parallel with the globalisation process, a process of financialisation of the economy in advanced economies took place. Financialisation is defined in several ways by scholars from the political sciences, sociology and economics. Most of these definitions, however, converge towards the identification of the financialisation process in a political economy phenomenon where there is a growing dominance of capital financial systems over bank-based financial systems (Krippner, 2005), or more broadly, the increasing role of financial motives, financial markets, financial actors and financial institutions in the operation of domestic and international economies (Epstein, 2005: 3–4). This process culminated, according to the Bank for International Settlements, in about 2 trillion dollars each day of volume of foreign exchange transactions in 2006, just before the crisis. This is more or less the gross domestic product (GDP) of a country the size of France. In contrast, in 1989, this volume was about 500 billion dollars per day.

The political and economic roots of the financialisation process, that brought about a new financial-led growth regime under the process of globalisation, identified also as financial capitalism, can be found in the 1970s. However, they were manifested openly politically in the 1980s. The financial sector has been an early and eager promoter of deregulation in the 1980s in the UK and the USA under the Thatcher and Reagan administrations (Boyer, 2000; Petit, 2009), respectively, which Jessop (2002) identifies as transition phases to the post-Fordist financial-led regime. Jessop (2002) argues that new accumulation strategies emerged during that period. They involved multinational firms, international financial discipline, a more authoritarian state and a form of popular capitalism. The previous Fordist strategy was replaced by an internationally oriented and financially aggressive strategy, deregulated and concentrated dually on Wall Street and in the City of London. Reaganomics and Thatcherism were strategies that aimed to restructure the accumulation system through the deregulation of the financial system (Peck and Tickell, 1992) at the expense of the social compromise realised after the Second World War. The result was uneven development (Peck and Tickell, 1992), with regions and countries divided between financial services and technology-oriented ones, and increasing trends in inequalities and income disparities, particularly in the USA and the UK, the countries which were keener on financialisation, as Figure 4.1 shows.

Moreover, after the fall of the Soviet Union, Alan Greenspan, who rose to oversee the US Federal Reserve during the Reagan administration, believed that the world economy could expand greatly through globalisation of the financial sector (Greenspan, 2007; Semmler and Young, 2010). Many other economies then followed the American example of a financial-led regime of accumulation, which used other institutional forms such as flexible labour and the nexus of compressed wages in order to increase firms' competitiveness under the condition of globalisation (Tridico, 2012). Shareholders sought higher dividends because they invested their own capital in firms, taking on a higher level of risk. Because economic growth and productivity of advanced economies in the post-Fordist market have not been greater than in the Fordist market, as Figure 4.1 shows, it follows that wages should be compressed in order for shareholders to obtain higher dividends. Labour flexibility and wage contraction were functional to obtain this result, at least in the short run.

Figure 4.2 shows the financialisation of the OECD economies since 1988. The variable of comparison here is the value of market capitalisation in the stock exchange as a percentage of GDP.[2] One can observe a huge increase among all the countries, particularly the USA, the UK, Switzerland, Australia and Canada. The highest percentage of financialisation in terms of GDP belongs to Switzerland. However, in terms of absolute value, the USA is the most financialised market, followed by the UK. The USA promoted neoliberalism as a main ideological paradigm for globalisation and financialisation through global, multilateral and bilateral measures under pressure from all the major international financial institutions, multinational corporations and Wall Street institutions (Epstein, 2005).

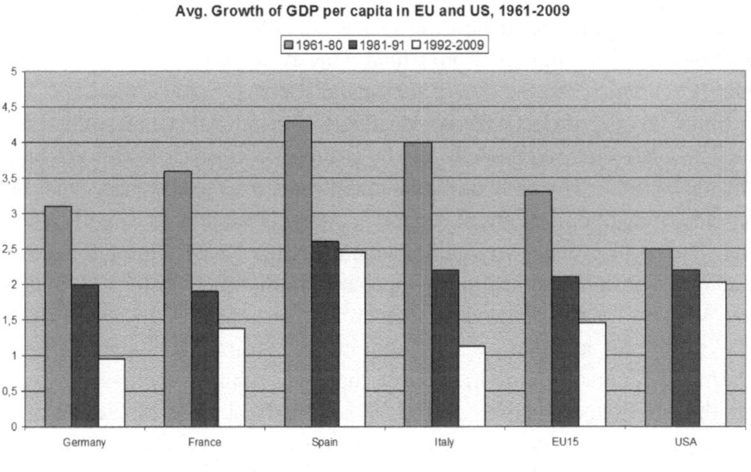

Figure 4.1 GDP growth in the EU and the USA

Source: Eurostat, online database: http://ec.europa.eu/eurostat

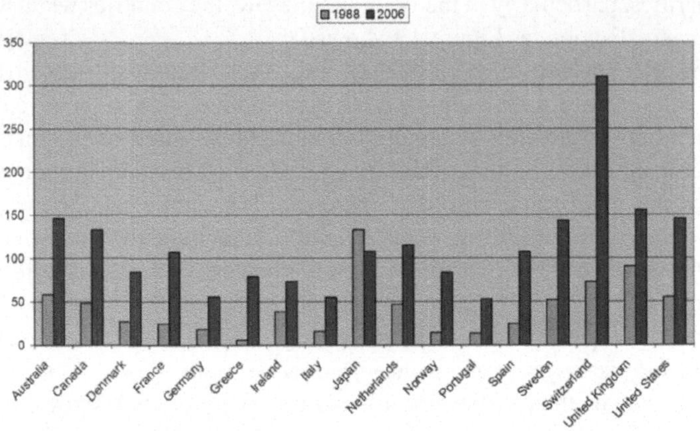

Figure 4.2 Financialisation: market value of listed companies in stock exchanges, 1988–2006 (% of GDP)

Source: World Bank (2010) Statistical Indicators (online database): www.worldbank.org

The trend of hyper-financialisation spread around the world, first to Europe and then to emerging markets. Financialisation is beneficial, Wall Street executives argued, to facilitate innovation and economic growth, despite a paucity of evidence supporting the claim. Quite the opposite is true, as clear evidence of a correlation between financialisation and inequality exists, manifested in the compressed wage share (Basili et al., 2006; Petit, 2009). Wages after the 1970s in advanced economies and particularly in the USA almost stagnated, and profits soared dramatically (EuroMemorandum, 2010; Tridico, 2012; Wolff, 2010). Simultaneously, inequality increased sharply (Engelen et al., 2008; OECD, 2010; Wolfson, 2010). In order to keep consumption up, the USA manoeuvred economic policies: it used cheap money, which allowed bubbles in the housing sector and private debt to soar and allowed a huge amount of cheap imports from China. This eventually produced a huge current account (CA) deficit: on the eve of the financial crisis in 2007, the US CA deficit was USbn$700 (5% of US GDP), of which 80% depended on Chinese exports (IMF, 2009). The USA financed the CA debt by issuing US bonds, which were bought in turn by the Chinese. The issue of global imbalances emerged strongly, and it is seen as a co-determinant of the current economic crisis (Obstfeld and Rogoff, 2009).

The sharing of productivity gains, which was the basis of the Fordist compromise, came to an end, and inequality increased dramatically, bringing about a need among workers for the demand of finance for consumption. In fact, income inequality is more marked than consumption inequality among advanced economies. In other words, consumption inequality, thanks to finance, increased by only 6% during the big financialisation period (1980–2007), despite the fact that, during the same period, income inequality increased by 23% (Tridico, 2012). This process, particularly in the USA, brought about a soaring of profits and a dramatic increase in finance compensation with respect to the rest of the economy (as shown by Figure 4.3).

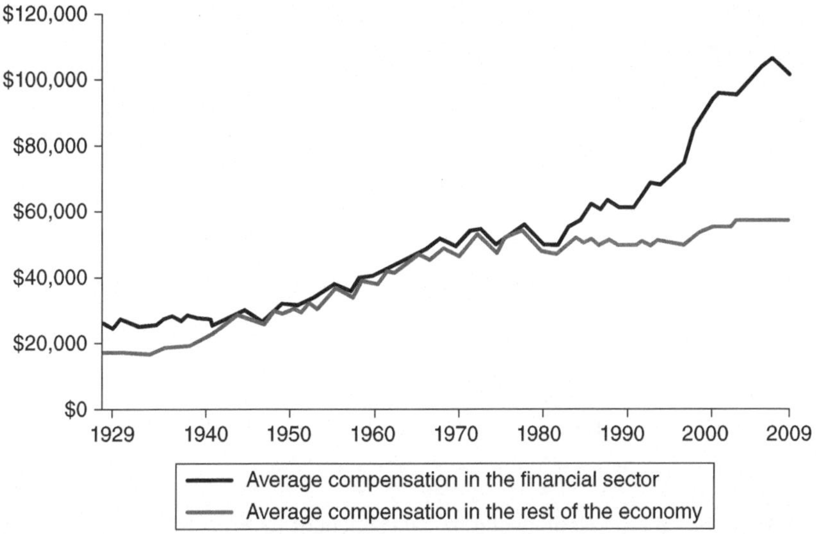

Figure 4.3 US average compensation

Source: Financial Crisis Inquiry Commission (2011)

In the financial sector, short-term results and stakeholder dividends are favoured over long-term results and productivity. The ratio between managers' compensation and the average wages of blue-collar workers increased steadily in the 1980s and in the 1990s. At the beginning of the last bubble in 2003, the ratio was 1 to 369, and at the eve of the financial crisis in 2007, it skyrocketed to 1 to 521 thanks to bonuses and compensation, which do not find a proper justification (ILO, 2010).

A similar process and a transition towards a financial-led post-Fordism regime, although less severe than in the USA and UK, are exhibited by other European countries, particularly in Mediterranean economies such as Italy and Spain (Jessop, 2002), where severe fiscal and monetary policies, along with industrial restructuring, generated precarious jobs and higher inequality, particularly since the 1990s (Fitoussi, 1992).

Wage shares declined dramatically, with negative consequences on the aggregate demand, as Figure 4.4 suggests. The figure reports the average data aggregate by group of countries. Anglo-Saxon economies (later included in the liberal competitive market economy model) and Mediterranean economies suffered the most from the restructuring process that occurred from the 1980s and intensified during the 1990s and 2000s.

Welfare states during globalisation

Globalisation, along with financialisation, poses several challenges to national economies and governments. One of the most important, as we will see below, is

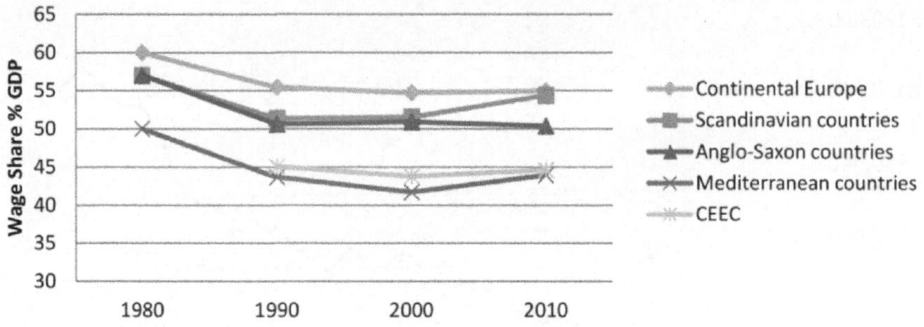

Figure 4.4 Wage share in advanced economies, unadjusted, 1980–2010, by group of countries

Source: Own elaboration on the ILO (2013)

Note: The unadjusted wage share is calculated as total labour compensation of employees divided by value added.

the pressure on labour relations and its consequences in terms of inequality, both within countries and between countries, and its impact on welfare-state sustainability (Hay and Wincott, 2012).

In this context, the debate is very lively, and it has produced two main interpretations of the problem. The first one states that globalisation reduces the share of welfare states because it constitutes a cost for firms. Higher levels of welfare states produce higher income tax levels, social costs and contributions, which reduce prospective profit and increase costs for firms. Firms would hence be pushed to go abroad unless government retrenched welfare-state spending and reduced taxes. Hence, in order to maintain higher levels of investments, firms and employment in the country, the welfare state needs to be reduced under the process of globalisation, with negative consequences for inequality. This interpretation is well known as 'the efficiency thesis'. This thesis was developed within the neoclassical (or neoliberal) paradigm, and it argues that globalisation has forced (or should force) states to retrench social welfare in order to achieve a market-friendly environment and attract increasingly mobile international capital and competitiveness (Allan & Scruggs, 2004; Blackmon, 2006; Castells, 2004).

The efficiency thesis is contrasted with 'the compensation thesis', which argues that, because globalisation increases inequality, welfare states need to increase. In other words, globalisation pressured governments to expand welfare expenditures in order to compensate for the domestic 'losers' in the globalisation process (Brady et al., 2005; Rodrik, 1998; Swank, 2002). In a way, it can also be argued following the compensation argument that welfare expansion would allow states to further pursue globalisation. An extensive interpretation would then see welfare expansion not as a result but as a condition of globalisation, so that in order to continue (or to start) with the process of globalisation, policy makers must expand social safety nets. Empirical evidence concerning the relation between globalisation (intensification) and welfare (expansion/retrenchment) is often found to be inconsistent and mixed.

However, it is true that with the introduction of outsourcing practices and foreign direct investment outflows, globalisation has improved the bargaining position of capital relative to labour in higher-income countries. As Feenstra (1998, p. 46) observes, the impact of globalisation on changing the bargaining position of labour and capital has far-reaching consequences. The decline in union power, particularly within trade-oriented industries, may well account for a portion of the increased wage inequality in the USA and in other countries (Borjas and Ramey, 1995). The decision of firms to move capital and production across countries has distributional effects: the position of low-skilled workers in industrial countries is worsened by a combination of globalisation and new technology (Tisdell and Svizzero, 2003). The first increases the bargaining power of capital against labour, with the consequence that it is easier for capital to obtain tax reductions and welfare retrenchment. States are willing to embark on tax competition among them in order to keep investments and production at home. The second has a direct and negative impact on unskilled labour and income distribution without welfare support and social institutions.

This argument was already very clear to Adam Smith in his *AnInquiry into the Nature and Causes of the Wealth of Nations*, published in 1776, as the following passage, which helps to understand the tensions between globalisation and welfare, suggests:

> The proprietor of stock is properly a citizen of the world, and is not necessarily attached to any particular country. He would be apt to abandon the country in which he is exposed to a vexatious inquisition, in order to be assessed a burdensome tax, and would remove his stock to some country where he could either carry on his business or enjoy his fortune at his ease. A tax that tended to drive away stock from a particular country, would so far tend to dry up every source of revenue, both to the sovereign and to the society. Not only the profits of stock, but the rent of land and the wages of labour, would necessarily be more or less diminished by its removal.
>
> (Smith, 1976 [1776]: 848–849)

Inequality during globalisation and particularly during the 1990s and the 2000s increased in most advanced and emerging economies. A simple look at the Gini coefficients across countries shows the worsening of income distribution within countries. The reasons for this are various (Atkinson, 1999; Galbraith, 2012; Milanovic, 1998; Tridico, 2010).

However, most of the arguments raised by the literature in the last several years have to do with the new socio-economic model built around the world in the last two decades as a consequence of the new macroeconomic consensus, which brought about a new and higher level of financialisation in the system under the process of globalisation (Arestis et al., 2013; Galbraith, 2012). The new macroeconomic consensus is strictly linked to, if not completely correspondent

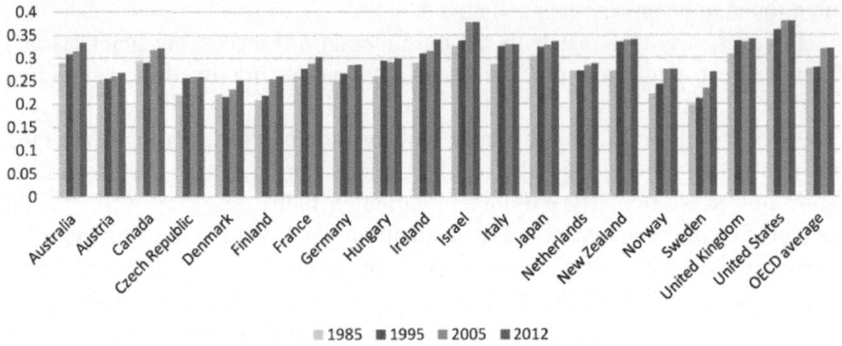

Figure 4.5 Inequality (Gini coefficients) among OECD countries

Source: OECD database (various years)

with, the Washington consensus doctrine, which called for the implementation of some institutional forms that better suit the globalisation process, such as the financialisation of the economy and the introduction of labour flexibility in the economy (see Tridico, 2012). Acemoglu (2011) argues that the policies over the last two decades in particular were more closely aligned with the preferences of a minority of high-income voters; instead of redistributive policies favouring low- and middle-income constituents, politicians implemented financial deregulation policies favouring influential high-income constituents (many of whom worked in, or directly benefited from, the financial sector).

Financialisation and labour flexibility are two institutional forms that go hand in hand and that were introduced across the world by countries in different degrees in order to guarantee the expansion of the globalisation process. Labour flexibility increased everywhere in Europe and in advanced economies in the last 20 years. However, some countries, such as Germany, Austria, Belgium and France, still have more rigid labour markets. Other economies, such as Denmark, Sweden, Finland and the Netherlands, introduced higher levels of flexibility along with higher levels of security. Countries such as the USA, the UK and Ireland increased (or maintained) a very flexible labour market. Finally, Mediterranean countries such as Italy, Spain and Greece and most former communist economies in Europe combined very hybrid situations (of liberal and corporative elements) with an increasing level of labour flexibility. Interestingly enough, these four groups of countries share similar levels and similar group classifications as far as financialisation is concerned. The highest level of financialisation is found to be in the last two groups, and the lowest level of financialisation in the first two groups, so that a clear and positive correlation, as Figure 1.6 suggests, can be found between labour flexibility and financialisation.

Employment protection legislation (EPL) is the indicator of the OECD, which measures the level of worker protection in the labour market and consequently the level of labour flexibility. This indicator shows the level of protection offered by

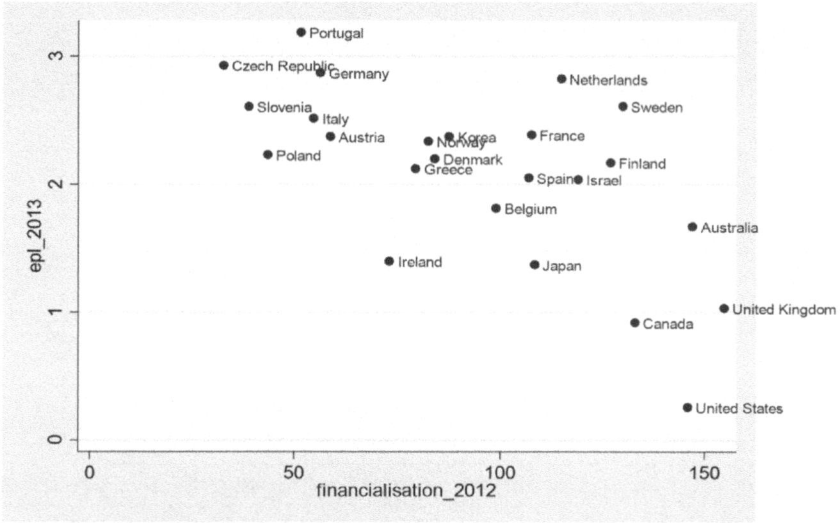

Figure 4.6 Correlation scatter between financialisation and labour flexibility (employment protection legislation)

Source: Own elaboration on the OECD database (various years) and World Bank database: www.worldbank.org

national legislation with respect to regular employment, temporary employment and collective dismissal – in other words, regulation that allows employers the freedom to fire and hire workers at will (OECD, 2004).

A flexible labour market with compressed wages and poor consumption needs to be supplemented by available financialisation and credit, hence, to have developed financial tools to sustain consumption, which otherwise was compressed by low and unstable wages (Brancaccio and Fontana, 2011). In this context, a large number of financial tools were invented to finance consumption, postpone payments, extend credit and create extra consumption (Tridico, 2012). That said, it is difficult to establish a causal relation: we cannot be certain whether financialisation required labour flexibility or if increased labour flexibility brought about hyper-financialisation. A simple correlation between these two complementary institutional forms of neoliberalism seems more likely (Figure 4.7).

Labour flexibility allows for reduction of labour costs and thus wage saving at the expense of wage earners, i.e. consumers. In such a situation, inequality increases and aggregate demand could be restricted because consumption decreases. It is very interesting to notice an inverse relationship between inequality and the EPL index (labour flexibility): the lower the EPL (higher flexibility), the higher the inequality. Continental and Scandinavian European countries have a higher EPL (lower flexibility) and lower inequality, while Anglo-Saxon and Mediterranean countries generally show the opposite values of higher inequality and lower EPL (higher flexibility) (see also Tridico, 2013).

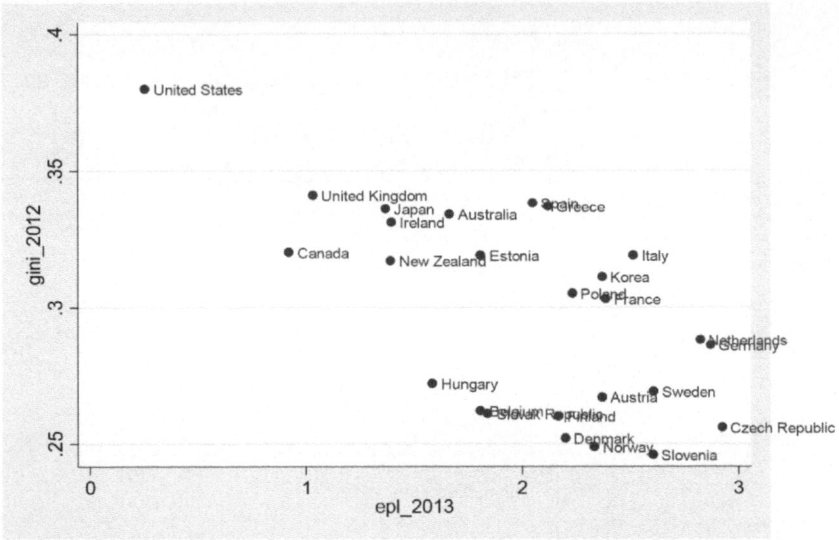

Figure 4.7 Correlation scatter between inequality and employment protection legislation
Source: Own elaboration on the OECD database (various years) and World Bank database: www.worldbank.org

As a result, it can be seen from Figure 4.8 that high financialisation is typically associated with high Gini coefficients and higher labour flexibility. More interesting, however, is the parallel trends of these variables: when financialisation increases, one notices both increased flexibility and inequality. In other words, as was argued elsewhere (Tridico, 2012), the rise of inequality generated in the labour market during globalisation led to an increased demand for credit, which translated into a credit expansion, and the increase of supply was provided for by accommodating monetary policies and financial deregulation.

However, what determines whether inequality increases or decreases under the condition of globalisation seems to be the pattern of the socio-economic model that each country built during the decades after the Second World War. More specifically, what is most relevant is the set of policies that each country is currently able to implement in order to cope with the challenges of globalisation in terms of both income distribution and competitiveness (Rodrik, 1999) – in particular, the institutions and conflict management policies that countries put in place during the last two decades, social protection against unemployment and lower wages, social expenditure against poverty, public expenditure and programmes on health and disease, social policy for housing, and so forth. In this context, our contribution is relevant. A proxy of these patterns can be offered by the relationship among OECD countries – which are considered the most advanced market economies between inequality and welfare expenditures. As Figure 4.9 shows, there seems to be a clear relationship between inequality and welfare expenditure in the sense that countries that spend more on welfare have a generally lower level of inequality.

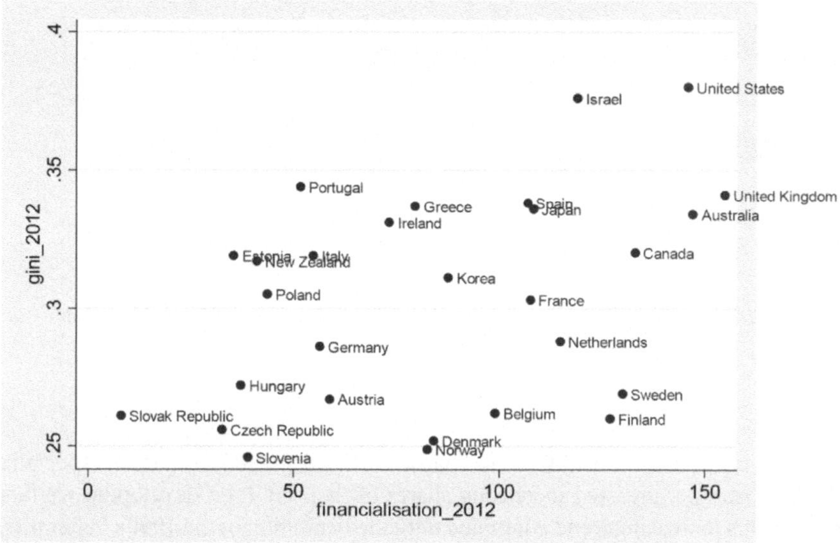

Figure 4.8 Correlation scatter between financialisation and inequality in 2012

Source: Own elaboration on the OECD database (various years) and World Bank database: www.worldbank.org

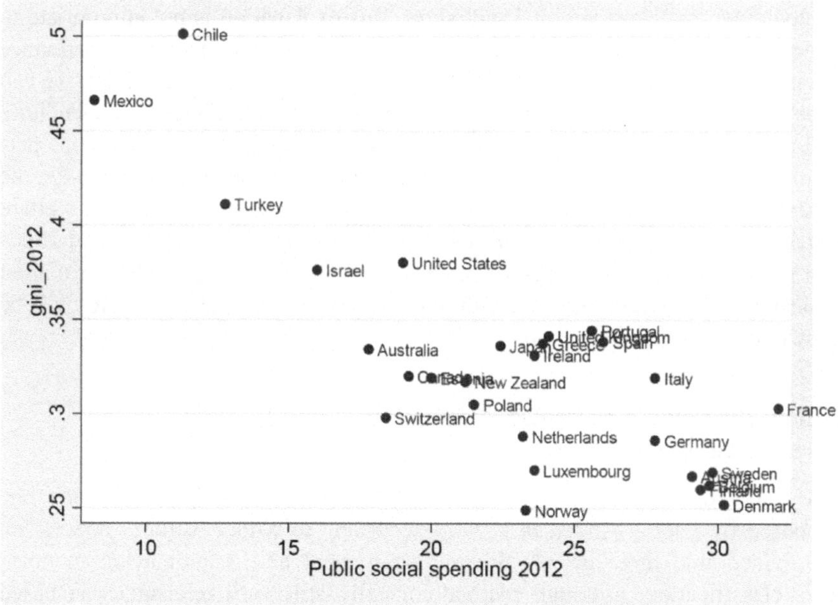

Figure 4.9 Gini coefficients and public social expenditure (% GDP) in 2010

Source: Own elaboration on the OECD database (various years) and OECD (2012)

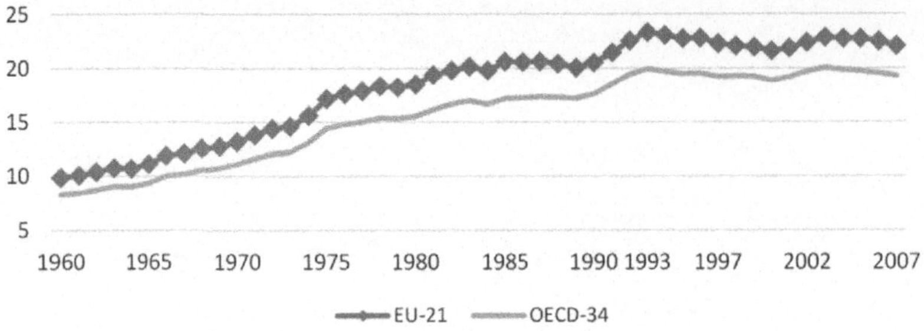

Figure 4.10 Expansion and retrenchment of welfare states since 1960 (public social expenditure, % of GDP)

Source: OECD (2012)

After the Second World War, and particularly since 1960, countries, especially those in Europe, invested increasing shares of their GDP on developing welfare states. This increasing trend continued until the beginning of the 1990s. After that, and particularly after the peak reached in 1993, governments started to retrench welfare states, and the percentage of welfare expenditure was lower at the eve of the financial crisis in 2007 than in 1993.

The efficiency thesis at first glance seems to provide a strong explanation here: advanced economies that embarked on globalisation had to reduce their welfare expenditure in order to satisfy firms' needs and requests and to increase their competitiveness. However, as I will show, this explanation is not appropriate to understand which countries in the end had actually better economic performance in terms of GDP dynamics and labour market performance. In particular, we can observe that countries that reached a relatively higher level of welfare expenditure and where cuts did not occur or occurred relatively less had better economic performance during the crisis that started in 2007 and continued until today. On the contrary, countries that at the eve of the crisis were found to have poorer welfare states and cut welfare expenditure more profoundly during the 1990s and 2000s had worse economic performance in terms of GDP dynamics and labour market indicators (like employment growth and unemployment). These results will be shown in the following section.

A new classification: welfare capitalism versus financial capitalism

The standard classification of socio-economic model, widely used, is the one proposed by Esping-Andersen (1990), according to whom welfare models can be divided into three groups, liberal, continental and Scandinavian models.[3] This classification, although methodologically still very relevant, was based on data from before 1990. Therefore, Hay and Wincott (2012) proposed a new one which takes into consideration the evolution of these models in the last two

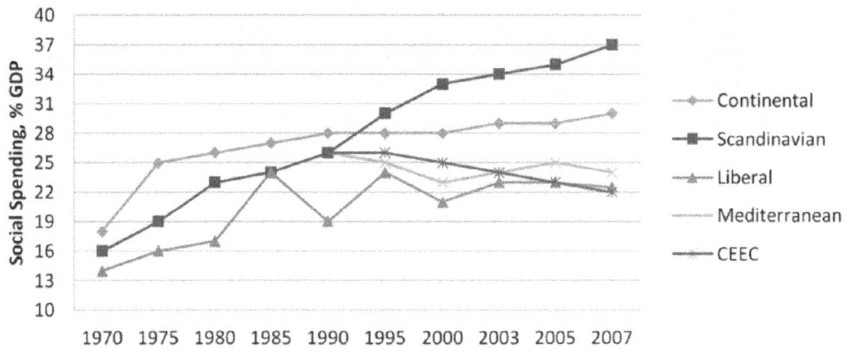

Figure 4.11 Welfare expenditure by models, 1970–2007

Source: Own calculation on the OECD database (various years). See also Adema and Ladaique (2009)

Notes: Social spending (% of GDP) is the sum of 'social benefits in-kind' and 'social transfers other than in-kind', as defined as well before (OECD definition). Continental: Belgium, Germany, Luxembourg, the Netherlands, Austria; Scandinavian: Denmark, Finland, Sweden, Norway; liberal: UK, Ireland, USA, Australia, Canada, New Zealand; Mediterranean: Greece, Spain, Italy, Cyprus, Malta, Portugal; CEEC: Czech Republic, Estonia, Latvia, Lithuania, Poland, Slovenia, Slovak Republic, Romania and Bulgaria.

decades. They extended this classification to five models: the three models used by Esping-Andersen plus the Mediterranean group and the Central and East European Countries (CEEC) group, claiming that a strong difference can be observed among these groups in general patterns. Moreover, since 1990, welfare patterns are diverging even more with the Scandinavian model, which seems to clearly have followed a compensation thesis in order to cope with the challenge of globalisation; the continental model, which maintained stable or slightly increased the level of welfare spending in the same period; and the other three groups, the liberal, the Mediterranean and the CEEC, which converge among themselves in the sense that they reduced the level of welfare spending clearly following a sort of efficiency thesis during the last two decades of globalisation, as Figure 4.11 suggests.

As we can see, some countries reacted to challenges of globalisation and financialisation by mplementing the 'efficiency thesis', according to which globalisation needs to be accompanied by the retrenchment of welfare states in order for firms to be competitive. These countries, however, did not achieve better economic performance and particularly during the current economic crisis suffered the most (these countries belong to the liberal and Mediterranean market economy models) (Figure 4.12). Moreover, their income distribution worsened and inequality increased.

On the contrary, countries that implemented the 'compensation thesis' (i.e. expanded welfare state) had better economic performance and better income distribution. Figure 4.13 indicates these conclusions. Moreover, the compensation approach contributed also to maintain lower levels of inequality. This emerges

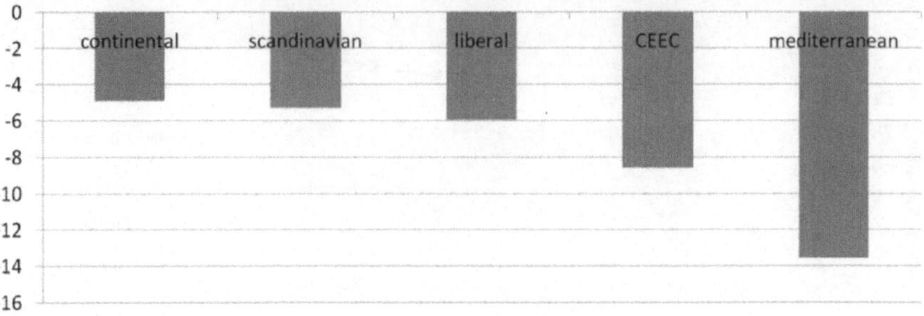

Figure 4.12 Performance index by group of countries $(g + n) - U$, average 2007–2013

Note: The performance index here is built simply by aggregating GDP and labour market performance in the following way: (g, average GDP growth in 2007–2013, + n, average employment growth in 2007–2013) – U, unemployment rate (average 2007–2013).[4] Source: Own elaboration on the World Economic Outlook at International Monetary Fund, online database (www.imf.org), and OECD database (various years)

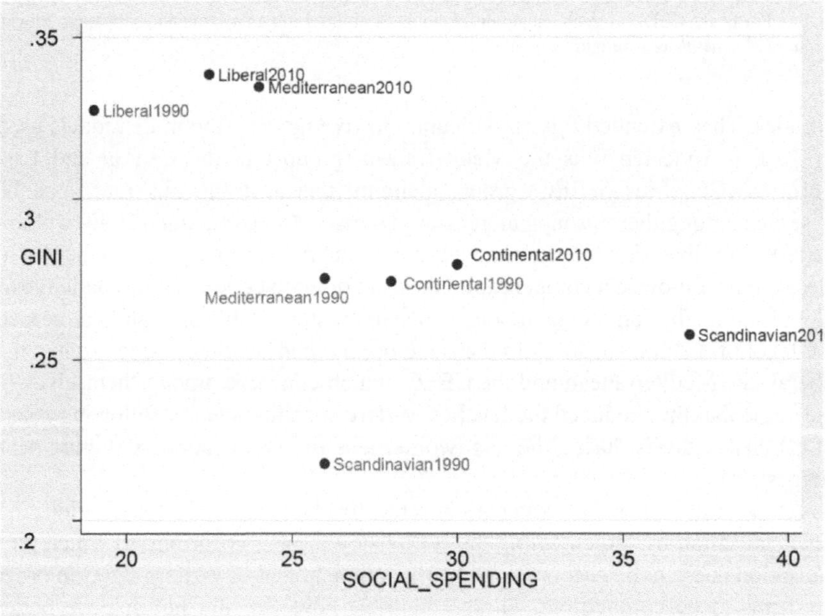

Figure 4.13 Inequality and social spending by welfare models in 1990 and in 2010

Source: Own elaboration on the OECD database (various years)

Note: Because of the lack of historical data, it is not possible to reconstruct variables for the CEEC group.

clearly when we group countries in the respective 'old classification', with simple calculations, and we account for the average values of inequality (Gini coefficients in 1990 and 2010) and welfare (social spending in 1990 and in 2010).

Given all that, several lessons can be learned.

1 First of all, it appears clear that some countries that were rightly included by the Esping-Andersen (1990) classification in the continental model, such as Italy, can no longer be included in this model. On the contrary, Italy, along with Greece, Portugal and Spain, constitutes a specific model, which has a pattern closer today to the liberal model rather than to the continental model. When data are available, the same pattern is also confirmed for Cyprus and Malta.
2 Second, there is a strong and steady correlation between welfare spending and inequality. Countries in the Scandinavian and continental models maintain higher levels of social spending along with lower levels of inequality. On the contrary, the countries of the liberal and Mediterranean models, which in the last two decades retrenched the welfare state or did not increase it, also experienced increasing inequality.
3 Third, the evolutionary path of welfare models under the condition of globalisation and financialisation presented a challenge for all countries involved in the process. Some countries, typically the Mediterranean countries, did not manage to increase welfare spending, and they ended up with both higher inequality levels and the worst performance in terms of GDP and labour market performance. The case of Scandinavian economies shows exactly the opposite: the challenges and the threats to income distribution and competitiveness of globalisation could be better coped with by increasing welfare spending.
4 Fourth, countries that are winners in the process of globalisation are also countries that did not embrace *tout court* financialisation along with globalisation and managed not to retrench welfare states. The persistence and/or the expansion of the welfare state found to be in place in Scandinavian and in continental European models functioned under the condition of globalisation to produce better performance during the years of the crisis (2007–2013). As the empirical evidence suggests, investing in social dimensions is the best policy option not only because it allows us to reduce or to keep lower inequality levels but also because it produces better performance in terms of GDP growth and labòur market performance (employment growth and unemployment). Hence, from a potential trilemma (globalisation, welfare and financialisation), it is better to adopt globalisation and welfare because any other solution would contribute to poorer socio-economic performance.
5 Last but not least, the evolution of welfare states, particularly the evolution that occurred during globalisation, leads us toward a new classification of only two socio-economic models among advanced economies that are quite polarised from each other: the financial capitalism regime versus the welfare capitalism regime. Countries that rely more on the financial nexus, having higher levels of financialisation in the economy, as measured by the market capitalisation index shown in Figure 4.2 above, fall clearly into the financial capitalism category. These countries have also relatively lower levels of welfare spending. Countries that rely more on the welfare nexus, having higher levels of welfare spending and lower levels of market capitalisation index, fall clearly into the welfare capitalism category. The financial capitalism

category clearly embeds the liberal and Mediterranean groups, while the welfare capitalism category clearly embeds the Scandinavian and continental groups (Table 4.1).

Figure 4.14 illustrates well this type of classification with a clear polarisation between the two categories, which also suggests the end of 'the three worlds of

Table 4.1 Welfare capitalism versus financial capitalism

		Welfare spending (% GDP)		
		Very high	*Middle*	*Very low*
	Very high			Liberal model
Financialisation (market capitalisation index, % GDP)	*Middle*	Scandinavian model		Mediterranean model
	Very low	Continental model		

Source: Own elaboration

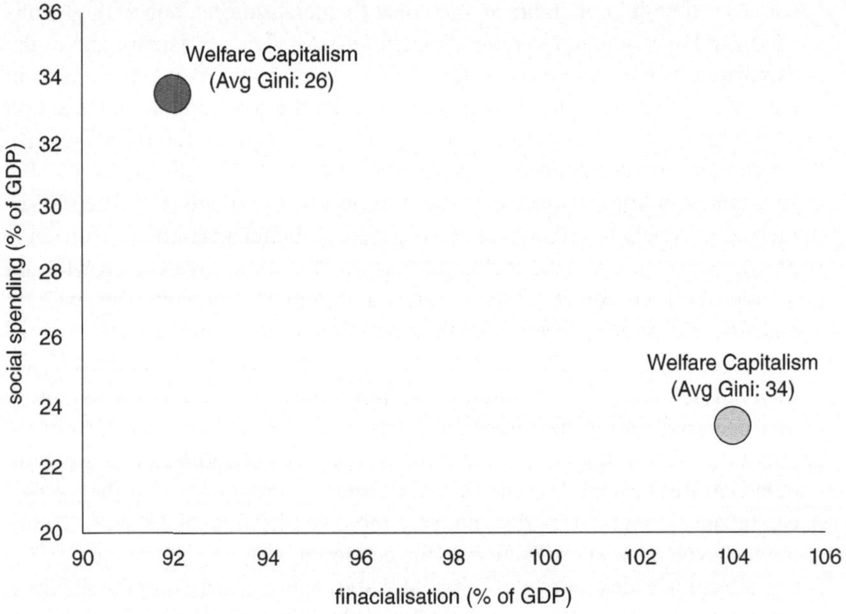

Figure 4.14 Poles apart: welfare capitalism and financial capitalism (data 2010)

Source: Own elaboration

welfare capitalism', described by Esping-Andersen. Countries of the continental and Scandinavian models are aggregated in the welfare capitalism type, sharing higher levels of social spending, lower levels of inequality (indicated in brackets with the average Gini coefficient), and from middle (the Scandinavian group) to very low levels (the continental group) of financialisation. On the contrary, the liberal and the Mediterranean models are aggregated in the financial capitalism type, sharing lower levels of social spending, higher levels of inequality (indicated in brackets with the average Gini coefficient) and from very high (the liberal group) to middle levels of financialisation. In terms of performance, the welfare capitalism regime proved to be superior to the financial capitalism regime not only as far as inequality is concerned but also in terms of economic performance (GDP and labour market).

Conclusions

In this paper, after describing the challenges that globalisation and financialisation posed to the labour sphere and to labour relations, in terms of inequality and income distribution, I came up with a new type of classification of socio-economic models: the welfare capitalism model and the financial capitalism model. Countries of the continental and Scandinavian models may be aggregated in the first category, sharing similar values of the relevant variables (welfare spending, financialisation and Gini coefficients), while liberal and Mediterranean models fall into the second category, sharing similar values of the same relevant variables. Countries of the welfare capitalism category exhibit better economic performance (i.e. a better performance index) and lower inequality; on the contrary, countries of the financial capitalism category have worse economic performance (a lower performance index) and higher inequality.

Notes

1 This paper was written during visiting research at the Vienna University of Technology in winter 2013–2014, financed by the COST Action IS0902 'Systemic Risks, Financial Crises and Credit – the roots, dynamics and consequences of the Subprime Crisis', which I gratefully acknowledge. I wish to thank Antonella Mennella and Bernhard Rengs for their comments, and Hardy Hanappi for his support, comments and discussion, which inspired the paper while I was in Vienna. Finally, I wish to thank also Paolo Pini for the comments on a previous version. The usual disclaimer applies.

2 Market capitalisation (also known as market value) is the share price multiplied by the number of shares outstanding. Listed domestic companies are the domestically incorporated companies listed on the country's stock exchanges at the end of the year. Listed companies do not include investment companies, mutual funds or other collective investment vehicles.

3 Esping-Andersen (1990) ranks welfare models mainly according to the level of social spending, to the level of (de)commodification of welfare and to degree of extension of welfare among citizens.

4 Taking into consideration, as a performance index, g, n and U contributes to avoid biases and to look at the economic performance from a wider perspective: in fact, some countries can have relatively better GDP dynamics but very bad employment performance (and vice versa).

References

Acemoglu D., (2011), *Thoughts on Inequality and the Financial Crisis*, Presentation held at the American Economic Association. http://economics.mit.edu/files/6348 (accessed 7 November 2013).

Adema W., and Ladaique M., (2009), 'How expensive is the welfare state? Gross and net indicators in the OECD Social Expenditure Database (SOCX)', *OECD Social, Employment and Migration Working Papers, No. 92*. http://www.oecd-ilibrary.org/social-issues-migration-health/how-expensive-is-the-welfare-state_220615515052(accessed 11 September 2016).

Allan J. P., and Scruggs L., (2004), 'Political partisanship and welfare state reform in advanced industrial societies', *American Journal of Political Science*, 48(3), 496–512.

Arestis P., Charles A., and Fontana G., (2013), 'Financialization, the great recession, and the stratification of the US labor market', *Feminist Economics*, 19(3), 152–180.

Atkinson A., (1999), *Is Rising Inequality Inevitable? A Critique of the Transatlantique Consensus*. WIDER Annual Lectures No. 3, Helsinki.

Basili M., Franzini M., and Vercelli A., (2006), *Environment, Inequality and Collective Action*. Routledge, Abingdon.

Blackmon P., (2006), 'The state: back in the center of the globalization debate', *International Studies Review*, 8(1), 116–119.

Borjas G.J. and Ramey V.A., (1995), "foreign competition, market power, and wage inequality,"*The Quarterly Journal of Economics*, 110(4): 1075–1110.

Boyer R., (2000), 'Is a finance-led growth regime a viable alternative to Fordism? A preliminary analysis', *Economy and Society*, 29(1), 111–145.

Brady D., Beckfield J., and Seeleib-Kaiser M., (2005), 'Economic globalization and the welfare state in affluent democracies, 1975–1998', *American Sociological Review*, 70, 921–948.

Brancaccio E., and Fontana G., (2011), 'The global economic crisis' (introduction). In Brancaccio E., and Fontana G., (eds). *The Global Economic Crisis. New Perspective on the Critique of Economic Theory and Policy*. Routledge, Abingdon.

Castells M., (2004), 'Global informational capitalism'. In Held D., and McGrew A. G., (eds). *The Global Transformations Reader: An Introduction to the Globalization Debate*. Blackwell, Malden, MA.

Engelen E., Konings M., and Ferandez R., (2008), 'The rise of activist investors and patterns of political responses: lessons on agency', *Socio-Economic Review*, 6(4), 611–636.

Epstein G., (2005), *Financialisation and the World Economy*. Edward Elgar, Cheltenham.

Esping-Andersen G., (1990), *The Three Worlds of Welfare Capitalism*. Polity, Cambridge.

EuroMemorandum, (2010), *Confronting the Crisis: Austerity or Solidarity*. European Economists for an Alternative Economic Policy in Europe – EuroMemo Group 2010/11, www.euromemo.eu (accessed 11 September 2016).

Feenstra R. C., (1998), 'Integration of trade and disintegration of production in the global economy', *Journal of Economic Perspectives*, 12(4), 31–50.

Financial Crisis Inquiry Commission, (2011), *Final Report of the National Commission on the Causes of the Financial and Economic Crisis in the United States*. Official Government Edition. U.S. Government Printing Office, Washington, DC.

Fitoussi J. P., (1992), *Il Dibattito proibito*. Il Mulino, Bologna.

Galbraith J. K., (2012), *Inequality and Instability*. Oxford University Press, Oxford.

Greenspan A., (2007), *The Age of Turbulence: Adventures in a New World*. Allen Lane, New York.

Hay C., and Wincott D., (2012), *The Political Economy of European Welfare Capitalism*. Palgrave Macmillan, Basingstoke.

ILO, (2010), *Global Employment Trends*. International Labor Organization, Geneva.

ILO, (2013), *Global Wage Report 2012/13 Wages and Equitable Growth*. ILO, Geneva.

IMF, International Monetary Fund (2009), *World Economic Outlook*. online database: www.imf.org (accessed 22 September 2016).

Jessop B., (2002), *The Future of the Capitalist State*. Polity Press, Cambridge.

Krippner G. R., (2005), 'The financialization of the American economy', *Socio-Economic Review*, 3(2), 173–208.

Milanovic B., (1998), 'Explaining the increase in inequality during the transition', *Policy Research Working Paper Series 1935*, The World Bank, Washington, DC.

Obstfeld M., and Rogoff K., (2009), 'Global imbalances and the financial crisis: products of common causes'. *CEPR Discussion Paper No. 7606*, London, CEPR.

OECD, (2004), *Employment Outlook (Chapter 2) Employment Protection Regulation and Labour Market Performance*. OECD, Paris.

OECD, (2012), *Social Expenditure Database*. www.oecd.org/els/social/expenditure (accessed 11 September 2016).

OECD, (various years), *Employment Outlook* (online database).

Peck J., and Tickell A., (1992), 'Local modes of social regulation? Regulation theory, Thacherism and uneven development', *Geoforum*, 23(3), 347–363.

Petit P., (2009), 'Financial globalisation and innovation: lessons of a lost decade for the OECD economies'. *CNRS Working Paper*, Paris, Centre National de la Recherche Scientifique.

Rodrik D., (1998), 'Why do more open economies have bigger governments?', *Journal of Political Economy*, 106, 997–1032.

Rodrik D., (1999), *Making Openness Work*. John Hopkins University Press, Washington, DC.

Semmler W., and Young B., (2010), 'Lost in temptation of risk: financial market liberalization, financial market meltdown and regulatory reforms', *Comparative European Politics*, 8(3), 327–353.

Smith A., (1976 [1776]), *An Inquiry into the Nature and Causes of the Wealth of Nations*. Oxford University Press, Oxford.

Swank D., (2002), *Global Capital, Political Institutions, and Policy Change in Developed Welfare States*. Cambridge University Press, New York.

Tisdell C., and Svizzero S., (2003), 'Globalization, social welfare, and labour market inequality', *Working Paper no. 20*, The University of Queensland, St Lucia.

Tridico P., (2010), 'Growth, inequality and poverty in emerging and transition economies', *Review of Transition Studies*, 16(4).

Tridico P., (2012), 'Financial crisis and global imbalances: its labor market origins and the aftermath', *Cambridge Journal of Economics*, 36(1), 17–42.

Tridico P., (2013), 'The impact of the economic crisis on the EU labour market: a comparative perspective'. *International Labour Review*, 152(2).

Wolff R., (2010), *Capitalism Hits the Fan. The Global Economic Meltdown and What to Do About It*. Pluto Press, New York.

Wolfson M., (2010), 'Neoliberalism and the social structure of accumulation', *Review of Radical Political Economics*, 35(3), 255–263.

5 Achievements and challenges of the Chinese model of capitalism

How much can be explained by Confucianism?

Klaus Nielsen

Introduction

Since the economic reforms of the late 1970s, China has experienced continuous high growth rates and a transformation of a historically unseen scale and scope. Hundreds of millions of people have been lifted out of poverty and the material infrastructure has undergone an astonishing renewal. Growth rates were maintained after 2007 by means of a massive fiscal stimulus programme. There is certainly potential for continued high growth rates but major challenges are on the horizon. China will experience the most radical demographic change in the next decades with an enormous rise in dependency rates in the next 30–40 years. China faces enormous environmental and social challenges with air pollution, toxic rivers, weak food security, huge income inequality, exploitation of workers, lack of social security and a highly inefficient health system. Further, corruption is endemic, not the least in the form of land seizures by local government officials. The challenges are caused by outdated and inefficient institutions, such as weak property rights, the system of fixed residency (*hukou*) and a politicized legal system, which are only partly and imperfectly offset by benevolent discretionary action by the central leadership.

This chapter takes a cultural economic approach to an analysis of these achievements and challenges. It is assumed that everywhere economic action and business practices are heavily influenced by the taken-for-granted effects of deep-rooted cultural characteristics. Evidence of the importance of culture on human behaviour is manifold. One striking example is the radically different responses to similar events in different cultures. For instance, a comparison of the aftermath of the flooding caused by the Katrina hurricane in New Orleans in 2005 with the Tohoku earthquake and tsunami in Japan 2011 reveals huge differences. Whereas the aftermath of the Katrina disaster was characterized by chaos and individual acts of enrichment and violence, the natural disaster in Japan was followed by civic cooperation and restraint illustrated by patient queuing.

In this chapter it is analysed to what extent the deep-rooted norms and values of Confucianism impact on economic relations and the behaviour of economic agents in China today. It is assumed that basic Confucian values, such as the importance of the family, group mentality, stability, loyalty to superiors, paternalism and reciprocity, underpin business practices and economic governance. Culturalist explanations of the successful economic development of Chinese societies are not without their critics (Dirlik, 1997). Further, Confucianism has been under attack by the Chinese Communist Party and it may recently be losing some of its grip as a result of capitalism, individualism, materialism and the huge structural transformation in recent decades.

The chapter aims at an interpretation of the achievements and challenges of the Chinese model of capitalism which stresses the role of Confucian culture underpinning the growth process. Further, it analyses to what extent Confucianism is at odds with the requirements and pressures of the modernization of Chinese society, as claimed by Max Weber in his seminal book, *The Religion of China*. In this chapter, we argue that, although the impact of Confucianism is ambiguous, it has mostly facilitated and supported the emergence of the highly successful capitalism in China.

However, the ongoing modernization of China puts pressure on the Confucian cultural heritage. New middle-class norms stress quality of life and self-determination in ways that challenge the behavioural norms. Further, the introduction of a full-blown capitalist economy has led to business scandals, exploitation, corruption and corporate excesses. The widespread dissent, protests and even riots that have emerged in recent years can be interpreted as anger over violations of basic Confucian values. Together, the protests inspired by the Confucian heritage and the emerging individualism and middle-class norms put pressure on the current model of development.

The chapter is based partly on reviews of the literature on Confucianism and its economic effects, and partly on interviews with professionals and managers in China as well as observation field notes from six study trips to China in 2010–2014. The primary data are collected in the Northern Chinese provinces of Heilongjiang, Jilin, Liaoning and Shandong and in Sichuan in Central China. Supplementary data from newspapers and other contemporary sources are included in order to counterbalance the potential impact on the findings of the northern bias in terms of data collection. While the chapter is based on the collected data, it does not include thorough documentation but will rather present some major conclusions illustrated by selective evidence.

The paper is structured as follows. The next two sections provide a brief summary of the major traits of Confucianism and a historical perspective on the status of Confucianism in Chinese society. Then, Max Weber's famous analysis of Confucianism as a hindrance for the development of capitalism in China is revisited. The following sections outline the Confucian characteristics of the contemporary Chinese model of capitalism by way of distinguishing between the factors that underpin and facilitate the economic growth process and the factors that impede growth. Then, this is discussed in relation to the ongoing modernization of Chinese society. The emergence of crony capitalism with neglect of environmental and social costs and extreme exploitation of labour had led to conflicts and protests against what may be interpreted as a violation of basic Confucian values. The final section describes the recent restoration of Confucianism and discusses its significance.

Confucianism – a brief introduction

The ideas of the Chinese philosopher Confucius (551–479 BC) did not gain official recognition in China until centuries after his death (Schuman, 2015). However, his followers were successful in establishing Confucian ideology as a powerful system of moral, political and social principles governing nearly every aspect of Chinese life since the Han era (206 BC–AD 220). As a philosophy considering proper behaviour and human relationships, Confucian influence has expanded to and penetrated many other Asian countries, including Japan, Korea, Singapore and Vietnam, and is today probably more strongly embedded outside of China, mainly in Korea but also in Taiwan (Schuman, 2015; Yao, 2000).

Confucian thought stresses the importance of five relationships and five virtues representing the social sphere and individual morality, respectively. Confucianism emphasizes harmony, hierarchy and development of moral potential and kinship (Buttery and Leung, 1998). It focuses on five core relationships in society: emperor–subject, father–son, husband–wife, elder–younger brother and friend–friend. All these relationships involve a set of defined roles and mutual obligations. Each individual should conform to his or her proper role and act properly. With the exception of the last relation, all the others are hierarchical and dominant–subservient in nature. The other side of Confucian ideology is represented by five virtues (benevolence, righteousness, propriety, wisdom and trustworthiness) which nurture the inner character of the person and further his or her ethical maturation.

Thus, if one side of Confucianism is the conformity and acceptance of social roles, the other is the cultivation of conscience and morals through education and reflection in a lifetime commitment to character building. It generates a high ideal for family interaction, i.e. that family members treat each other with love, respect and consideration for the needs of all, and it prescribes a lofty idea for the state, i.e. that the governor is the father to his people and looks after their basic needs (Wang et al., 2005). These two conforming and reforming sides of Confucianism define principles for appropriate individual behaviour in relation to others in a social hierarchy.

In more than two millennia Confucianism was entrenched in Chinese society as organizational principles and behavioural guidelines officially sanctioned and supported by education. However, Confucianism lost its official recognition and privileged position with the collapse of Imperial China in the early 20th century. Confucianism was seen as part of the reason for the stark decline of China. Its rigid, traditional view of social interaction was deemed incompatible with the requirements for adapting to the challenges of the modern world.

After the Communist revolution, the official status of Confucianism reached its nadir. Confucianism can be seen as a foundation for the success and acceptance of Communism in China with its stress on subservience, stability and benevolent leadership. However, it was seen by the new Communist rules as preserving the status quo and hindering the required societal changes. In particular, during the Cultural Revolution, vestiges of Confucianism were vilified and purged as an ideology that hindered the creation of 'the new socialist man'. Since then Confucianism has experienced a quiet revival from absence of opposition through passive acceptance to tentative official recognition. Since 2014, the Communist Party has officially endorsed Confucius and other classical Chinese thinkers, while tightening restrictions on Western influence in art, academia and religion (Page, 2015). Some observers interpret this as an opportunistic means to mobilize support for the anti-corruption campaign (Schuman, 2015), but it signifies a significant change of discourse and can be seen as a reflection and recognition of the role of Confucianism in facilitating and supporting the momentous economic growth in China in recent decades.

Revisiting Weber's *The Religion of China*

Max Weber argued in *The Religion of China* (Weber, 1951, first published in 1915) that, while several factors provide China with good material conditions for the development of a capitalist economy, they are outweighed by the legacy of Confucianism, which he saw as a religion. According to Weber, Confucianism does not facilitate but rather hinders/obstructs the emergence and functioning of capitalism. His analysis of China provides the antithesis to his analysis of the puritan protestantism which he claimed provided the ideal spiritual foundation for a well-functioning capitalist system. His analysis can be briefly summarized in four points.

First, Confucianism is not disposed to methodical control and rationalization of life, due to its world-accommodating nature. Instead of changing the world, adjusting oneself to it is seen as virtuous. Second, because of its veneration for traditions and respect for ancestors, Confucianism is inherently sceptical toward technical inventions which disturb established patterns of behaviour. Third, extended kinship groups protect their members against economic adversities and decrease the motivation for payment of debts and work discipline. Fourth, Confucian ethics rejects professional specialization, expert bureaucracy and special training due to the notion that 'a cultured man' is seen as an end in itself and not just a means for a specified useful purpose or a functional end. Weber sees instrumental rationality like specialization, professionalization and bureaucratization as crucial features of the modern age, and he stresses that the lack of emphasis on law and professional specialization is an element of Confucianism which constitutes barriers to the rise of capitalism in China.

How Confucianism underpins the economic growth process

There are several features of Confucianism that have facilitated the extraordinary economic success story of contemporary China. Confucianism impacts on economic behaviour and relationships in various ways. Many scholars have argued that Confucianism is the bedrock upon which the economic success of China and other Chinese societies rests (Chan, 2008; Hang, 2011; Wu & Leung, 2005; Yin, 2003). This section covers the main factors but is by no means exhaustive.

First, the crucial role of hierarchy and harmony in Confucian thought implies loyalty and obedience to superior authority. Subordination and acceptance of all kinds of authority are considered natural, including corporate management and the leading role of the Chinese Communist Party. This has no doubt facilitated implementation of policies at the macro level and corporate leadership at the micro level. Chen et al. (2014) show how affective trust mediates the relationships between benevolent and moral paternalistic leadership and employee performance. Another effect is a low inclination to dissent and rebel in case of adversity. Kung and Ma (2014) conclude, in a historical study comparing incidents of peasant rebellions in natural disasters in different regions of China, that the inclination to rebel was significantly lower in regions where Confucianism was strongly embedded compared to regions where this was less so.

Second, Confucianism implies a strong work ethic. The obligations of subordinates include persistence, perseverance and willingness to endure hardship in their work efforts. This has served the Chinese economy well. Chinese workers are generally hard-working and willing to work long hours. There is also a widespread acceptance of precarious working conditions. This is most pronounced for migrant workers. The result is an extraordinary large pool of numerically flexible, cheap, hard-working labour willing to take on all kinds of tasks and working conditions. The advantages for companies in terms of cost competitiveness are obvious.

Third, self-reliance of the extended Chinese family based on mutual obligations facilitates capital accumulation in several ways. Self-reliant families guarantee free access of (often well-educated) labour for capital, facilitate small-scale entrepreneurship and take care of most of the core tasks of the welfare state without any costs for capital or the state.

Fourth, thrift is a Confucian virtue that complements economic and social reproduction in the family. China has an extraordinary high private savings ratio. This is to some extent a necessity in the absence of a welfare state but Confucian norms include a predisposition for thrift. High savings are necessary in order to secure financing of the costs involved in the mutual family obligation, as outlined above. Small-scale entrepreneurship prospers in China in spite of lack of access to finance. This is facilitated by thrift, as indicated by a willingness to save a large share of earned income to save for the start of own businesses. The mirror image of virtuous thrift in Confucian thought is a negative view of unnecessary spending. Conspicuous consumption is considered a vice.

Fifth, there are both positive and negative incentives for virtuous behaviour. Having a sense of shame, which is inherent in Confucianism, supplements the positive incentives. Virtuous behaviour is facilitated by the negative incentive to avoid the embarrassment of feeling shame. Shame is not only an internal phenomenon but may have public manifestations, e.g. managers are publicly shamed in business scandals.

Sixth, one of the defining characteristics of Confucian societies is the extraordinary importance attached to education (Frederickson, 2002, pp. 618–619). Confucian ethics advocates respect for learning, teachers and scholars. Great importance is placed on formal education and knowledge-based learning (Han, 2013), examinations, academic achievements and diplomas (De Bettingies & Tan, 2007, p. 20). Education is assumed to reap huge cultural and social benefits. It also has obvious economic benefits.

Seventh, group orientation rather than individualism is a strong, highly significant trait of Confucianism. Group identity dominates individual identity. This trait obviously facilitates teamwork, including associated reward mechanisms. Responsibility to the collective strengthens commitment at the work place. Organizational citizenship behaviour prevails. Zhuang et al. (2005) show a perhaps surprising effect of such behaviour. Chinese employees are more willing to engage in whistleblowing against their peers than employees in the USA. However, they are reluctant to blow the whistle in case of a superior's misbehaviour; in this respect they are not significantly different from employees in the USA.

Eighth, *guanxi* is the widely used Chinese term for a special type of group-oriented behaviour in Chinese societies that involves intense networking, reciprocity and trust. It has some resemblance to social capital but represents more encompassing, intensive and long-term commitments (Parnell, 2005). *Guanxi* is a person's social nexus encompassing family, friends, school and university alumni and acquaintances in positions of influence. The bonds it creates must be maintained by courtesy visits, banquets and gift giving and politeness rituals must be followed strictly. To a large extent business deals take place in the context of *guanxi* and several scholars attribute the success of Chinese entrepreneurs to the benign characteristics of *guanxi* (Buttery & Wong, 1999; Guo & Miller, 2010; Park & Luo, 2001; Yang &Wang, 2011). Hsu (2005) compares the effect on *guanxi* versus an apparent similar phenomenon in Russia, *blot*. Whereas *guanxi* builds trust and reaches out, *blot* has led to predatory behaviour. *Guanxi* has both positive and negative economic consequences. It provides access to resources within a context of trust, reciprocal obligations and informal governance of exchanges that compensates for the absence of appropriate legal, regulatory and financial institutions. Some scholars identify advantages that go beyond such compensatory functions. One of the benefits of *guanxi* is the information offered on government policies, market trends and business opportunities. They also improve efficiency by reducing transaction costs (Fan, 2002). Davies et al. (1995) suggest an underlying structure of four factors: it facilitates procurement, enables information gathering, reduces bureaucracy and smoothens transactions. Others focus on its less benign effects, which will be covered in the next section.

How Confucianism impedes economic growth

There has been a tendency in the research literature to stress the positive impacts of the Confucian framing of economic behaviour and relationships. However, the impacts are not uniquely positive. Traditional Chinese culture is only partly conducive to entrepreneurship (Liao & Sohmen, 2001). In this section we will focus on some of the traits of Confucianism that impede rather than foster economic growth.

First, subordination, obedience and respect for authority and tradition have not only economically positive impacts. They also result in lack of initiative and creativity. The acceptance of a superior's leadership prerogative often makes subordinates abstain from making proposals for solving problems. Chinese employees often show less proactive participation and less independent and critical thinking than their Western counterparts (Wang et al. 2005, p. 320). This hampers innovation and efficiency (Jacobs et al., 1995) as well as the advocacy part of organizational citizenship behaviour (Bolino et al., 2006).

Second, Confucianism underpins the tendency to rely on networks and authority rather than legal rules and formal contracts. Often formal contracts are made but neither adhered to nor enforced. This reflects a general management style known as 'ruling by man' rather than 'ruling by law' (Wang et al., 2005, pp. 320–321). There is a dislike of formal contracts and a lack of standard procedures and policies for decision making (Jacobs et al., 1995). In business transactions, 'ruling by man' implies deal making and problem solving through personal interactions instead of following business regulations (Kirby & Fan, 1995). This makes business transactions beyond the boundaries of *guanxi* networks difficult and costly. It also means that top decision makers have the final authority with few legal constraints and their decisions are unquestionable. For instance, interviewees reported how managers often consider formal rules and regulations, including employment contracts, as something that can be ignored or changed unilaterally if required.

Third, in employment relations, 'ruling by man' gives managers discretion that often has negative consequences on professionalism and competence. Wang et al. (2005, p. 321) outline the following manifestations:

(a) employee selection is based more on *renqing* (human feelings) and *guanxi* than on personal competence;
(b) promotion is conducted on the basis of loyalty and social acceptance;
(c) compensation is largely based on seniority rather than performance; [and]
(d) performance evaluation is largely qualitative and tends to be subjective.

This is not only based on the side of Confucianism that stresses the importance of hierarchy and harmony. It also reflects the stress on the importance of character building and strengthening of morality of leaders rather than professional skills in education, work and governance.

Fourth, although the reliance on *guanxi* in business relations does constitute a flexible and adaptable vehicle for business transactions based on in-group loyalty and trust, it may also impede economic growth. Fan (2002) concludes that the benefits of *guanxi* are exaggerated. The benefits for business are seen as outweighed by the time-consuming and expensive efforts required to develop and maintain *guanxi* (Fock & Woo, 1998). Further, *guanxi* as a personal asset cannot be a source of competitive advantage. It does not live up to the criteria by being valuable, rare, non-imitable or non-substitutable (Fan, 2002, pp. 553–554). Park and Luo (2001) show that *guanxi* clearly contributes to sales growth but does not improve net profits. *Guanxi* is important in relation to establishing external relations and legitimacy but does not improve internal operations.

Rather, the high costs to cultivate and maintain *guanxi* offset the benefits from market expansion.

Fifth, there are obvious negative effects of *guanxi* in government–business relationships. *Guanxi* encourages nepotism, favouritism, 'under-the-table' dealings, bribes and other forms of corruption that seem to pervade China's business environment. The *guanxi* between a business person and a government is inherently corrupt and ethically questionable (Fan, 2002). Luo (2008) analyses the intertwinement between *guanxi* and corruption. The study concludes that 'guanxi is implicated in almost all big corruption cases. One particular feature is that corruption has evolved from individual wrongdoings into institutionalized corruption that often involve a complicated guanxi network between high-ranking officials and private businessmen' (Luo, 2008, p. 192). For instance, case studies have shown that *guanxi* between environmental regulators and industrial enterprises strongly influences the implementation of environmental policies and results in less stringent enforcement of legislation at the local level (De Bettingies & Tan, 2007, p. 23).

Sixth, an important aspect of guanxi is gift giving and reciprocity linked to the Chinese concept of *mianzi* (face). *Mianzi* involves 'giving face' and 'maintaining face' or 'protecting face' (Hwang, 1990). To 'give face' means to show respect for your counterpart's status and reputation. To 'maintain or protect face' means to stay trustworthy and honour one's obligations in social interactions. Giving favours to the weaker parts of a relationship demonstrates power or capacity beyond one's peers and indicates a gain in 'face'. Reciprocity implies an obligation to return a favour whenever called upon. Subordinates can always give superiors face by asking favours from them, although this is limited by the code of reciprocity. The outcome of this spiral of 'giving face' and reciprocity is a costly drain on business in terms of gift giving and favours in various forms.

Confucian dynamics

Most contributions to the literature give priority to either the positive or negative effects of Confucianism on economic growth. Hofstede and Bode (1988) are different in the sense that they see Confucianism as a combination of values oriented toward the future (persistence/perseverance, ordering relationships by status and respecting this order, thrift, having a sense of shame) and values oriented toward the past (personal steadiness, protecting your face, respect for tradition, reciprocity of greetings, favours and gifts). Hofstede and Bode attempt to make sense of societies influenced by Confucianism in relation to the four cultural dimensions identified in Hofstede (1984): power distance, individualism/collectivism, masculinity/femininity and uncertainty avoidance. Hofstede and Bode found that societies influenced by Confucianism are characterized by high power distance as well as high collectivism and low individualism, whereas they do not show significant characteristics in relation to masculinity/femininity and uncertainty avoidance. Further, they introduced a new variable 'long-term orientation' which is seen as relatively high in societies influenced by Confucianism (Buttery & Leung, 1998). Dunning and Kim (2007) test propositions about whether power distance and collectivism, respectively, lead to a strong perception of *guanxi* and find strong support.

Hofstede and Bode introduce the concept of 'Confucian dynamism' which, in their view, has facilitated the stellar performance of Chinese economies in China and beyond. Such dynamism depends on the specific context and is associated with the relative strength of the Confucian values oriented toward the future and the relative weakness of values oriented toward the past. Whereas the values oriented toward the future stimulate growth, the backward-oriented parts of Confucianism have contrary effects. Cases where the future-oriented values are stronger than the past-oriented values show more economic dynamism than cases where the Confucian values oriented toward the past are more entrenched. This opens up a perspective of social engineering (Yin, 2003). Economic growth can be facilitated by strengthening some aspects of Confucianism while suppressing other parts. Other scholars have criticized Hofstede and Bode for the introduction of the dimension 'long-term orientation', and hence 'Confucian dynamics' concept, as such, and argue that Confucianism is a package that comes as a whole, i.e. it is impossible to separate the positive and negative economic impacts of Confucianism (Fang, 2003).

Modernity

The concept of Confucian dynamism signals the actual or at least potential of accommodating Confucianism with the requirements of the modern world. This runs counter to Weber's characterization of Confucianism (Nuyen, 1999). We shall take a closer look at the conflicts and the compatibility of Confucianism with modernization or modernity.

Modernity originates from the Enlightenment and as such it is not a novel phenomenon. Weber took account of the rise of modernity as it manifested itself in the late 19th and early 20th century. Still, a century later modernization is an on-going process with uncertain outcomes. Protests against manifestations of modernity and counteracting movements prosper currently with the resurgent societal role of religion and vestiges of the pre-modern world persist.

Modernity is a wide-ranging concept taking account of the ensemble of particular socio-cultural norms, attitudes and practices linked to a modern society. Modernization entails the emergence of a multitude of emerging phenomena, such as questioning or rejection of tradition; the prioritization of freedom and formal equality; faith in inevitable social, scientific and technological progress and human perfectibility; rationalization and professionalism; a movement toward profit orientation, capitalism, and the market economy; industrialization, urbanization and secularization; the development of the nation state and its constituent institutions (e.g. representative democracy, public education, modern bureaucracy) and forms of surveillance; sexual freedom and increased role of women in all spheres of life. Perhaps the most important aspect of modernity, however, is increasing importance of the individual, eventually replacing the family or community as the fundamental unit of society.

Confucianism and modernity

China has arguably undergone a rapid modernization process since the economic reform process started in 1979 and the consequent opening up for foreign investment and Western cultural influence. This raises a number of questions related to the Confucian cultural legacy: how has modernization impacted on this legacy? Has Confucianism hindered or facilitated the modernization process? Has Confucianism shaped the manifestations of emerging modernity in China, and if so, how? In order to provide preliminary answers to these questions we shall start by evaluating how 'modern' Confucianism is.

It is evident that Confucianism is modern in some respects and distinctly unmodern in others. A strong belief in human perfectibility is part of the Confucian legacy. This constitutes a favourable environment for technical progress, organizational change and institutional reform which fits well with modernity. In addition, the impact of Confucianism on economic behaviour and relationships, as outlined above, and, in particular what Hofstede and Bode called Confucian dynamism, facilitates in many ways the development of capitalism. Other aspects of modernity are at least not incompatible with Confucianism. This is the case with some of the institutions normally associated with modernity, such as representative democracy (Ackerly, 2005; Xu, 2006). However, Confucianism is indeed unmodern in many respects. The reverence for tradition and stability imply resistance to the dynamics of social change that characterizes modernization. The obedience of subordinates in hierarchies runs counter to the ideal of formal equality and freedom. Further, rationalization and professionalism are challenged by the requirements of *guanxi* and the 'ruling by man instead of ruling by law'.

There are pressures for change in relation to all the dimensions of modernity in modern China. Some of these pressures are being suppressed or modified by the Chinese Communist Party. Some of them challenge deep-rooted Confucian values.

Individualism is definitely on the rise as an effect of Western cultural influence and increasing middle-class affluence. This is perhaps particularly significant among the young, urban professionals who were interviewed as part of this research project. New middle-class norms and aspirations are manifest, as articulated by a young female professional (married to a middle-ranked party official):

- As all our friends we would move abroad if possible, preferably Japan and alternatively Canada, Australia or the USA.
- Why?
- Because quality of life is so poor in China. The pollution, especially air quality, is intolerable. The low food security is a major concern. Welfare is poor with insecure pensions and malfunctioning health system that requires access through personal network to get proper treatment, money is not enough. Life is stressful, not the least for school children and parents.

The underlying preferences are not unlike similar groups in Western countries and other emerging economies. However, in China the rise of individualism is restrained by the strong, socially and culturally entrenched, role of the family.

Concerns for the family take precedence and put limits on individualist behaviour. Part of it is sheer necessity in the absence of proper welfare-state services and unavailability of credit for business start-ups. Typically, parents not only finance their offspring's education, including studying abroad, and the purchase of their first flat. They often also provide financial support for starting up a small business enterprise. As everyone who has been around in a big city in early morning will be aware, grandparents also have family obligations. They compensate for the inadequate supply of public childcare by picking up their working offspring's children and caring for them until their parents come back from home. On the other hand, grown-up children expect and are expected to take care of their parents when they get old. One of the economic consequences is a constraint on geographical mobility. Proximity of parents (and grandparents) is important for working adults, and they do not seem to imagine the possibility of moving too far away when their parents become old or experience bad health. In many interviews I searched for expressions of discontent for being restricted in terms of individual freedom by the burdens of reciprocal family support as is common in Western countries, but found none. These reciprocal obligations are apparently perceived not merely as a necessity but as a deep-rooted expression of filial piety.

Another impact of modernization is a tendency for at least the group of young professionals that I interviewed to become less subservient and less constrained by the Confucian respect for authority and belief in hierarchy and harmony. Education and Western influence provide them with a broader outlook which makes them more inclined to express open dissent and to demand influence and self-determination. Still, this tendency is muted but it is obvious that changes are in process.

In addition, several studies show scepticism toward inherited forms of group orientation, most prominently in the form of *guanxi*. Recent empirical studies show reservations toward this deeply ingrained practice. Andersen and Lee (2008) conducted a survey of managers in Hong Kong and young middle-class people in China. Both groups understood and used *guanxi* but did not like it or enjoyed its use. Both groups anticipate a diminishing use of *guanxi* when China's regulatory and market environment improves. It seems to be a predominant perception that *guanxi* is wasteful, inefficient and responsible for the widespread corruption. According to a Chinese professor in management:

> guanxi takes too much time and is very costly. People waste valuable time by nurturing business contacts and links to government officials. Further, the costs of building and maintaining connections reduce the profit margin of many companies. This creates severe deadweight losses in firms and in the economy as such.

The negative perceptions of *guanxi* are particularly prominent among the younger generation. Studies show that young Chinese are more sceptical in this respect than older Chinese (Lin & Ho, 2009). Attitudinal differences between young and old regarding practices based on Confucian values and norms are not restricted to differences in relation to *guanxi*. This was evident in the conducted interviews and is supported by other indicators and other studies. The evidence makes it reasonable to conclude that the younger generation, the new middle class and well-educated professionals are carriers of modernization which to a certain extent challenges inherent cultural traits of Confucianism. Experiences through foreign travel, overseas studies and the (albeit controlled) internet led to new lifestyle aspirations and a desire for greater self-determination and influence on decision making in companies and government. Traditional values such as filial piety are becoming modified under the impact of modernization (Hwang, 1999). On the other hand, some of the unmodern Confucian traits such as family orientation and the stress on harmony and stability are widely accepted and culturally and socially entrenched, which shapes the modernization process and can be expected to result in a specific Chinese form of modernity.

Crony capitalism, exploitation and immoral profit seeking

In one respect the emergence of modernity has been extremely fast, freewheeling and largely unrestrained by cultural inhibitions. Capitalism and markets have been promoted without any constraints. This has been successful in terms of decades of extremely high growth rates but it has also resulted in the emergence of one of the most unequal societies in the world (*World Bank*, 2013, pp. 46–54) and a variety of capitalism characterized by widespread cronyism, extreme exploitation of labour and unregulated profit seeking which is as far removed from the morality advocated by Confucianism as possible. Confucianism has the potential of providing a mental framework for an indigenous Chinese form of corporate social responsibility. A study of owners of manufacturing or business firms who harbour Confucian moral values concludes that they give priority to moral principles over material gain in cases where there is a conflict or tensions between morality and profit (Cheung & King, 2004), in accordance with the explicit priority of righteousness over profit in classical Confucian texts (De Bettingies & Tan, 2007). However, manifold recent business scandals show widespread disregard of corporate social responsibility and evidence of immoral profit seeking.

Ip (2009) takes stock of the moral doldrums created by socially irresponsible profit seeking though a brief account of three major scandals where unscrupulous profit-maximizing behaviour has led to environmental degradation, product safety issues and extreme exploitation of labour and violation of labour rights.

Air pollution and toxic rivers have recently become major issues of concern. These are among the most visible, but far from the only incidents of large-scale ecological degradation in China. The absence of a coherent system of environmental legislation combined with weak and ineffective enforcement led to neglect of environmental protection in favour of unrestrained economic growth. Corruption in local government, feeble central control and business–government cronyism further exacerbate the problems.

Product safety is another major concern (Khan et al., 2009). Negligence in health dangers puts consumers at risk. This is an effect of efforts to cut corners in the pursuit of maximum profit in an environment of weak regulation and *guanxi* corruption. Ip (2009) and Lu (2009) list a number of scandals and crises: tainted pet food, contaminated toothpaste, toxic toys, defective tyres and fake medicine. The mess is linked to weak regulation and lack of enforcement. However, irresponsible and immoral capitalist profit seeking reinforces the problem. In the last decade, China has tightened monitoring of safety and quality of food and pharmaceutical products. However, public trust in the capability and willingness of the government to take the safety issues seriously is low and difficult to regain. The continued emergence of new food safety scandals (*The Guardian*, 2013) contributes to an open cynicism among the professionals and managers interviewed in the context of this study.

> I worry a lot about food security. After the last scandal with contaminated vegetables I avoid street vendors and only buy foreign products. I use a lot of time on precautions and efforts to reduce risk.

Widespread violation of labour rights is another consequence of legally and morally unrestrained profit seeking. Working and employment conditions vary from relatively high salaries, employment security and the associated social security (the so-called 'iron rice bowl') in state-owned enterprises to low wages, precarious working conditions and absence of security in private companies. This is particularly the case for the estimated 200 million workers who have migrated from poor rural villages to urban areas to take up low-paying, dirty, unsafe and unhealthy jobs in the manufacturing and construction industries (Ip, 2009, p. 212). The violations of the migrant workers' rights are extensive and frequent, partly because they are the most marginalized and powerless group. The violations include withheld or delayed payment of wages; longer working hours than stipulated in state regulations; failure to pay overtime pay; physical and verbal abuse from employers and security staff, and appalling conditions in their living quarters (Ip, 2009, p. 213). In addition, migrant workers are not covered by accident insurance and only few have medical insurance. Their plight is worsened by their status as rural rather than urban citizens (the so-called *hukou* system), which implies that they have no access to social services and medical care and their children have only access to education in the rural areas from which they originate (*World Bank*, 2013, pp. 32–33).

However, also workers in state-owned enterprises experience serious labour issues. Coal miners earn relatively high wages but endure extremely dangerous working conditions. According to official Chinese statistics the number of deaths from mining accidents is enormous, i.e. the number of deaths per ton of coal is a hundred times higher than in the United States.

Other labour issues include forced labour and human trafficking, which are not unusual in China. The arrests and convictions of several hundred people, including local Communist Party officials, responsible for organizing slave labour in Shanxi and Henan provinces (BBC News; see Ip, 2009) appear to be only the top of the iceberg.

Emerging conflicts and protests

The costs of socially irresponsible corporate behaviour have become more evident and the underlying dissatisfaction with the situation has seemingly increased. However, dissatisfaction is not only tacit and underlying. Increasingly it takes the form of open dissent, conflict and protests. Recent years have seen protests against government inactivity in relation to pollution and the collusion between business interests and local governments. Other issues such as access to education and pension rights have also given impetus to public expressions of dissatisfaction (*Financial Times*, 2016a; *The Economist*, 2014). However, by far the most prevalent causes for conflicts and protests in recent years are labour disputes, and to an even larger extent, land grab by local governments and developers.

Labour protests have become far more frequent recently. According to official statistics, the number of major disputes increased from 23 in 2007 to 209 in 2012 (*Financial Times*, 2015a). The increased frequency of labour unrest is linked to the increasing relative economic power of labour as a result of early signs of depletion of the reservoir of cheap migrant labour, but the underlying cause is the extreme exploitation and the violations of labour rights. The labour disputes range from protests against closure of plants (*Financial Times*, 2016b) by relatively privileged workers in state-owned industries to suicides and threats of mass suicide by migrant workers as desperate protests against the slave-like employment conditions (*Daily Telegraph*, 2012).

However, the most frequent and most disruptive and violent protests have been rural protests against widespread land grab (*World Bank*, 2013, pp. 30–31). All land is owned by the state. Peasants have property in terms of the right to use their piece of land and ownership of its proceeds. They own their house and the associated equipment and livestock. However, the state, or, in practice, the local government has the formal ownership and the ultimate right to expropriate all land at a price corresponding to its value in agricultural production. After the advent of the financial crisis in 2008 the revised Chinese economic growth strategy gave priority to infrastructure and construction projects. This resulted in a building boom and rapid extension of urban space. Local governments expropriate peasant land for what is seen by the expropriated part as a compensation which is far too low, failing to take account of their investments in the place, providing them with no opportunities to acquire new land or accommodation of similar standard. The land is then resold to developers for a much higher price. The differential contributes a crucial part of the local government budget, and deals are often associated with kickbacks to local officials.

More than four million rural inhabitants have lost their land to local governments every year since 2008 (*The Guardian*, 2014). The land grab has fuelled anger and widespread protests in many rural areas. Frustrated by futile attempts to restrain local governments, petitions have been made to the central government in Beijing. In 2010, a total of 180,000 petitions related to alleged land grab were made (Hodgson & Huang, 2013). At least 39 farmers resorted to suicide in desperation/protest against eviction (*New York Times*, 2015). Even violent riots are not uncommon. In Chengdu alone, several violent incidents are reported every day (*Financial Times*, 2015b). Recent riots in Wukan and Fuyou resulted in many deaths of protesters as well as government officials and policemen (Hodgson & Huang, 2013; *Financial Times*, 2015b).

More Confucianism as solution

The entrenched crony capitalism is partly a consequence of the dark side of *guanxi* and, as such, of the Confucian cultural heritage. However, the emerging business scandals and public protests can also be seen as caused by too little Confucianism. Immoral profit seeking can be seen as a result of too much unrestrained modernity and too little Confucianism. The perpetrators seek economic gain and shun their responsibilities to subordinates. They fail to adhere to the five virtues. They are no Confucianism 'gentlemen'. Corruption, exploitation of labour and land grab are caused by violations of the Confucian requirements of mutual obligations, reciprocity and paternalism. In other words, part of the reason for the anger and protests is the breakdown of the implicit Confucian contract of hierarchy and harmony because of the superiors' moral deficiencies. Institutional reform is probably the most important part of the cure but moral restoration, business ethics and corporate social responsibility may also have a role to play (Han, 2013).

Recent political initiatives point in this direction. The Chinese Communist Party has recently restored Confucianism as a moral foundation, seeking a fresh source of legitimacy by reinventing the party as inheritor and saviour of a 5,000-year-old civilization. Since 2014, the party has publicly ordered its officials nationwide to attend lectures on Confucius and other classical Chinese thinkers. Confucianism is being reintroduced in the education system. Textbooks are being rewritten, curricula revised and teachers retrained to inject a solid dose of Confucian thinking in the education system (Page, 2015). Even 'traditional' civil servant examinations have been introduced in parts of China (Hang, 2011, p. 439). At the same time the access and use of Western textbooks and cultural influence is being reduced.

It remains to be seen if the restoration of Confucianism is here to stay or rather a brief interlude similar to episodes in the past. Is it a means to counter the spread of Western political ideals of individual freedom and democracy in a reversal of cultural values and ideology, or is it a temporary fix to boost the legitimacy of the regime? Or, is it a serious attempt to inject much-needed Chinese-style moral restoration, business ethics and corporate social responsibility?

References

Ackerly, B.A. (2005). Is liberalism the only way toward democracy? Confucianism and democracy. *Political Theory*, 33: 547–576.

Andersen, A.R., and Lee, E.Y.C. (2008). From tradition to modern attitudes and applications of guanxi in Chinese entrepreneurship. *Journal of Small Business and Enterprise Development*, 15(4): 775–787.

Bolino, M.C., Turnley, W.H., and Bloodgood, J.M. (2002). Citizenship behavior and the creation of social capital in organizations. *Academy of Management Review*, 27(4): 505–522.

Buttery, E.A., and Leung, T.K.P. (1998). 'The difference between Chinese and western negotiations. *European Journal of Marketing*, 32: 374–389.

Buttery, A.E., and Wong, Y.H. (1999). The development of a guanxi framework. *Marketing Intelligence and Planning,* 17(3): 147–154.

Chan, G.K.Y. (2008). The relevance and value of Confucianism in contemporary business ethics. *Journal of Business Ethics*, 77: 347–360.

Chen, X.-P., Eberly, M.B., Chiang, T.-J., Farh, J.-L., and Chng, B.-S. (2014). Affective trust in Chinese leaders: linking paternalistic leadership to employee performance. *Journal of Management*, 40(3): 769–819.

Cheung, T.C., and King, A.Y. (2004). Righteousness and profitableness: the moral choices of contemporary Confucian entrepreneurs. *Journal of Business Ethics*, 54: 245–260.

Daily Telegraph. (2012). "Mass suicide" protests at Apple Manufacturer Foxconn, 11 January.

Davies, H., Leung, T.K.P., Luk, S.T.K., and Wong, Y. (1995). The benefits of 'guanxi': the value of relationships in developing the Chinese market. *Industrial Marketing Management*, 24: 207–214.

De Bettingies, H.-C., and Tan, C.K. (2007). Values and management education in China. *International Management Review,* 3(1): 17–37.

Dirlik, A. (1997). Critical reflections on "Chinese capitalism" as a paradigm. *Identities: Global Studies in Culture and Power*, 3(3): 303–330.

Dunning, J.H., and Kim, C. (2007). The cultural roots of guanxi: an exploratory study. *The World Economy*, 30: 329–341.

Fan, Y. (2002). Questioning guanxi: definition, classification and implications. *International Business Review,* 11: 543–561.

Fang, T. (2003). A critique of Hofstede's fifth national culture dimension. *International Journal of Cross Cultural Management*, 3(3): 347–368.

Financial Times. (2015a). Toil and trouble, 8 June.

Financial Times. (2015b). Dying for land, 7 August.

Financial Times. (2016a). China university quota cuts prompt protests, 24 May.

Financial Times (2016b). China police round up protesting coal miners, 15th March.

Fock, K.Y., and Woo, K. (1998). The China market: strategic implications of guanxi. *Business Strategy Review*, 7(4): 33–44.

Frederickson, H.G. (2002). Confucius and the moral basis of bureaucracy. *Administration and Society*, 33(6): 610–628.

Guo, C., and Miller, J.K. (2010). Guanxi dynamics and entrepreneurial firm creation and development in China. *Management and Organisation Review*, 6(2): 267–291.

Han, P.-C. (2013). Confucian leadership and the rising Chinese economy: implications for developing global leadership. *The Chinese Economy*, 46(2): 107–127.

Hang, L. (2011). Traditional Confucianism and its contemporary relevance. *Asian Philosophy*, 21(4): 437–445.

Hodgson, G.M., and Huang, K. (2013). Brakes on Chinese development: institutional causes of a growth slowdown. *Journal of Economic Issues*, 47(3): 599–622.

Hofstede, G. (1984). *Culture's Consequences: International Differences in Work-Related Values (2nd ed.). Beverly Hills, CA: Sage.*

Hofstede, G., and Bode, M.H. (1988). The Confucius connection: from cultural roots to economic growth. *Organizational Dynamics*, 16: 5–21.

Hsu, C. L. (2005). Capitalism without contracts versus capitalists without capitalism: comparing the influence of Chinese guanxi and Russian blat on marketization. *Communist and Post-Communist Studies*, 38: 309–327.

Hwang, K.-K. (1990). Modernisation of the Chinese family business. *International Journal of Psychology*, 25: 593–618.

Hwang, K.-K. (1999). Filial piety and loyalty: two types of social identification in Confucianism. *Asian Journal of Social Psychology*, 2: 163–183.

Ip, P.K. (2009). The challenge of developing a business ethics in China. *Journal of Business Ethics*, 88: 211–224.

Jacobs, L., Guopei, G., and Herbig, P. (1995). Confucian roots in China: a force for today's business. *Management Decision*, 33(10): 29–34.

Khan, S., Munir, A.H., and Mu, J. (2009). Water management and crop production for food security in China: a review. *Agricultural Water Management*, 96(3): 349–360.

Kirby, D.A., and Fan, Y. (1995). Chinese cultural values and entrepreneurship. A preliminary consideration. *Journal of Enterprising Culture*, 3(3): 245–260.

Kung, J.K-s., and Ma, C. (2014). Can cultural norms reduce conflicts? Confucianism and peasant rebellions in Qing China. *Journal of Development Economics*, 111: 132–149.

Liao, D., and Sohmen, P. (2001). The development of modern entrepreneurship in China. *Stanford Journal of East Asian Affairs*, 1: 27–33.

Lin, L.-H., and Ho, Y-L. (2009). Confucian dynamism, culture and ethical changes in Chinese societies: a comparative study of China, Taiwan and Hong Kong. *The International Journal of Human Resource Management*, 20(11): 2402–2417.

Lu, X. (2009). A Chinese perspective: business ethics in China now and in the future. *Journal of Business Ethics*, 86: 451–461.

Luo, Y. (2008). The changing Chinese culture and business behaviour: the perspective of intertwinement between guanxi and corruption. *International Business Review*, 17: 188–193.

New York Times. (2015). Choosing death over eviction, 15 September.

Nuyen, A.T. (1999). Chinese philosophy and western capitalism. *Asian Philosophy*, 9(1): 71–79.

Page, J. (2015). Why China is turning back to Confucius. *Wall Street Journal*, 20 September.

Park, S.H., and Luo, Y. (2001). Guanxi and organizational dynamics: organizational networking in Chinese firms. *Strategic Management Journal*, 22: 455–477.

Parnell, M.F. (2005). Chinese business guanxi: an organisation or non-organisation? *Journal of Organisational Transformation and Social Change,* 2(1): 29–47.

Schuman, M. (2015). *Confucius and the World he Created*. New York: Basic Books.

The Economist. (2014). Labour unrest. Danger zone, 26 April, p. 57.

The Guardian. (2013). Food scandals are undermining trust in China's new regime, 12 May.

The Guardian. (2014). Champion of Chinese farmers' rights jailed for forgery, 28 June.

Wang, J., Wang, G.G., Ruona, W.E.A., & Rojewski, J.W. (2005). Confucian values and the implication for international HRD. *Human Resource Development International*, 8(3): 311–326.

Weber, M. (1951, first published in German 1915). *The Religion of China. Confucianism and Taoism*. New York: Free Press.

World Bank. (2013). *China 2013: Building a Modern, Harmonious, and Creative Society*. Washington, DC: World Bank.

Wu, W.-P., and Leung, A. (2005). Does a micro–macro link exist between managerial value of reciprocity, social capital and firm performance? The case of SMEs in China. *Asia Pacific Journal of Management*, 22: 445–463.

Xu, K. (2006). Early Confucian principles: the potential theoretic foundation of democracy in modern China. *Asian Philosophy*, 16(2): 135–148.

Yang, Z., and Wang, C.L. (2011). Guanxi as a governance mechanism in business markets: its characteristics, relevant theories, and future research directions. *Industrial Marketing Management*, 40: 492–495.

Yao, X. (2000). *An Introduction to Confucianism*. Cambridge: Cambridge University Press.

Yin, L.C. (2003). Do traditional values still exist in modern Chinese societies? The case of Singapore and China. *Asia Europe Journal*, 1: 43–59.

Zhuang, J., Thomas, S., and Miller, D.I. (2005). Examining culture's effect on whistle-blowing and peer reporting. *Business and Society*, 44(4): 462–486.

6 Economies of scope

Explaining liberal authority and its consequences in the Eurozone

Charlie Dannreuther

Introduction – the problem with neoliberalism

For some time before the financial crisis, critiques of "neoliberalism" abounded in popular and academic debates. For some neoliberalism was seen to be the advance of free markets into areas where states once protected social rights; for others it was the disciplinary ideology that asserted the power of markets over people and nature, even producing neoliberal subjects. The notion that markets exercised power was not a new one by any means. Indeed a core assumption of political and institutional economy is that markets do not "clear" automatically, that they need regulating or support from state or public-sector authorities. Neoliberalism (or ordoliberalism) described the productive role of the free market through moralising, demonising, and disciplining everyday lives. Post-crisis neoliberalism described the assertion of austerity to push through health-sector reforms and as a meme that validated regional under-development, and anti-democratic and authoritarian policies imposed by the EU and Germany on smaller Eurozone member states.

Increasingly, however, the term "neoliberalism" has lost its power as both a mobiliser for political action and a way of capturing diverse material realities (Venugopal, 2015). Too many complex decisions in too broad a range of experiences are laid at the foot of neoliberalism. If abstract market freedoms are the mechanism for neoliberalism then how is power exercised? Can over-simplistic determinism can get in the way of much-needed scrutiny or even contain opposition? For example, some member states have demanded more exemption from Transatlantic Trade and Investment Partnership for their health services than others. The increasingly slack usage of neoliberalism as a descriptor has allowed the signifier to float away from the signified, making it harder for those opposing the privatisation of health (for example) to identify links with those challenging austerity. Like its associated term "globalisation," neoliberalism has been a victim of its own success.

The aim of this chapter is not to deny these phenomena. Rather we aim to reinterpret them through the framework of economies of scale and economies of scope, concepts more closely associated with mainstream management science. The reasons for this are twofold. First, describing the problem in the same language as the perpetrator may allow an alignment of facts to demonstrate internal contradictions in capital accumulation. Second, by examining how management science assumptions have been accepted uncritically in international political economy, we may also be able to problematise and even reinterpret key trends and events and so generate different political responses.

The chapter proceeds in the following stages. First we examine the political economy of scale and scope. This section introduces Chandler's concepts of scale and scope and argues that they warrant further investigation. Specifically, the notion of economies of scope and its relationship with concepts like representation needs further unpacking. The following section looks at how economies of scale have been used to justify and explain European integration in the past and have tended to be functionalist in their representation of European society. The fourth section demonstrates how this was possible due to the limited representation of the economy to core corporatist actors at the expense of the more diverse and less homogeneous grouping of the *petite bourgeoisie*. The rest of the chapter explores the redefinition and reassertion of the *petite bourgeoisie* as small and medium-sized enterprises (SMEs), the reframing of SMEs as delivering economies of scope for financial markets, and the subsequent support for development of capital markets to support these relations. Finally the chapter concludes on the political economy of scope.

Economies of scale and scope

If markets are not exercising control there are many explanations for who or what is. Sociological approaches highlight the role of social forces, ideas, or hegemonic class relations. For institutional economists who see markets as institutions (rather than institutions as markets), "lock-in" may be determined by technology and change by entrepreneurial individuals. Both refer to history and to institutional methods to explore how the market is coordinated by a "visible hand." Alfred Chandler exemplified this approach with his empirically rich analyses of the birth of the modern corporation. The "M corporation" succeeded by combining economies of scale (in manufacturing) and economies of scope (in marketing) with capable management (Chandler, 2009). Economies of scale described the reduction of unit costs through increased volume. Greater production runs required greater capital investment but could dramatically drive down unit costs. Economies of scope referred to the reduction in costs by exploiting diversity. A marketing department might be used to sell five products rather than one, or a railway built to carry raw materials to a plant might be opened up to passenger trains.

These concepts are familiar to students of political economy. Economies of scale could also describe the extension of the working day described by theories of labour value theory as the increase in absolute surplus value. Economies of scope described the benefits of joint production of, for example, market regulation in a shared set of political institutions or a new flexible form of technology. This might be familiar as a change in the relative surplus value in the market. Improving management capabilities will be familiar to any public-sector worker in the relentless pursuit of improved performance delivery, or the decentralisation of decision making within a devolved political structure.

For Chandler it was only when the mass production technologies that delivered economies of scale were married with the marketing and distribution techniques that delivered economies of scope that the managerial corporation came to prevail (manufacturing, marketing, and management made this the "M corporation"). Entrepreneurs who invested in management capability could obtain a first mover advantage if they could maintain levels of throughput that allowed the benefits of mass production manufacturing techniques to generate vast profits.

While Knight focused on the role of the entrepreneurial manager, he is perhaps better remembered for his distinction between risk and uncertainty (Knight, 2012). This distinction rests on the identification of a homogeneous grouping from which statistically credible probabilities of prices and demand can be calculated. Like Chandler, this would require a well-organised corporation with expert (or competent) managers to coordinate the process. Like Chandler, there were also economies of scale and scope to be realised in Knight's risk/uncertainty distinction. A production line that generated low unit costs could assume high levels of statistical accuracy. Calculating these unit costs would inform decisions about capital investment. The greater the homogeneity of the grouping, the greater the predictability and so the greater the potential for securing the benefits of both scale and scope.

This explains the investment in the social institutions and welfare compromises that companies committed to in the golden years of capitalism. Economies of scale were organised by negotiating collective wage agreements with labour unions that enabled corporations to survive fluctuations in demand. Negotiating at the national level would reduce the costs of plant-level negotiations, realising economies of scale, while the use of trade unions to also organise a range of other labour-related activities (apprentices, working conditions, social events) offered economies of scope. Historically, in small-scale societies the differentiation between goods and assets and the institutions that regulated and supplied them was limited. But as they grew gaps emerged in the assets available (schools) and in the supply of key public (security) and private (food) goods that necessitated the growth of the state. Industrial scale was accompanied by industrial society with its needs and institutions, hence the emergence of Fordism.

Chandler explicitly rejected any analytical claim to explaining the political or labour consequences of his analysis. But his ideas have been taken up broadly: *Visible Hand* has in excess of 6,700 citations on Google Scholar. For example, in central contribution to the debate about globalisation, scale and scope were used to explain the emergence of the modern nation state:

> the development of scale economies in both the economic system and the political order during the nineteenth and early twentieth centuries dramatically reinforced and expanded the scope of this institutional isomorphism. A powerful structural convergence developed between the second industrial revolution economy, on the one hand, and the bureaucratic state, on the other.
>
> (Cerny, 1995: 598)

By the mid-1990s, however, the needs of society changed, creating a disjuncture between the goods and assets needed and those supplied by the state:

> In recent decades, however, an accelerating divergence has taken place between the structure of the state and the structure of industrial and financial markets in the complex, globalizing world of the third industrial revolution. There is a new disjuncture between institutional capacity to provide public goods and the structural characteristics of a much larger-scale, global economy. I suggest here that today's "residual state" faces crises of both organizational efficiency and institutional legitimacy.
>
> (Cerny, 1995: 598)

In this early piece on globalisation, the concepts of scale and scope explained the rise of regional trade areas in place of nation states, and the acceleration of corporate and financial market integration across the world. This important explanation of the phenomenon of globalisation relied heavily on economies of scale and scope to explain the emergence of regional trade areas with standardised market rules. Since that time, and often in direct response to the assumption of globalisation, a large literature emerged on the changing competences of public administration in the competitiveness literature, new public management literature, and practices designed to improve public-sector performance through benchmarking and good practice. But there was only scant discussion of the political economy of scope.

Yet economies of scope are central to understanding the changing forms of representation that have characterised late modern democracies in Europe because they describe the way that diversity is captured into the decision-making process. In the language of politics this is called representation. The "principal agent" form of representation described that the principal (voter) who delegated the representative function to a representative (politician, trade union, interest group) to act on his or her behalf was no longer credible. Since the 1970s new social movements, declining voter turnouts for national and EU elections, a refutation of traditional class cleavage for identity politics, and the assertion of marketing techniques in political campaigning all undermined the ability of representatives to speak with authority on behalf of their constituents, i.e. to represent them.

In its place new forms of representation came to dominate, described as "microcosmic" (Maclean, 1991). This form of representation has an empirical reality, like a photograph that attempts to capture a real or objective picture of the constituency. It is most closely associated with statistical representations of groups. A microcosmic form of representation offers far greater opportunities for control. This is evident even if we ignore all the costs of organised political activity and labour strikes that may secure expensive egalitarian policies. Representation can be delivered more cheaply through surveys and consultations designed to address specific policy issues than expensive forms of participatory democracy or electoral campaigns. Auditors can use predefined methods and recognised standards to compare the value and cost of new initiatives in ways that are far more predictable than the random outcome of elections. This enables significant economies of scale in representation. Microcosmic representation also allows for greater economies of scope. By reducing the role of the political agent to a supervisory one (Majone, 1994), technocratic decisions can prevail in the assessment of credible needs and voices. Accounting standards and procedures can deliver transparency by using techniques like cost–benefit analysis, by defining performance criteria, and by comparing these across different sectors of the public and then private sector (Henkel, 1991).

The next sections of the chapter aim to illustrate how this shift in economy of scope described changes in the political economy of the EU. First there is a description of how economies of scale have habitually been deployed to explain and justify economic integration in the EU, followed by a demonstration that these economies-of-scale arguments did not accommodate the diversity of national economies and relied instead on an understanding of diversity that was constrained within modern forms of political representation. The *petite bourgeoisie* is described as a case in point. The next section demonstrates how changes in financial technologies allowed more complex representations to be developed of the economy that allowed greater economies of scope to be realised through the securitisation of small business debt using credit scoring.

Scale and the EU

From the point of view of decreasing costs of trade, European integration is often presented as a success. The removal of first tariff barriers and then quotas under the Treaties of Paris and then Rome enabled large companies to retain extraordinary levels of throughput in the economies of France and Germany. Economies of scale were central to the rationale for further integration which made the arguments for further economic integration in the 1980s. The 1988 Ceccini Report, commissioned by Lord Cockfield to calculate the impact of the 1985 White Paper on completing the single market, asserted that "Economic gains from the 1992 programme could rise to 200 billion ECU or more, together with a substantial boost to employment" (CEC, 1988: 1). This gross figure was based on a series of measurements of the micro economic consequences of a single market in the EU, such as:

(a) the removal of frontier delays and costs,
(b) the opening of public markets to competition,
(c) the liberalisation and Integration of financial markets, and
(d) more general supply-side effects, reflecting changes In the strategic behaviour of enterprises in a new competitive environment.

(CEC, 1988: 5)

The gains calculated "from exploiting economies of scale more fully" were calculated at ECU 61 billion or gross domestic product (GDP) 2.1% (CEC, 1988: 10). Similar reports are regularly produced by the European Parliament Think Tank, which published its third edition of *Mapping the Cost of Non-Europe* in April 2015 (EP, 2015), although the same information is now presented regularly in a diagrammatic form (Figure 6.1) (EP, 2015: 11).

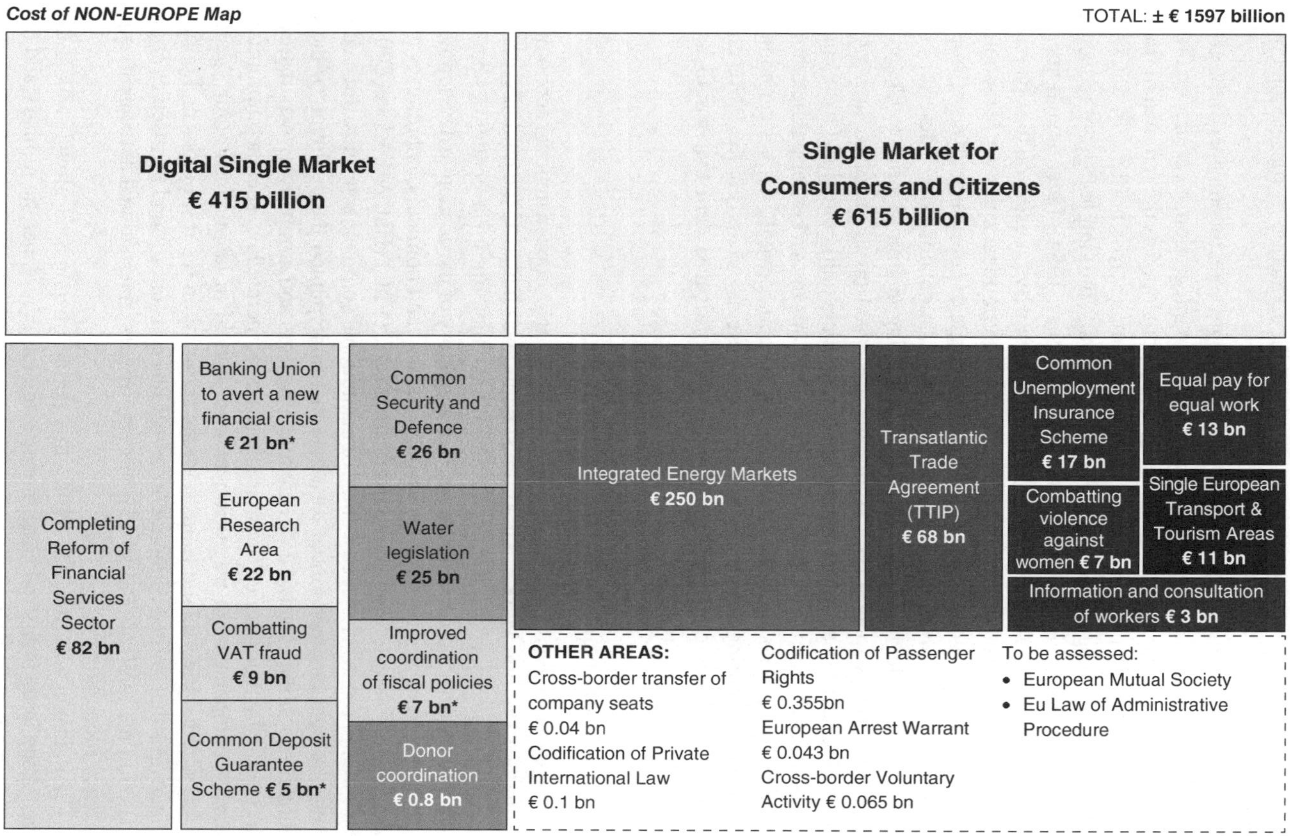

Figure 6.1 Cost of non-Europe

The point that Europe is cheaper than non-Europe has retained its power in the launch of many other EU agendas (e.g. cost of non-capital union). The benefit of such an argument is that it is clear, authoritative (in that authorities can support it) and links the benefits to integration directly to the reduction of transaction costs experienced by all economic actors in the EU.

This focus on reducing transaction costs is recognisable for students of the politics of European integration as a driver to European integration. Neofunctionalists, like Ernst Haas, argued that economies of scale developed as the removal of trade barriers generated opportunities for new transactions across borders. In this way much, if not all, integration could be justified through the simple logic of reducing costs to trade by achieving economies of scale (Haas, 1958). Later developments of the approach focused more on economies of scope by focusing on the upstream integration of market regulatory functions through political spillover (Tranholm-Mikkelsen, 1991). Indeed, the functionalist language of political analysis mirrored closely that of Chandler. Majone's construct of a "regulatory state" describes the input and output legitimacy of EU decision making in similar terms to Chandler (Majone & Baake, 1996). His arguments are based on the relative savings of EU-level regulation and the economies of scale that could be realised by a single market. At the same time the devolution of decisions to markets or public administrations through an agenda of multi-level governance would deliver economies of scope by capturing a diversity of interests. These discussions in the 1990s contributed to debates over reforms to the EU's political system that would later inform the Lisbon Treaty.

Scale without scope under the national fix

Modern corporations captured economies of scale and scope in national economies within the Common Market. This Fordist period was hailed as the golden years of industrial capitalism ("*les trente glorieuses*") in which European economies developed into modern industrialised form. The trajectory of the economic development of these markets was coordinated through societal and political compromises and successfully presented as "varieties of capitalism" (VoC) (Hall & Soskice, 2001). The VoC approach privileged a range of institutional complementarities, often confirmed in legal or other formal relations, that underpinned the evolution of these national economic systems. For example, investors and company owners/managers complied with rules defined in traditions of corporate law, social compromises between companies and wage earners were upheld in labour institutions, states clearly defined their relationships with the economy in the institutions and policy frameworks that guided economic interventions and states found themselves coordinated in the international system through treaties, international agreements and currency hierarchies.

The management of scope during this period of industrial growth was at the level of the large industrial conglomerate, the large bureaucratic ministry and the organised labour movement. Such analyses are often entered through an emphasis on one of these institutional complementarities such as corporate form, or the wage labour relation or the organisation of the political parties. In each, economies of scope were pre-aligned to readily organised groups. Diversity was predefined, evolving into a structure that could cooperate with others within the national institutional milieu.

By confirming the status quo through its functions, the VoC assumes conformity and coherence. Yet many such groupings were both arbitrary and the product of political conflict and more often than not the *petite bourgeoisie* under Fordism was defined as peripheral to capital accumulation. Indeed, Marx dismissed the lower strata of the middle classes because of their lack of capital and limited productive scale in the face of modern industry. Stuck between the main classes, the *petite bourgeoisie* could only hope to inspire a socialism based on corporate guilds for manufacture and patriarchy for agriculture (Marx & Engels, 2002). They were destined to a "miserable fit of the blues" (Marx & Engels, 2002: 60). This "miserable fit of the blues" took the form of a considerable body of the social support for National Socialism in 1930s Germany (Crossick & Haupt, 1997). Even before then, much liberal and radical commentary has been dismissive of the *petite bourgeoisie* for its "egoism and narrowness of spirit" (Crossick & Haupt, 1997).

Crossick and Haupt (1997) revealed more ambiguous structural constraints to the development of a coherent *petite bourgeoisie* class formation. The uncertainties of industrial transformation, local constraints and social formation around the family all contributed to the creation of a heterogeneous and disparate political group. They warned of "the false perspective obtained by analysing "a class" that appears to exist only at a time of extreme crisis, rather than recognising the fundamental functional division within it between entrepreneurs and workers" (Morris, 1996: 280).

The *petite bourgeoisie* only appear to get their act together under times of great societal duress: the presence of an organised *petite bourgeoisie* was therefore a signal of very bad times. Yet coherence had formed among the sector around the far right in the past, so under what conditions did this occur? The "social question" that characterised late 19th-century European politics was experienced as a drive for centralisation at the expense of the *petite bourgeoisie.*

> In Germany industry concluded the Stinnes-Legien Pact with the unions on 15 November 1918. Artisans therefore lost the political function they had enjoyed during the Kaiserreich as a buffer between capital and labour. Then the formation of the Weimar coalition, including the Social Democrats, compounded this feeling of exclusion and encouraged a nostalgia for the more authoritarian days before the war when artisans had had a more secure political role and their socialist enemies had been kept firmly out of power.
>
> (McKitrick, 1996: 403–404)

It was a similar experience in Sweden, where competition with larger units weakened the closer ties between shop owners and their employees. The Swedish Model, introduced by the Social Democratic party, shared a common ideology with the unions, cooperative movements and larger corporations. Shopkeepers were "squeezed between different interest groups" (Ericsson, 1996: 368). During the inter-war years, when economic and structural uncertainties prevailed, the *petite bourgeoisie* was therefore more politically exposed than the unionised workforce engaged in nationally significant production. Their recognition and valorisation in Germany was less the product of political patronage and more in the pursuit of economic necessity. Despite the ideology of self-sufficiency and liberalism that characterised many European *petite bourgeoisie*, it was often state intervention, rather than self-organisation, that led to their effective representation in political life.

Artisans or self-employed people were seen as simple commodity producers working usually in an individual capacity and in local markets. They had limited labour, often fewer workers than family members, and so offered few opportunities for increasing profitability through capital investment or achieving economies of scale or scope. The uncertainty associated with this small firm was one of contingency. Undefinable, unmanageable and individualist, the *petite bourgeoisie* inhabited a place where there was no universal truth because every experience was different.

Economies of scope were difficult to secure from this group, making it economically peripheral despite its social significance. Because of this, credit supplies to small firms in post-war Europe were therefore the consequence of either direct state intervention or indirect financial market regulation (Zysman, 1984). Germany's KfW benefitted from Marshall Aid and used these funds to offer cheap credit to small firms. For economies with limited industrial growth national banks injected credit to small villages through local branches (as in France) and locally sponsored banks delivered credit to Italian small firms in the post-1945 period (Weiss, 1984). Small firms were regulated through local chambers and corporations or through other state-sponsored regulations that demanded specific skills to be able to trade. But these organisations were based on archaic, not modern, assumptions and there was also a concern that the *petite bourgeoisie* would lapse into fascism (Weiss, 1986). Banks had to manage the risk of investing in small firms through expensive branch-based relationships between the bank manager and the small company, rather than realising effective economies of scale and scope. Most famous for this were banks in the UK where the larger liberal-market economy presented a significant and long-standing gap for those seeking finance between the sizes of bank loans and the equity markets. The policy solution was to pool the risk of lending to small firms between banks in the Industrial and Commercial Financial Corporation. These loans were limited and unproductive.

Neoliberalism and the politics of scope

From the mid-1970s to the late 1990s, Fordism transformed from a period of growth based on flexible specialisation to one dominated by a finance-led regime of accumulation. The economies of scope enjoyed during the mass production era that had relied on reducing labour costs through concerted labour market institutions were now no longer credible as manufacturing relocated internationally. Left behind in Europe were place-specific services that could add value but were less able to generate the levels of demand in consumer markets associated with mass production. But with more complex societies with differentiated needs, flexible forms of production line that enabled short-batch specialised production and a shift in economic emphasis to services such as marketing, these labour market institutions were seen as too inflexible to offer the economies of scope that would generate the wages to match labour wages with the required levels of consumption.

By the mid-1990s a range of circumstances had contributed to the assimilation of the *petite bourgeoisie* into the mainstream economy. First they were now called SMEs and associated with high-tech growth, entrepreneurial risk taking and economic dynamism. This was supported secondly by a policy framework introduced by a 1994 Commission White Paper based around the idea of competitiveness. While the European Employment Strategy had reinforced the notion that SMEs created jobs, the White Paper on competitiveness argued for widespread changes in societal institutions to facilitate the growth of a dynamic and flexible European economy. Thirdly the end of the Cold War was taken to confirm the victory of free markets and freedom over socialism and democracy. Finally the commitment to the Economic and Monetary Union placed a strait-jacket on member-state expenditure, limiting their ability to deliver wages through corporatist agreements with trade unions. SMEs presented an alternative representation of society that was pro-market, allowed under EU state aid regimes and disorganised. The flexibilility associated with these strategies failed to deliver high levels of growth but did enable the break-up of traditional social compromises based on wage labour relations.

These changes are often characterised as neoliberal: deregulated markets, individualisation, precariousness, financialisation are all associated with the promotion of SME policies. But they were not primarily concerned with liberalism so much as control through a new category of SME that would enable new economies of scope. The SME was a universal category that could capture the diversity of the EU economy on an infinite scale and in doing so demonstrate the potential for stable growth. For the rest of the chapter we explore this through the growth of financial practices and EU associated policy responses.

Scale and scope of the EU

The main obstacle to realising economies of scale and scope in financial services was the issue of control. IT technology did not present problems for scale or scope, as processing data on market behaviour could benefit from huge mainframes (scale) and the same computer can do a little or a lot of calculations without any additional costs (scope). Nightingale and Poll (2000) demonstrated that, despite investing over $1billion a year in IT systems, Chase bank was unable to manage the complexity of its new trading technologies because of issues of control. Scale and scope were possible even in a service corporation, but only because the development of new capabilities in control allowed this to happen. This control was defined as achieving "purposive influence towards a predefined goal" and to do this required "communication between processes" and a "feedback mechanism to guide and redirect future action" (Nightingale & Poll, 2000: 121).

During the 1990s the widespread extension of credit scoring offered a whole new income stream for banks. Small-firm bank accounts became more profitable for banks in the UK (even during the recession). But it was the ability to translate these debts into collateral that could then be securitised and sold for an additional income stream that was vital to the evolution of finance as a dominant regime of accumulation. As Eisenbeis observed in 1996:

> credit-evaluation systems . . . quantify the risks of small-business borrowers so it becomes possible both to value and to monitor the payment performance of portfolios of these assets so they can be securitized and funded in the open market. . . . then the value of the traditional banking charter decline[s] . . . and the door will rapidly open for non traditional suppliers of credit to tap this market.

Small firms were no longer a liability which needed public insurance to encourage lending. They had become a central opportunity for income generation for financial institutions. After the unstable years of SME-oriented manufacturing growth in the 1980s and early 1990s, the huge increases in wealth creation from credit scoring and securitisation presented the SME with a whole new opportunity. Rather than representing a client to whom to deliver services, the SME became a source of collateral through which to generate speculative returns. The fees alone from these activities are extraordinary. Bankscope UK data (2014) show net fees and commissions as increasing both before and after the financial crisis (Figure 6.2).

Like other sections of the *petite bourgeoisie* – homeowners with mortgages, people with loans for cars or breast implants – these heterogeneous middle classes were no longer peripheral to the regime of accumulation but pivotal. But their place in the production process was redefined by the technologies and capacities of the new banks. SMEs were not only producing goods and services that they sold to consumers. Their most important contribution to the accumulation process was to service debts that served as collateral for securitisation. As long as they serviced these reliably, banks could generate secondary, more lucrative, income from the fees derived from securitised asset sales.

Securitisation was not entirely due to the economies of scope in lending to small firms and other parts of the *petite bourgeoisie* sector. SMEs generating niche products in global markets, or innovating or offering services like marketing or legal support or nail polishing, all play a vital role in the financialised economy. But the main contribution of SME finance was that it demonstrated how economies of scope could be realised through the securitisation of debt. By demonstrating how banks could generate fees through creating asset-backed securities (ABS), the economies of scope of lending to SMEs, subprime borrowers, student loans, and almost anything as long as they also produced a debt with credit score was demonstrated.

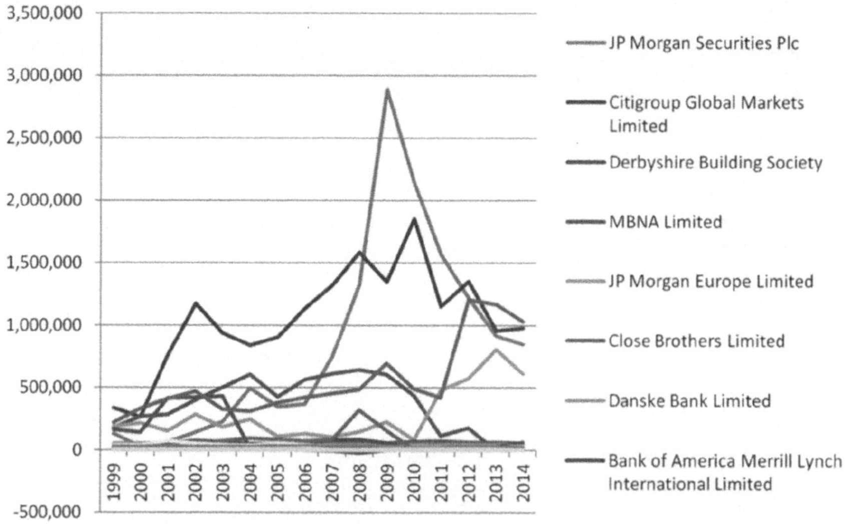

Figure 6.2 Bank fees and commissions

Financialisation of scale and scope and the case for capital market union

Recent calls for a capital market union by the Junker Commission and a wide range of financial elites (Bank of England to Association for Financial Markets in Europe) have placed special importance on the way that it will support small firms. Surveys of SME opinions have highlighted that the primary concern is demand in the economy. But the second concern has been a common call for credit availability. European SMEs are up to three times more likely to rely on bank finance than their US counterparts and significant variations in lending rates have emerged between core and periphery economies since the financial crisis (Figure 6.3).

The European Central Bank's (ECB's) solution to SME finance has been to promote the securitisation of SME debt (Coeuré, 2013; EIB, 2013; Bank of England/ECB, 2014) (Figures 6.4 and 6.5). This aims to allow banks to lend more while complying with Basel III, increase competition between banks and kick-start the EU's economy using private rather than public investment. The choice of this particular form of intervention is because of the lack of availability of SMEs to securitised issues and the relative abundance of this form of finance in the USA.

But another explanation may be the falling volume of sales of securities backed by SME debt (DB, 2014: 11) and the poor performance of the financial sector in comparison to its global competitors (Figure 6.6).

Asset securitisation was a core component of the failure of the US banking system – indeed, the name "subprime crisis" defines it in these terms. Furthermore, these off-book banking practices were largely unappreciated prior to the financial crisis, giving them the suspicious term of "shadow banking." Rather than

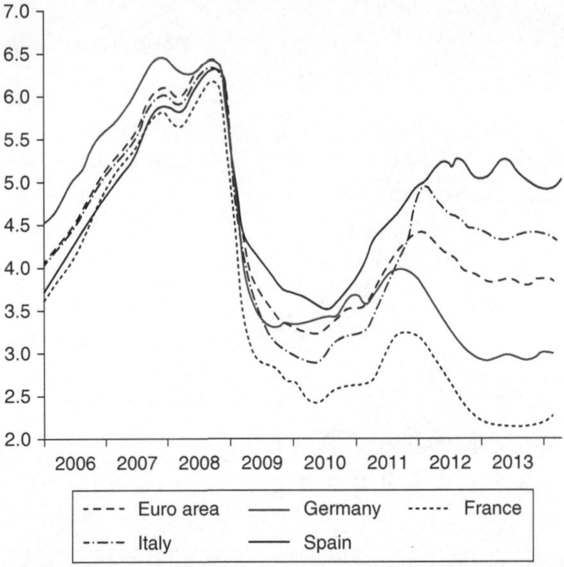

Figure 6.3 Indicator of the short-term cost of borrowing for non-financial corporations (ECB, 2012: 8)

Source: ECB and ECB calculations.

Notes: Short-term lending rates are a weighted average of loans with floating rates and with an initial rate fixation period of up to one year. Weights are based on new business volumes.

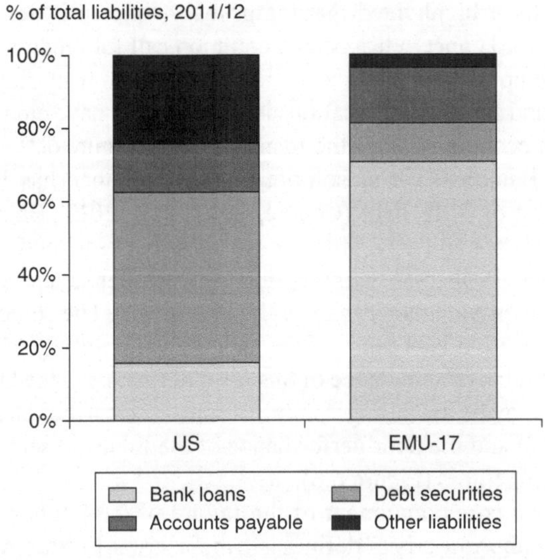

Figure 6.4 Bank versus capital market funding of non-financial corporations (DB, 2014: 5)

Source: Eurostat, Fed, DB Research

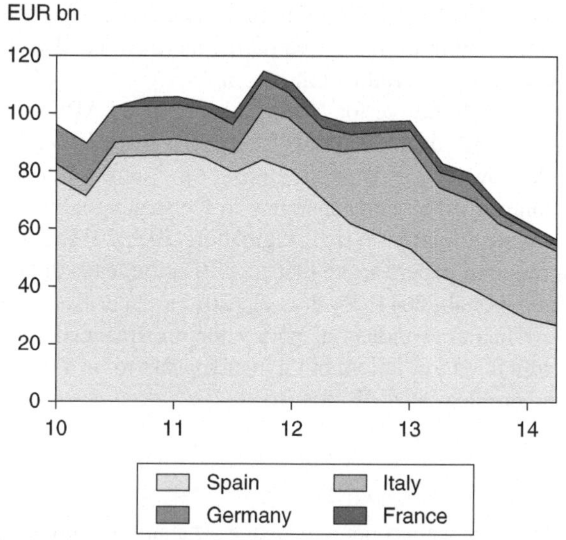

Figure 6.5 Outstanding amount of securities backed by loans to SMEs (DB, 2014: 11)

Source: AFME, Deutsche Bank Research

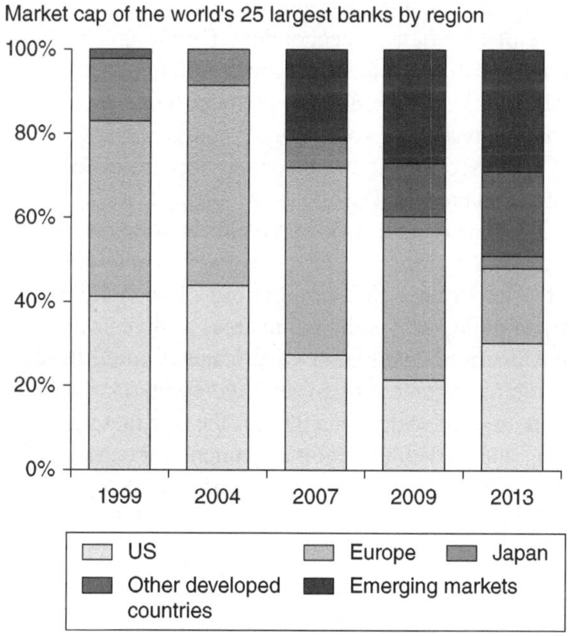

Figure 6.6 European banks losing ground

Source: Bloomberg, The Banker, Thomson, DB Research

Note: As of mid-June each year

introducing greater safeguards to protect against these practices, the goal of stimulating SME ABS markets has led the ECB to reduce them. Specifically the ECB lowered SME ABS minimum rating requirements (in December 2011, June 2012, July 2013) and lowered credit rating from 2xAAA to 2xAA in its Loan Level Data Transparency Initiative for ABS. It also reduced ABS (including SME ABS) "haircuts" (2xAA from 16% to 10%, 2xBBB from 26% to 24%) and so allowed banks to borrow, and so lend on, more for the same collateral.

Regulators have complained of poor transparency in fee structure, "incentive misalignment" and inadequate attention to risk origination (BIS, 2011; Burne & Kuriloff, 2015), while a range of papers argue that securitisation leads to opacity (Cheng et al., 2008; Petersen et al., 2011; Ryan et al., 2015). Securitisation may be politically expedient, a lucrative industrial policy for the financial services and a jumpstart for the capital market union, but it also appears to be a risky and improbable solution to the problem of SME finance.

Conclusion

This chapter has explored the political economy of scope. The aim was primarily to offer an alternative grounded explanation for neoliberalism by examining the way that the visible hand of modern corporation could exercise control by exploiting economies of scope. By focusing on Chandler's functionalist description of the M corporation, we could see how the representation of society contributed to authoritative structures.

In the international political economy literature, economies of scope have not received the same degree of attention as economies of scale or organisational capacity formation. Yet, as we can see, they have been central to understanding the dynamics of institutional evolution in the EU as a political economy. In this case we have examined how the representation of the *petite bourgeoisie* as SME could normalise a new form of credit scoring that would enable significant economies of scope through the securitisation process. Despite the problems associated with this approach to SME financing, considerable lock-in remains in policy arenas, in part because of their investment in the economies of scope that this involves.

This chapter shows the importance that assumptions of economies of scope have had for the delivery of policy across the EU in areas as diverse as including SME policy, competitiveness policy and good governance. Central to revealing assumptions of scope is the management of societal representation in the policy process. Focusing on economies of scale alone ignores the role that the control of diversity plays in securing and sustaining regional economic integration. By not recognising this, we also ignore the consequences that privileging specific forms of societal representation may have.

References

Bank of England/ECB. (2014). "The case for a better functioning securitisation market in the European Union." https://www.ecb.europa.eu/pub/pdf/other/ecb-- boe_case_better_functioning_securitisation_marketen.pdf (accessed 14 April 2015).

Bankscope. (2014). *Thomson One Banker*. Thomson Reuters. http://www.bvdinfo.com/en-gb/our-products/company-information/international-products/bankscope (accessed 10 September 2016).

BIS (Bank of International Settlement). (2011). *The Joint Forum – Report on Asset Securitisation Incentives*. Basel Committee on Banking Supervision. http://www.bis.org/publ/joint26.pdf (accessed 27 September 2016).

Burne, K., & Kuriloff, A. (2015). "Regulators want data on bond: trade FeesSEC, others scrutinize markups paid by retail bond investors." *Wall Street Journal*. http://www.dowjonesindex.today/stockmarkettoday---regulators---want---data---on---bond---trade---fees/ (accessed 23 January 2015).

CEC. (1988). *Europe 1992: The Overall Challenge SEC (88)524 Final*. CEC, Brussels.

Cerny, P. (1995). "Globalization and the changing logic of collective action." *International Organization* 49(4): 595–625.

Chandler, A. (2009). *Scale and Scope: The Dynamics of Industrial Capitalism*. Harvard University Press, Cambridge, MA.

Cheng, M., Dhaliwal, D., & Neamtiu, M. (2008). "Banks' assets ecuritization and information opacity." *Working Paper*, The University of Arizona. http://www.usc.edu/schools/business/FBE/seminars/papers/ARF_5---2---08_NEAMTIU.pdf (accessed 14 April 2015).

Coeuré, B. (2013). "SME financing, market innovation and regulation: Eurofi High Level Seminar organised in association with the Irish Presidency of the Council of the EU," Contribution to plenary Session 11: Challenges and feasibility of diversifying the financing of EU corporates and SMEs, Dublin, 11 April 2013. https://www.ecb.europa.eu/press/key/date/2013/html/sp130411.en.html (accessed 20 June 2016).

Crossick, G., & Haupt, H.-G. (1997). *The Petite Bourgeoisie in Europe 1780–1914: Enterprise, Family and Independence*. Psychology Press, London.

DB. (2013). *Bank Performance in the US and Europe: An Ocean Apart*. https://www.dbresearch.com/PROD/DBR_INTERNET_ENPROD/PROD0000000000320825.pdf (accessed 11 September 2016).

DB. (2014). *SME Financing in the Euro Area: New Solutions to an Old Problem*. https://www.dbresearch.com/PROD/DBR_INTERNET_EN-PROD/PROD0000000000344173/SME_financing_in_the_euro_area%3A_New_solutions_to_a.PDF (accessed 11 September 2016).

ECB. (2012). "Economic and monetary developments: monetary and financial developments." *ECB Monthly Bulletin* November. https://www.ecb.europa.eu/pub/pdf/other/mb201211_focus02.en.pdf (accessed 27 September 2016).

EIB. (2013). *SME Report 2013*. http://www.eib.org/infocentre/publications/all/sme---report---2013.htm (accessed 20 June 2016).

Eisenbeis, R.A. (1996). "Recent developments in the application of credit-scoring techniques to the evaluation of commercial loans." *IMA Journal of Mathematics Applied in Business & Industry* 7(4): 271–290.EP (European Parliament). (2015). *Mapping the Cost of Non-Europe*. http://www.europarl.europa.eu/RegData/etudes/STUD/2015/536364/EPRS_STU(2015)536364_EN.pdf (accessed 11 September 2016).

Ericsson, T. (1996). "Shopkeepers and the Swedish model: the petty bourgeoisie and the state during the interwar period." *Contemporary European History* 5(3): 357–369.

Haas, E.B. (1958). *The Uniting of Europe: Political, Social, and Economic Forces, 1950–1957*. No. 42. Stanford University Press, Stanford, CA.

Hall, P., & Soskice, D. (eds). (2001). *Varieties of Capitalism: The Institutional Foundations of Comparative Advantage*. OUP, Oxford.

Henkel, M. (1991). *Government, Evaluation and Change*. Jessica Kingsley, London.
Knight, F. (2012). *Risk, Uncertainty and Profit*. Houghton Mifflin, Boston (1921).
Maclean, I. (1991). "Forms of representation and systems of voting." In: Held, D. (ed.), *Political Theory Today,* pp. 172–198. Stanford University Press, Stanford, CA.
Majone, G. (1994). "The rise of the regulatory state in Europe." *West European Politics* 17(3): 77–101.
Majone, G., & Baake, P. (1996). *Regulating Europe*. Psychology Press, Abingdon.
Marx, K., & Engels, F. (2002). *The Communist Manifesto*. Penguin, Harmondsworth.
McKitrick, F. (1996). "An unexpected path to modernisation: the case of German artisans during the Second World War." *Contemporary European History* 5(3): 401–426.
Morris, J. (1996). "Introduction. The European petite bourgeoisie 1914–1945: encounters with the state." *Contemporary European History* 5(3): 279–283.
Nightingale, P., & Poll, R. (2000). "Innovation in investment banking: the dynamics of control systems within the Chandlerian firm." *Industrial and Corporate Change* 9(1): 113–141.
Petersen, M., De Waal, B., Senosi, M., & S. Thomas. (2011). "Profit and risk under subprime mortgage securitization." *Discrete Dynamics in Nature and Society* 1–64. doi:10.1155/2011/849342
Ryan, S., Tucker, G., Wu, J., & Ying, Z. (2015). "Securitization and insider trading" (March 2, 015). http://ssrn.com/abstract=2262446(accessed 11 September 2016).
Tranholm-Mikkelsen, J. (1991). "Neo-functionalism: obstinate or obsolete? A reappraisal in the light of the new dynamism of the EC." *Millennium—Journal of International Studies* 20: 1–2.
Venugopal, R. (2015). "Neoliberalism as concept." *Economy and Society* 44(2): 165–187.
Weiss, L. (1984). "The Italian state and small business." *European Journal of Sociology* 25(2): 214–241.
Weiss, L. (1986). "Demythologising the petite bourgeoisie: the Italian case." *West European Politics* 9(3): 362–375.
Zysman, J. (1984). *Governments, Markets, and Growth: Financial Systems and the Politics of Industrial Change*. Cornell University Press, New York.

7 Inequality dynamics, (unmet) aspirations and social protest

Svenja Flechtner

Introduction

A long-standing literature in the social sciences has discussed the occurrence and absence of social protest for decades and centuries. While it is understood that major social protest and revolutions will most often take us by surprise (Kuran 1993), even in the aftermath of events, explanations are not always straightforward. Most often, protest is supposed to be linked to economic and/or social inequalities. This premise, however, is challenged by recent experiences in different parts of the world: neither the Arab Spring countries nor Turkey, Brazil or Chile went through phases of increasing inequality before protests broke out – quite the contrary. In most Arab countries, for instance, income inequality has decreased, and populations in most Arabic countries have higher education levels than ever before (Campante and Chor 2012). Nevertheless, some groups and sometimes significant parts of the population are highly unsatisfied and have pronounced their dissatisfaction to a worldwide audience.[1]

Against this background, this chapter seeks to contribute a particular perspective to the quest for explanations of social protest: it asks how the ocurrence of social protest can be explained in situations in which inequality has *decreased.* More specifically, I take the empirical puzzle as point of departure for discussing the question of whether disappointed aspirations can be a motive and driver of social protests in societies where expectations and aspirations have been high for a while, but were then disappointed.

When Hirschman formulated his tunnel parable in 1973, he sought to explain why increasing inequality did not necessarily result in social protest and upheaval (Hirschman and Rothschild 1973). When expecting gains in the near future, he argued, people can interpret temporary inequalities as forecast of a wealthier future for themselves as well. Increasing inequality would only lead to social protest if people did not expect to catch up soon or if an expected catching-up effect did not happen after some time. The tunnel parable thus describes the other side of the coin of the dynamics that this chapter suspects to be responsible of the above-mentioned protests.

Although the tunnel effect is relatively widely known and cited, empirical tests of the hypothesis have remained scarce. The probably most prominent empirical applications refer to preferences for redistribution (Ferreira et al. 2010), subjective well-being (Smyth and Qian 2008) or, less directly, to the Easterlin paradox. At a theoretical level, the idea of the tunnel parable has been discussed with regard to aspirations by Ray (2010). Related to this, Genicot and Ray (2015) analyse how disappointed aspirations can result in frustration.

Having put these pieces together on a theoretical level, the chapter uses the case of Chile to discuss an applied case. In Chile, recent years have brought important improvements for many citizens. Reductions in inequality and poverty came with increased school enrolment and promises of more equal access to education and participation. However, ambitious aspirations of this generation began to crumble some years ago, when they realised that access to education was not as available as they had believed, and that social mobility remained low. In this case, the widespread impression that it was not a lack of self-efficacy, capacities and education that was to blame for slow social mobility, but rather socially rigid structures and pervasive inequalities provoked protest.

The remaining chapter is organised as follows. First, the economic literature about protests and the demand for change is analysed. Then Bandura's social cognitive framework is discussed against the background of the recently emerged aspirations literature and Hirschman's tunnel parable. The framework is then applied to the Chilean case.

Protest and inequality in the economic literature

The literature about the incidence of protest and the demand for change addresses individual preferences for change and redistribution. A large part of the extensive literature appears under the heading of "preferences for redistribution", assuming that people demand change and/or protest when resources are not distributed in a way that benefits them. The distribution of economic resources lies at the origin of action.

Some authors do not differentiate preferences and action clearly and, most often, the literature does not address questions of collective action explicitly. Many papers investigate preferences starting from questions like "Why do people not protest?" or "Why do people not vote for more redistribution?," without addressing the link between preferences and beliefs on the one hand and voting behaviour or social activism on the other. The literature can be divided into a large part in which the demand for change comes from a rational agent *vis-à-vis* economic distribution, and into another part in which people do not protest against unequal distributions because of cognitive distortions.

Rational choice-based contributions

In models based on rational choice, agents are assumed to consider their own current or future income position when building their redistributive preferences. Already at this point, theoretical predictions about the demand for redistribution suggest diverse and even contradictory results, depending on the time frame and the modelled characteristics of the agents.

A first stream of literature is based upon the median voter hypothesis (Alesina and Perotti 1996; Meltzer and Richard 1981; Milanovic 2000). The authors suggest that poorer income groups demand more distribution because of their self-interest: they would benefit from redistributive policies. Meltzer and Richard (1981) provided a seminal presentation of this argument, while Moene and Wallerstein (2003) developed it further by differentiating between different types of redistributive policies. The opposite prediction about people's preferences, yet through similar channels of argumentation, results from Bénabou and Ok's (2001) contribution about the "prospect of upward mobility" (POUM) hypothesis, probably the most renowned paper of this literature. They start from the observation that poor majorities might not have preferences for redistribution and argue that in the face of positive expectations about one's future income, it can be rational for poor voters not to be in favour of redistribution. The poor majority prefers not to put in place long-lasting redistributive policies because they expect their position to improve and then belong to the part that finances a redistributive project for the benefit of others. Their model refers to the case of democratic systems where voters can translate their preferences into action, but the general logic may be transferred to non-democratic societies in which people expect future benefits.

The POUM hypothesis does not directly depend on social mobility, but on people's expectations about it. In a sense, contradictory predictions of rational agent models can be accounted for by the inclusion or not of dynamic patterns of redistribution and future expectations. Piketty (1995) incorporated the importance of past experiences in his "theory of rational learning". People's attitudes toward redistributive policies are influenced by their social background and income, but also change over time when they experience upward and/or downward mobility. The political economy of revolution model of Acemoglu and Robinson (2006a, b) is based upon a similar logic: the distribution of income in a society provides the basis for revolutionary attempts on behalf on oppressed and underprivileged groups.

Approaches that base group action on individual interests have been criticised for fallacy of aggregation problems: aggregated groups may act in a way that contradicts the interests of their members (Apolte 2012; DellaVigna 2009). Apolte (2012) argues that, in fact, income distribution is not a sufficient, and maybe not even a necessary, condition for uprising, but that revolutionary interests of a small group can suffice and that dynamics and commitment structures between subgroups of society are the decisive element. "Taking this reasoning seriously implies that revolutions occur because the individually participating revolutionaries benefit from them, but they do not occur because there is a public good (in terms of a better government) to be supplied" (Apolte 2012, p. 568).

Most important for the question of this chapter are two points. First, from a rational choice perspective, it makes no sense to protest when inequality decreases and there is inclusive economic growth. This literature just simply does not seem to apply to the cases of interest here: in most of these countries, a medium-term downward tendency of inequality in the years prior to the protest can be observed. Figures 7.1 and 7.2 show that increased inequality before the incidence of protest does not seem to be a good explanation. For Latin America, a range of papers in recent years has tackled the (surprising) finding that, in the continent of traditionally high inequality, inequality began to fall some years ago (Cornia 2014; Gasparini and Lustig 2011; Gasparini et al. 2011; Lopez-Calva and Lustig 2009).

Second, the empirical evidence supporting the theoretical proposals is ambiguous at best. Papers dedicated to empirical testing of the POUM hypothesis did not support it for Latin America (Gaviria et al. 2007; Silva and Figeiredo 2013;). In an analysis of inequality and political implications in Latin America, Kaufman (2009) emphasises that poor people in Latin America do not necessarily vote in favour of redistribution or demand social change through protest (see also Moene and Wallerstein 2001, 2003).

Distortions and denials

A second stream of research explains the occurrence or absence of protest by cognitive distortions. Distorted views on current states of the world distort preferences for redistribution and may make agents favour redistributive policies whereas a rational agent in their situation would not favour or refrain from protesting against highly disadvantageous or unfair living conditions. Cognitive dissonance, such as known from Bénabou and Tirole (2006)'s "Beliefs in a just world and redistributive politics," makes agents suppress feelings about injustice and systematic unfairness in order to avoid cognitive dissonance. This is because people wish to maintain and transmit to their children a "just" view of the world and resort to information oppression or reinterpretation when everyday experiences contradict this justness. This mechanism allows individuals to believe in the (long-term) reward of personal effort, for example, in terms of economic mobility, even if reality tells quite a different story. As a consequence, the individual is able to motivate herself and her children towards education, effort, determination and perseverance (Bénabou 2008).

While this approach may be useful for explaining why protest does not arise, it cannot fruitfully be turned around for discussing why it sometimes does. Stating that the absence of cognitive distortions leads to protest may at best be a necessary, but not sufficient, explanatory condition. The same problem applies to non-cognitive distortions. Kuran (1993, 1995, 1998) has argued that under conditions where agents associated with revolutions and upheaval risk political pursuit, for instance under dictatorships, people might well have the wish to protest, but keep this information private. As a consequence, protest may fail to appear even when preferences for protest are privately shared by a large part of the population. But again, such approaches cannot inform the discussion of situations in which discontent arose under economically rather favourable conditions. The next section turns to an alternative explanation.

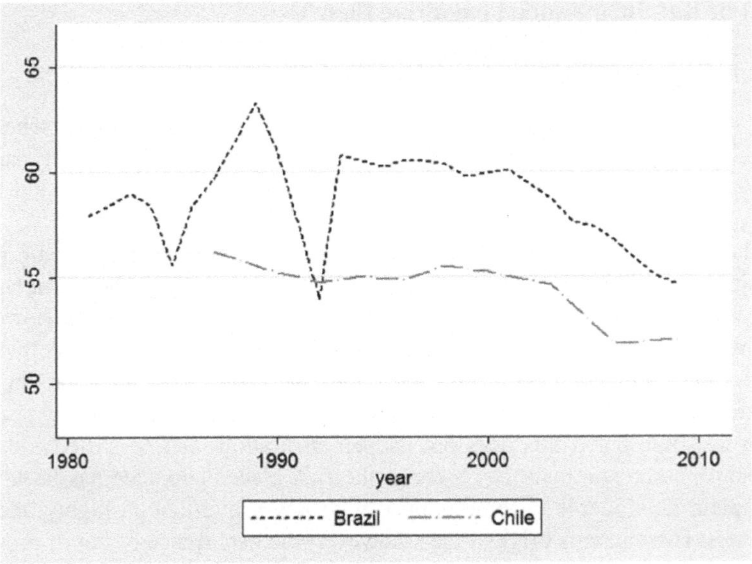

Figure 7.1 Gini coefficients in Chile and Brazil

Data source: World Bank (2013)

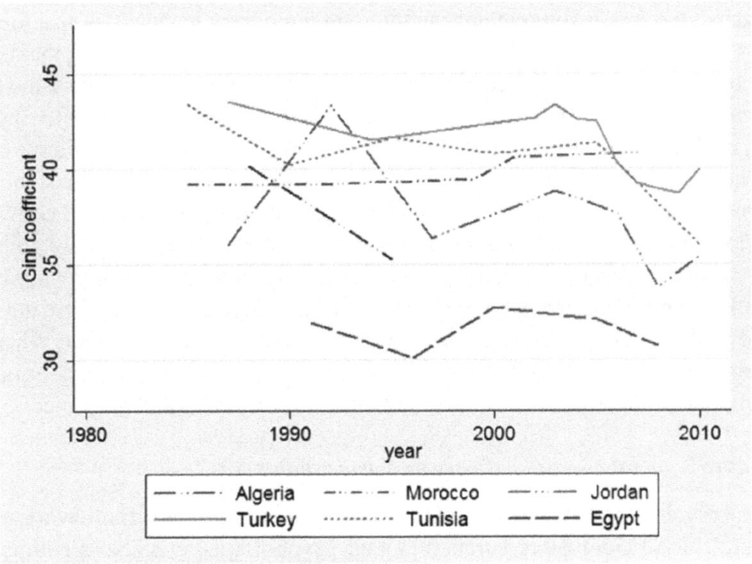

Figure 7.2 Gini coefficients in six Arab countries

Data source: World Bank (2013)

Unmet aspirations and the tunnel parable in light of Bandura's social cognitive theory

The tunnel parable and unmet aspirations

This section discusses a possible alternative explanation connecting Hirschman's tunnel parable with Bandura's social cognitive theory. The tunnel parable (Hirschman and Rothschild 1973) was written as a potential explanation for a *lack of* protest that would be expected in view of rising inequalities.

The story goes that car drivers in a traffic jam first become optimistic when cars in the neighbouring lane start moving, become they expect their own lane to start moving forward soon, too. If this does not happen after a while, however, they are more frustrated and pessimistic than before. Ray (2010) argues that this effect can be applied to aspirations: temporary inequalities and the improvements of the living conditions of others can be tolerated for a while if one expects to catch up soon, but if this does not happen, aspirations can be stifled and may be more pessimistic than they were in the first place. This idea has been used to explain how people become trapped with low aspirations in highly unequal societies. Hirschman's original idea, however, the occurrence or not of protests, has received much less attention (Genicot and Ray 2015; Ray 2010). The logic is straightforward: people who begin to perceive that the expected catching up does not arrive do not necessarily react with frustration and apathy, but may react with protest and upheaval.

Hirschman wanted to explain why increasing inequality did not necessarily result in social protest and upheaval. The argument is that, when people are expecting gains in the near future, they can interpret temporary inequalities as a forecast of a wealthier future. Growth tends to be uneven (Ray 2010), implying that not all members of a society will benefit from development and growth at the same time. Increasing inequality only leads to social protest if people do not expect to catch up soon or if an expected catching-up effect does not happen after some time.

The tunnel parable suggests precise relationships between aspirations, increasing inequality and economic development from a dynamic perspective. Growth or development in broader terms signalises in the first place that things are going on in a society, making everybody expect benefits. Increased inequality would then stimulate aspirations, except in societies with extreme polarisation, where the most disadvantaged group does not believe in future benefits at any moment. When not all parts benefit after a while, typically again because of high inequality or polarisation, initial hopes can be reversed and result in frustration and grievance.

Bandura's social cognitive theory and aspirations

Social psychologist Albert Bandura's social cognitive theory framework establishes a broad field of research in social psychology. It is also an important reference for economic research on aspirations and aspiration failures (Bernard et al., 2014, 2016). In this field, economists are interested in how people's aspirations, through the channels of decision making and actions, may contribute to the (re)production of inequalities. The basic idea is that people's evaluations of what they view as possible and achievable determine their aspirations and thereby their actions (Ray 2006). When agents underestimate their possibilities or capacities, they will underinvest in terms of education, capital investment or effort, for instance. Since aspirations determine effort levels, they will consequently achieve relatively low goals, which apparently confirm the adequateness of the chosen aspiration level (Dalton et al. 2016; Heifetz and Minelli 2006). Since such underestimations of possibilities and capacities are typically correlated to experiences of poverty and deprivation (Appadurai 2004), the described downward spiral mechanism lends itself to the perpetuation of poverty. In general, low aspirations have received major attention in this context. The question of too high aspirations, which are however not followed by corresponding achievements, has not been addressed. Thus, although Bandura's theory has found its way into the aspirations literature, its whole potential has not been used to inform research on aspirations.

Social cognitive theory explains aspirations along two dimensions, *self-efficacy* and *locus of control*, which permit a differentiated understanding. The first one, perceived self-efficacy, refers to "the conviction that one can successfully execute the behaviour required to produce [specific] outcomes" (Bandura 1977, p.79). This belief strictly refers to the individual's belief about her own capacity and has to be differentiated from outcome efficacy: an individual might believe that an action will lead to a specific outcome, but be doubtful about her own capacity to perform this action (Bandura 1977).

The second term, locus of control beliefs, goes back to Rotter (1966). It has received a great deal of attention and belongs to the most researched concepts throughout social sciences. The original term coined by Rotter was "internal versus external control of reinforcement" and referred to the degree to which an individual believes that outcomes are contingent on a person herself or rather on luck, destiny or powerful others.

Bandura (1997b) identifies four different ideal-type combinations (Figure 7.3) of perceived self-efficacy, which can be rather high or low, and locus of control beliefs, the poles of which are internal and external. Depending where on the continuous axes an individual is placed, she ends up in one of four ideal-typical fields. Resignation, apathy and fatalism arise when control beliefs are external (little control over one's life) and self-efficacy beliefs are low (1). The individual has little faith in both her own capacities and external possibilities. Low self-efficacy beliefs combined with internal locus of control beliefs, in turn, lead to self-devaluation, despondency, self-criticism and depression (2). Here, the individual believes that her external environment generally allows people to be in control of their fate, but that she specifically lacks the required capacities or abilities. Optimistic aspirations and engagement are the result of internal locus of control beliefs and high self-efficacy beliefs (4). Finally, external locus of control beliefs and high self-efficacy beliefs may provoke grievance, protest and social activism (3) (Bandura 1997b). The interest of this paper is in the dynamics that lead members of a society to be in field (3).

		locus of control beliefs	
		external ----------	---------- internal
perceived self-efficacy	low	Resignation, apathy (1)	Self-devaluation, self-criticism, depression (2)
	high	protest, grievance, social activism (3)	high aspirations, productive engagement (4)

Figure 7.3 Combinations of perceived self-efficacy and locus of control beliefs according to Bandura

Source: Own representation based on Bandura (1977, 1997b)

High aspirations occur, according to Bandura's typology, when people believe that a specific outcome or goal – in broad terms, prospects for the future – is possible thanks to both societal conditions and their personal capacity. For instance, an individual has positive aspirations regarding future social mobility when she believes that in the society she lives in, social mobility is possible, and that she possesses the characteristics or abilities required for the corresponding activities. Protest, in contrast, results from the combination of external locus of control beliefs and high perceived self-efficacy. In other words, people believe in their personal capacity, but societal conditions do not allow them to make use of them – rigid social hierarchies, high inequality or repressive regime are only some possible reasons.

When do individuals hold high self-efficacy beliefs and perceive control to be external? According to Bandura, there are four main sources of self-efficacy beliefs. The first and strongest one is *mastery experiences* (Bandura 1997a). Personal experiences of achievement provide the most direct evidence of one's capacities with regard to specific tasks or goals. The second source of high self-efficacy beliefs is through *vicarious experiences*, provided by social models. Successes and failures of people who are very similar to us lead us to believe that our capacities are such that similar successes or failures would arise if we were the agent. Furthermore, self-efficacy beliefs can stem from *social persuasion* and, for the sake of completeness, *physiological and emotional states*.

Regarding the origins of external control beliefs, early experiences of low or no control over situations or life courses more generally seem to play an important role (Chorpita and Barlow 1998). Also, a link between control and economic development can easily be established: according to Kuran (2004), economic development is not only influenced by desires, but also by perceived economic opportunities. When the economy goes well, an individual can generally pursue more options than when a recession restricts one's control over one's economic life.

Connecting these ideas with Hirschman's tunnel parable, we can easily formulate Hirschman's ideas in the language of social cognitive theory. Hirschman argued that rising inequality might at first suggest growth and development and stimulate beliefs in social mobility prospects in a dynamic society. In other words, locus of control beliefs are stimulated. If people then realize or come to believe that society is more rigid than they thought after some time or that they are left behind, however, their perception might shift and their control beliefs vanish.

Generalising this idea, shifts towards protest can come via different paths. One is when an individual with initially productive aspirations comes to realise that the possibilities she expected at a societal level have changed or do not exist as assumed, while beliefs in her personal capacities remain unchanged. This is the path of the tunnel parable. Also, people might develop their self-efficacy beliefs further, for example, through higher educational attainment, while beliefs about possibilities at societal levels remain pessimistic or are increasingly regarded pessimistically as self-efficacy increases.

An illustration with the Chilean case

The educational landscape in Chile

In August 2012, the Chilean weekly magazine *Qué pasa* published an article titled "Great expectations (. . .) Is a new time bomb being activated?"[2] They were referring to parental expectations about their children's education. This section first summarizes some findings about expectations and educational aspirations in Chile and then attempts to interpret these against the previously presented framework: are expectations justified with regard to access to and opportunities within the educational system, and do educational achievements play the expected role for social mobility? Where can the findings be placed in Bandura's framework, and are tunnel effect symptoms visible?

According to a study by Urzúa (see Urzúa 2012b) with data from SIMCE, the Chilean Education Quality Measurement System, educational aspirations of parents increased greatly over a short period: in 1999, 48% of Chilean parents with children in fourth grade thought that their children would complete a university degree, whereas 85% reported that they believed so in 2010. Researchers recognise the beneficial effects of aspirations and expectations for goal setting, which is the primary aspect of economic aspirations research, but warn of a "crisis of frustrated expectations" as well (Alonso and Rivas 2012, p.24). According to (Urzúa 2012a, p.46), many Chilean parents "bought" the idea that higher education would guarantee prosperous labour market outcomes for their children.[3] The (misleading) idea that every student who is committed to primary and secondary education can make it at university is referred to as a "Chilean dream".

The expectation of around 85% of parents of fourth-graders that they will pass a tertiary degree cannot be motivated through the labour market and demand for labour. Urzúa (2012b) sees a potential source of unrealistic aspirations in public discourse and public policies: the emphasis on university studies occurred at the expense of social prestige even of non-university degrees, for instance at technical institutes. Furthermore, the rapid increase in schooling, often through private schools, leads to a situation in which students learn that their secondary education did not prepare them for university entrance exams only when they receive the results of these exams (Alonso and Rivas 2012).

Chile experienced substantial educational expansion throughout the second half of the 20th century, and even more so in comparison with its Latin American neighbours. Gross secondary enrolment increased from 19% to 83%, and tertiary enrolment increased from 1% to 38% between 1950 and 2000. Secondary education was increased most notably during the 1970s, whereas the expansion of the post-secondary sector is more recent – it accelerated in the 1990s (Torche 2008).

In a study on returns to tertiary education in Chile, Urzúa (2012a) did not find evidence to supporting the theory that broad-based access to universities, largely financed through scholarships and student credits, would have led to increased social mobility, better labour market chances and decreased poverty. While the study is to some extent inconclusive because of the impossibility of assessing what labour market outcomes for university graduates would have been had they not obtained their degrees, the author emphasises that tertiary education might have been beneficial for some graduates in terms of earnings, but on the other hand, the conclusion that it has not created improvements for a significant part of graduates cannot be rejected. Quality seems to be an issue, as well as recognisable information about university quality on the market in order for students to make informed educational choices. For instance, rapid increases in tertiary enrolment were not necessarily acompanied by constantly high levels of learning and teaching quality, which affects interactions on the labour market (Urzúa 2012b).

As with stable inequality, educational achievements have remained closely connected to family income and background (Echenique and Urzúa 2013). In 2009, the average years of education of adults aged 25 to 65 was 8.9 in the poorest quintile, as opposed to 13.7 in the richest quintile. This income difference is much larger than that between genders (10.9 for women, 11.1 for men). During recent years, education levels increased for all income groups. In Chile, in contrast to most of Latin America, the gap between the richest and poorest quintile has decreased over the last decades, particularly during the 1990s and in the 2000s (Cruces et al. 2014). Gaps are becoming smaller, especially for younger people.

Reyes et al. (2013) investigate returns to post-secondary degrees in Chile. On average, according to their results, higher incomes can be earned with a post-secondary degree as compared to secondary degrees. However, within this average, there is a significant proportion of individuals yielding negative monetary returns to post-secondary education. For the 2000s, Torche (2008) found that social mobility and fluidity in Chile were not as rigid as would be expected from inequality indicators. She attributed this to Chile's inequality pattern: the top income decile is highly concentrated, while there is less inequality among the remaining parts of Chilean society. Social mobility among this part is relatively high (Torche 2005). In retrospect and from a more recent perspective, however, Echenique and Urzúa (2013) found that inequality and segregation, at least in the capital city Santiago, remained stable.

Interpretation in light of the proposed framework

When increased self-efficacy encounters perceptions of external control, process and unrest can arise. People perceive barriers to their advancement, which they do not attribute to their lack of personal capacities or abilities, but to factors external to them, like social rigidity or lack of opportunities. In Chile, educational expectations were boosted through large expansions in the educational system, which can be interpreted as perceptions of increased self-efficacy: growing parts of the population and, notably, of parents came to believe that their children were able to succeed in the educational system, and that this success would allow them to live under better conditions than the parents themselveshad done.

These expectations, however, were stifled in recent years through two factors: access constraints to the educational system and lack of social mobility and low returns to (higher) education. Parents and students learned that, despite high successes and educational abilities, they were not as much in control of their future earnings as they had come to believe: rigidity in terms of access in a highly privatised educational sector, as well as limits to social mobility, shifted the *perceived* locus of control from an internal position – where everything is believed to be possible in a phase of educational optimism – to a rather external position. The point here is not that actual changes have occurred regarding the opportunity structure. This might have been the case, but what is more important is the shift in people's perceptions.

Finally, perceptions of high self-efficacy encountered perceptions of control, which after a period of optimism and high aspirations ended in a society with still high inequality and limited opportunities. After aspirations had been high and optimistic for years, however, parts of Chilean society were not willing to shift their aspirations downward, but reacted with protest to the disappointment of unmet aspirations.

An initial *lack* of aspirations, as most often discussed in the aspirations trap literature, is not the prevalent case in Chile's educational system over recent years. The tunnel parable seems to be a fruitful metaphor for the observed dynamics: the catching-up moment did not arrive, and this incited protests.

Concluding remarks

It was the goal of this chapter to discuss a possible explanation for the protest in several societies just after inequality had declined and economic prospects looked promising at the outset. Recent social protests in Arab Spring countries, Brazil or Chile do not fit theories that explain the occurrence of social protest with the rise of economic inequalities and discontent. This chapter therefore discussed how, instead, decreasing inequality and, more generally, favourable economic environments can provoke dynamics fostering people's aspirations and resulting in unrest when these aspirations remain unsatisfied after a while. A theoretical discussion was developed connecting Hirschman's tunnel parable with Bandura's social cognitive theory.

The case of Chile illustrated how educational expansions and a public discourse on social mobility prospects through educational achievements encouraged aspirations in a large proportion of Chilean families. Parents developed very ambitious aspirations for their children and were willing to invest quite a lot into their education, but were disappointed when returns turned out to be less promising and slower than expected. While it is true that inequality declined and opportunities for middle classes and even poorer parts of the population grew, they did not keep up with the rhythm of aspirations. Despite offering an explanation for the arousal of protest under these conditions, the Chilean case thus shows that raising people's aspirations can be a double-edged sword when aspirations grow faster than real possibilities.

Notes

1 In Chile, a series of student-led protests agitated the country mostly between 2011 and 2013. Protests in Egypt, Tunisia and other Arab countries became famous as the "Arab Spring" as of early 2011. In Brazil, protests around the rise of bus price tickets and, at the same time, in the context of the 2014 Confederations cup became known as "Brazilian Spring." In Turkey, the Gezi Park protests in 2013 initially addressed urban development plans and then turned into large events with violent responses from the government.

2 The original full text on the title page is: "Grandes esperanzas. En 10 años se duplicaron las expectativas de los padres sobre la educación de sus hijos: Un 85% espera que al menos ingresen a la educación superior. ¿Se está activando una nueva bomba de tiempo?"

3 Original: "Aparentemente, las familias 'compraron' la idea de que la educación superior aseguraría un futuro laboral próspero para sus hijos."

References

Acemoglu, Daron; Robinson, James A. (2006a): De Facto Political Power and Institutional Persistence. In *American Economic Association Papers and Proceedings* 96(2), pp.325–330.

Acemoglu, Daron; Robinson, James A. (2006b): *Economic Origins of Dictatorship and Democracy*. Cambridge: Cambridge University Press.

Alesina, Alberto; Perotti, Roberto (1996): Income Distribution, Political Instability, and Investment. *European Economic Review* 40(6), pp.1203–1228. DOI: 10.1016/0014-2921(95)00030-5.

Alonso, Nicolás; Rivas, Sebastián (2012): El despegue de las expectativas. In *Qué pasa*, 8/10/2012, pp.22–29.

Apolte, Thomas (2012): Why is there no revolution in North Korea? *Public Choice* 150(3–4), pp.561–578. DOI: 10.1007/s11127-010-9716-4.

Appadurai, Arjun (2004): The Capacity to Aspire: Culture and the Terms of Recognition. In Vijayendra Rao, Michael Walton (Eds): *Culture and Public Action*. Stanford, California: Stanford University Press; Stanford Social Sciences, pp.59–84.

Bandura, Albert (1977): *Social Learning Theory*. Englewood Cliffs, NJ: Prentice Hall.

Bandura, Albert (1997a): Exercise of Personal and Collective Efficacy in Changing Societies. In Albert Bandura (Ed.): *Self-Efficacy in Changing Societies* (Reprinted). Cambridge: Cambridge University Press, pp.1–45.

Bandura, Albert (1997b): *Self-Efficacy. The Exercise of Control*. New York: W.H. Freeman.

Bénabou, Roland (2008): Ideology. *Journal of the European Economic Association* 6(2–3), pp.321–352.

Bénabou, Roland; Ok, Efe A. (2001): Social Mobility and the Demand for Redistribution: The POUM Hypothesis. *Quarterly Journal of Economics*, pp.447–487.

Bénabou, Roland; Tirole, Jean (2006): Belief in a Just World and Redistributive Politics. *Quarterly Journal of Economics* 121(2), pp.699–746.

Bernard, Tanguy; Dercon, Stefan; Orkin, Kate; Seyoum Taffesse, Alemayehu (2014): *The Future in Mind: Aspirations and Forward-Looking Behaviour in Rural Ethiopia*. Centre for the Study of African Economies, University of Oxford. Paper presented at the World Bank ABCDE Conference 2014, 3 June 2014.

Bernard, Tanguy; Dercon, Stefan; Seyoum Taffesse, Alemayehu (2016): Beyond Fatalism: An Empirical Exploration of Self-Efficacy and Aspirations Failure in Ethiopia. *Centre for the Study of African Economies (CSAE) Working Paper* 2011–03. Available online at http://www.csae.ox.ac.uk/workingpapers/pdfs/csae-wps-2011-03.pdf (checked on December 3, 2016).

Campante, Filipe R.; Chor, Davin (2012): Why was the Arab World Poised for Revolution? Schooling, Economic Opportunities, and the Arab Spring. *Journal of Economic Perspectives* 26(2), pp.167–188. DOI: 10.1257/jep.26.2.167.

Chorpita, Bruce F.; Barlow, David H. (1998): The Development of Anxiety: The Role of Control in the Early Environment. *Psychological Bulletin* 124(1), pp.3–21. DOI: 10.1037/0033-2909.124.1.3.

Cornia, Giovanni Andrea (Ed.) (2014): *Falling Inequality in Latin America. Policy Changes and Lessons*. UNU-WIDER studies in development economics. Oxford: Oxford University Press.

Cruces, Guillermo; García Domench, Carolina; Gasparini, Leonardo (2014): Inequality in Education: Evidence for Latin America. In Giovanni Andrea Cornia (Ed.): *Falling Inequality in Latin America. Policy Changes and Lessons*. UNU-WIDER studies in development economics, pp.318–339. Oxford: Oxford University Press.

Dalton, Patricio S.; Ghosal, Sayantan; Mani, Anandi (2016): Poverty and Aspirations Failure. *Economic Journal* 126(590), pp. 165–188. DOI: 10.1111/ecoj.12210.

DellaVigna, Stefano (2009): Psychology and Economics: Evidence from the Field. *Journal of Economic Literature* 47(2), pp.315–372. DOI: 10.1257/jel.47.2.315.

Echenique, Juan A.; Urzúa, Sergio (2013): Desigualdad, Segregación y Resultados Educationales. Evidencia desde el Metro de Santiago. *Centro de Estudios Públicos: Puntos de Referencia* 359.

Ferreira, Francisco H.G.; Leite, Phillippe G.; Ravallion, Martin (2010): Poverty Reduction Without Economic Growth? *Journal of Development Economics* 93(1), pp.20–36. DOI: 10.1016/j.jdeveco.2009.06.001.

Gasparini, Leonardo; Lustig, Nora (2011): The Rise and Fall of Income Inequality in Latin America. Society for the Study of Economic Inequality (Ecineq Working Paper, 2011–2013). Available online at http://www.ecineq.org/milano/WP/ECINEQ2011-213.pdf, updated on August 2011, checked on 6/29/2013.

Gasparini, Leonardo; Cruces, Guillermo; Tornarolli, Leopoldo (2011): Recent Trends in Income Inequality in Latin America. *Economía* 11(2), pp.147–190.

Gaviria, Alejandro; Graham, Carol; Braido, Luis H.B. (2007): Social Mobility and Preferences for Redistribution in Latin America. *Economía* 8(1), pp.55–96.

Génicot, Garance; Ray, Debraj (2015): *Aspirations and Inequality*. Unpublished manuscript, October 2015. Available online at http://www.econ.nyu.edu/user/debraj/Papers/GenicotRayAsp.pdf, checked on April 20 2016.

Heifetz, Aviad; Minelli, Enrico (2006): Aspiration Traps. Available online at http://www.openu.ac.il/Personal_sites/Aviad-Heifetz/Aspiration-Traps.pdf, checked on March 3/2006.

Hirschman, Albert O.; Rothschild, Michael (1973): The Changing Tolerance for Income Inequality in the Course of Economic Development. *The Quarterly Journal of Economics* 87(4), p.544. DOI: 10.2307/1882024.

Kaufman, Robert (2009): The Political Effects of Inequality in Latin America: Some Inconvenient Facts. *Comparative Politics* 41(3), pp.359–379.

Kuran, Timur (1993): The Unthinkable and the Unthought. *Rationality and Society* 5(4), pp.473–505. DOI: 10.1177/1043463193005004005.

Kuran, Timur (1995): *Private Truths, Public Lies. The Social Consequences of Preference Falsification*. Cambridge, MA: Harvard University Press.

Kuran, Timur (1998): Social Mechanisms of Dissonance Reduction. In Peter Hedström, Richard Swedberg (Eds.): *Social Mechanisms. An Analytical Approach to Social Theory*. Cambridge: Cambridge University Press (Studies in rationality and social change), pp.147–171.

Kuran, Timur (2004): Cultural Obstacles to Economic Development: Often Overstated, Usually Transitory. In Vijayendra Rao, Michael Walton (Eds): *Culture and Public Action*. Stanford, CA: Stanford University Press; Stanford Social Sciences, pp.115–137.

Lopez-Calva, Luis F.; Lustig, Nora (2009): The Recent Decline of Inequality in Latin America: Argentina, Brazil, Mexico and Peru (Ecineq Working Paper, 140).

Meltzer, Allan H.; Richard, Scott F. (1981): A Rational Theory of the Size of Government. *Journal of Political Economy* 89(5), pp.914–927.

Milanovic, Branko (2000): The Median-Voter Hypothesis, Income Inequality, and Income Redistribution: An Empirical Test with the Required Data. *European Journal of Political Economy* 16(3), pp.367–410. DOI: 10.1016/S0176-2680(00)00014-8.

Moene, Karl Ove; Wallerstein, Michael (2001): Inequality, Social Insurance, and Redistribution. *American Political Science Review* 95(4), pp.859–874.

Moene, Karl Ove; Wallerstein, Michael (2003): Earnings Inequality and Welfare Spending: A Disaggregated Analysis. *World Politics* 55(4), pp.485–516. DOI: 10.1353/wp.2003.0022.

Piketty, Thomas (1995): Social Mobility and Redistributive Politics. *Quarterly Journal of Economics* 110(3), pp.551–584.

Ray, Debraj (2006): Aspirations, Poverty and Economic Change. In Abhijit V. Banerjee, Roland Bénabou, Dilip Mookherjee (Eds): *Understanding Poverty*. Oxford: Oxford University Press, pp.409–421.

Ray, Debraj (2010): Uneven Growth: A Framework for Research in Development Economics. *Journal of Economic Perspectives* 24(3), pp.45–60. DOI: 10.1257/jep.24.3.45.

Reyes, Loreto; Rodríguez, Jorge; Urzúa, Sergio (2013): Heterogeneous Economic Returns to Postsecondary Degrees: Evidence from Chile. *Journal of Human Resources* 51(2), pp. 416–460.

Rotter, Julian B. (1966): Generalized Expectancies for Internal Versus External Control of Reinforcement. *Psychological Monographs: General and Applied* 80(1), pp.1–28.

Silva, Cleiton Roberto da Fonseca; Figeiredo, Erik Alencar de (2013): Social mobility and the demand for income redistribution in Latin America. *CEPAL Review* 110.

Smyth, Russell; Qian, Xiaolei (2008): Inequality and Happiness in Urban China. *Economics Bulletin* 4(23), pp.1–10.

Torche, Florencia (2005): Unequal but Fluid: Social Mobility in Chile in Comparative Perspective. *American Sociological Review* 70(3), pp.422–450.

Torche, Florencia (2008): Social Mobility and Education in Contemporary Chile. In Hiroshi Ishida (Ed.): *Social Stratification and Social Mobility in Late-Industrializing Countries*. Sendai, Japan: SSM (SSM Research Series).

Urzúa, Sergio (2012a): La rentabilidad de la educación superior en Chile. Revisión de las bases de 30 años de políticas públicas. *Estudios Públicos* 125 (summer).

Urzúa, Sergio (2012b): Opinión: Fin de la inocencia. *Qué pasa*, 8/10/2012, pp.30–31.

World Bank (2013): GINI Index. Available online at http://api.worldbank.org/datafiles/SI.POV.GINI_Indicator_MetaData_en_EXCEL.xls, checked on 6/12/2013.

8 Any alternatives left?

From green narratives of change to socio-ecological transformative utopias – a political economy framework

Annika R. Scharbert, Bernhard Leubolt and Manuel Scholz-Wäckerle

Introduction

Humanity is currently facing challenges in a multitude of realms: political, economic, ecological, social and cultural. In the academic literature, this is exemplified through the increasing attention to limits, reaching back to the original *Limits to Growth* (Meadows *et al.* 1972) and recently has been receiving renewed interest within the context of planetary boundaries (Rockström *et al.* 2009; Steffen *et al.* 2015). The concept of socio-ecological transformation is increasingly discussed in academia but also in civil society and by policy makers. In our contribution, we aim to elaborate on some of these issues in the context of the global political economy, namely how biophysical limits are dealt with in the international policy area. To explore this, we employ the examples of "planetary boundaries" and green growth.

We offer a set of heuristics to provide a holistic analysis of socio-ecological transformation. These heurists enable a different kind of political economy analysis through, firstly, focusing on the social structure of the economy. Institutional change (or inertia, for that matter) is, in the Veblean tradition, related to habits and modes of human behaviour. The crucial element in this process is given by the habits of thought that are forced to adapt to a continuously changing institutional landscape. This forms an integral part of any analysis of socio-ecological transformation; in our case, this is especially applied to the manner in which social science is conducted. Secondly, the co-evolution of nature–society relationships needs to be considered when understanding the economy as an open system. This aspect implies that economic processes are ontologically part of evolutionary change and are thereby irreversible by nature. Thirdly, power relations cannot be disregarded. The starting point for an analysis of transformation dynamics is given by conflict and power relations rather than harmony and consensus in both the institutionalist and Marxist tradition.

By focusing on power and the role of (social) science we employ a Gramscian understanding of hegemony to elaborate on current issues in the policy arena, incorporating both coercive and non-coercive elements. Thus, hegemony is framed as a combination of consensus and coercion and we subsequently focus on the role of social science and its role in shaping policy. The emphasis lies on how knowledge is crucial to the framing of the issue at hand. Then we introduce the above-mentioned heuristics for the analysis of socio-ecological transformation. The Gramscian approach to hegemony is outlined and then we move on to examples in the global political economy: the focus lies on the concept of planetary boundaries and the green economy respectively, while always considering the role of social science in shaping and changing these.

Preliminary heuristics for socio-ecological transformation

Current discussions on the state of the planet, its species and civilizations are dominated by a number of salient issues that are fundamentally connected to a variety of spheres – namely the political, the social, the economic, the cultural and the environmental. We assume that the problems in these spheres are real and not simply social constructions that emerge *ex nihilo*. In this paper, we aim to disentangle some of these realities that are crucial for transforming political economy. In particular we consider the appearance of the concept of "planetary boundaries" proposed by Rockström *et al.* (2009) as a central turning point for future debates in political economy. Rockström *et al.* (2009) have received serious criticism, relating to the lack of fundamental social foundations as at least an equal boundary to operate in a safe space on planet Earth (e.g. Raworth 2012). The concept of planetary boundaries represents a prototype example in political economy since it polarizes researchers (compare Stirling 2014: 85). In light of these oppositions it is even more difficult to find an appropriate economic theory capable of delivering heuristics of socio-ecological transformation. The complexity of the given problem indicates shortages in most of the individual economic schools; respectively it is the environmental, the economic, the social or the political component that is missing. We identify three theoretical preliminaries in this sub-section that are significant for addressing a theory of socio-ecological transformation for further, more explicit analyses of urgent political economic problems emerging from environmental degradation: we are dealing with: (1) the social structure of the economy; (2) the co-evolution of society–nature relationships; and (3) the omnipresence of power relations.

Firstly, we assume that there are some institutional interdependencies between individual actors and social structures. Institutional economists have emphasized that these interdependencies lead to changes in the economy and some of them have even labelled this process evolutionary (Veblen 1898). Thorstein Veblen argued that institutional evolution occurs through cumulative causation of habits of thought. The major driving force behind this process is given by the dichotomy of instrumental versus ceremonial proclivities. These proclivities are conceived as instincts by Veblen that can either be supportive in terms of progress, as is the case with the "instinct of workmanship," "parental bent" or "idle curiosity", or obstruct constructive properties along "practices of exploit, prowess or mastery (warfare), ownership (material acquisition), and in pecuniary control of industry" (Tool 1977: 825–826). Institutionalists basically argue that the latter human urges or drives are not subject to practical reason but are instead of ceremonial character and can inhibit change, i.e. enforcing institutional inertia. Tool (1977: 825) explains:

> Veblen, as did Karl Marx before him, sought inclusive and continuously applicable theory to explain that change. The evolutionary development of institutional forms appeared to him to parallel the Darwinian account of the evolutionary development of life forms. Veblen sought to identify those modes of thought and behavior which promote or provide for the continuity of culture and those that tend to impair or obstruct developmental cultural continuity.

The dynamics emerging from the coexistence of ceremonial and instrumental character are always conflict-laden and transform political economy, because the former is based in authority and the latter "denotes performance based upon belief informed by causal reasoning", as Klein and Miller (1996: 268) highlight. The crucial element in this process is given by the habits of thought that are forced to adapt to a continuously changing institutional landscape. As emphasized by Brown (1991: 699), the Veblenian habits of thought evolve out of a combination of experience and the societal setting.

Secondly, we assume a co-evolutionary process of society–nature relationships. We follow Kapp (1977), who makes a decisive argument for the economy as an open system. As Berger and Elsner (2008: 83) outline, Kapp's open-system approach emphasizes the "interaction with the natural and the social systems and focuses both on physical and biological, and institutional interactions between the economic system and its environment". He looks into the direct consequences of physical and biological theories of open systems for economics, such as the entropy law. The latter implies that "the economic process, from a physical point of view, basically is an entropic transformation since it transforms low into high entropy, which is irrevocable waste" (Berger and Elsner 2008: 84). This aspect implies that economic processes are ontologically part of evolutionary change and are thereby irreversible by nature and non-replicable in terms of perfect copies. Nicolas Georgescu-Roegen emphasized that life accelerates entropic transformation, and (even more drastically) that:

> [t]he present biological spasm of the human species – for spasm it is – is bound to have an impact on our future political organization. . . . My reason for the last statement is that, like Marx, I believe that the social conflict is not a mere creation of man without any root in material human conditions.
>
> (Georgescu-Roegen 1971: 306)

Georgescu-Roegen (1971) is rather pessimistic about the potential elimination of conflict on multiple levels of social, economic and political organization in the future. He believes in the material basis of social conflict and for that very reason deemed it counter-intuitive that its elimination can be made on behalf of human decision or by the social evolution of mankind. However, Georgescu-Roegen (1971: 316–322) brought some significant conclusions forward related to his historical materialism and the dialectic nature of accumulation processes in political economy. First of all, the idea of boundaries of economics should be given up and, therefore, also the boundaries of the economic process, a notion that was firstly addressed by the German historical school but made prominent by Marx and Engels. In contrast, "[t]he non-Marxist economists apparently believe that by proving the existence of some natural boundaries for the economic process they will implicitly expose the absurdity of historical materialism and, hence, its corollary: scientific socialism" (Georgescu-Roegen, 1971: 316). In a quite similar vein, Kapp (1977: 528) argues that:

> the disruption of the environment and its protection raise problems of such complexity that no single academic discipline within its present boundaries can hope to make significant contributions to their solution without at least a basic familiarity with the knowledge of other relevant social and natural sciences. For this reason it is necessary that social and natural scientists concerned with environmental problems and policies engage in transdisciplinary research.

Kapp (1977) emphasizes the power of proper institutionalization processes in reducing the mentioned complexity.

Thirdly, we assume an omnipresence of power relations and derive this concept from a synthesis between institutionalist and Marxist positions. The starting point for an analysis of transformation dynamics is given by conflict and its power relations rather than harmony and consensus, as indicated by institutionalists (Gruchy 1973) as well as Marxists (Hobsbawm 2012). This aspect is revealed by the agonistic nature (Mouffe 2000) of political struggle that leads to dynamic change and transformation in the political economy. Institutionalists conceive power as tridimensional, stemming from economic, political and legal sources. Gruchy (1973) outlines that industrial capitalism brought forward two areas of economic activity, where:

> [t]here is an inner area or sector of large-scale oligopolistic industrial enterprises and an outer sector of small-scale mainly competitive enterprises. The outer area functions very much as does a market economy in the manner indicated in all standard economics textbooks . . . In the inner heartland of the economy relations between the giant corporations and the state are close, and profit maximization is secondary to the expansion of sales and the enhancement of the corporation's power and prestige.
>
> (Gruchy 1973: 629–630)

The calculus of utility maximization fits perfectly for small-scale enterprises, because "economic power is largely contained by the market system" but "in the inner sector corporate power extends to the oligopolistic markets, the consumer in them, and the state" (Gruchy 1973: 629–630). Thereby, the neoclassical economic apparatus comes too short in their political economic analysis, because it builds upon the competitive economy where the size of enterprises is reduced and political as well as legal power is minimalized in order to build a system with almost no economic power. However, the political economy of today is highly influenced by large corporations that act as political units via their high market power and this is especially true for cases within the energy transition (Stirling 2014). Essentially, "[t]hese enterprises assume the character of a political unit that differs in form and degree but not in kind from the state" (Gruchy 1973: 630). Facing these circumstances, environmental movements seem to be too marginal to invoke any change at all. In particular, social movements face significant problems in eventually making the transition from cultural change to institutional change (Castells 2009: 300). But, as highlighted by Laclau and Mouffe (2014) with reference to the Foucauldian understanding of power "wherever there is power there is resistance" if we recognize that there is a large variety in the form this resistance takes (Laclau and Mouffe 2014: 136).

To summarize, we argue that a successful analysis of socio-ecological transformation needs to cover three sub-areas: the social structure of the economy, the co-evolution of society–nature relationships and power relations. In contrast, the planetary boundaries concept commits the fallacy of scientific reductionism that atomizes and isolates the objects of investigation from each other in almost meaningless quantifications, if not charged with accountable narratives. Instead, we argue in favour of a strategic-relational approach (Jessop and Sum 2013: 48–50) where small-scale cultural changes can be transformed into more large-scale institutional environments. However, for this very reason it is first of all important to look into the hegemonic structure of this transformation process in order to develop proper strategic actions thereafter.

Ecological crisis: material basis and normative solution

The subsequent section provides a summary and analysis of the forms that sustainable development takes on the international level. We highlight two different, albeit related, concepts: that of planetary boundaries on the one hand, and, on the other, green growth. Planetary boundaries seem to offer a justification for environmental policy making grounded in objective, natural scientific terms. The second example we employ is that of green growth – a political strategy introduced by the United Nations Environment Programme (UNEP) at the Rio + 20 Conference in 2012. Political strategies that aim to combine (consumer) capitalism, growth and wealth accumulation as well as sustainability come to the forefront of our critical analysis. Here, we answer a call made by Blühdorn and Welsh to explore different avenues of analysis: "As the reassuring belief in the compatibility and interdependence of democratic consumer capitalism and ecological sustainability has become hegemonic, different and perhaps counter-intuitive lines of enquiry are not particularly popular" (Blühdorn and Welsh 2007: 186). In the sections below, we specifically outline the role social science can play in providing viable utopias; that is, engage in counter-hegemonic activities to question the current understanding of and approach to transformation in light of socio-ecological crises.

A Gramscian understanding of power – who is hegemonic in the global political economy?

In order to sustain itself over time, a system has to be constantly reproduced. There are a number of approaches to understand this process; here, we adhere to a Gramscian understanding of hegemony. Hegemony has been described by Gramsci as a condition in which the most powerful group in society is able to include vast majorities, who accept and reproduce the dominant mode of living. As such, hegemony becomes the organizing principle of daily routines and common sense.[1] Hegemony is not a static concept but is actively formed by particular forces that continuously construct and maintain the social system, through the interplay of coercion and consensus forming. In this sense, power is not understood as brute force but as combined with a process of opinion moulding. Hegemony, then, depends on the interplay of material and coercive capabilities, ideas and institutions and is characterized by the articulation and justification of a specialized set of interests as general interests.

It follows that hegemony is characterized by economic and ideological components, while always including coercive force, such as the military or the police (Hobsbawm 2012). Coercive, economic and politico-cultural forms of hegemony presuppose each other (Candeias 2007: 19). Therefore a capitalist economic system presupposes and also influences specific modes of political and cultural behaviour. Nevertheless, the state of hegemony as effective and inclusive leadership by a specific societal group is very difficult to obtain and even more difficult to sustain. If economic and cultural inclusion is lagging behind, coercive elements tend to be fortified (Leubolt 2015: 100–101). Hegemony is organized by the dominant power bloc, i.e. a specific social group (e.g. a class fraction). If successful, the power bloc is able to organize a historical bloc, as:

> an historical congruence between material forces, institutions and ideologies, or broadly, an alliance of different class forces politically organized around a set of hegemonic ideas that gave strategic direction and coherence to its constituent elements. Moreover, for a new historical bloc to emerge, its leaders must engage in conscious planned struggle.
>
> (Gill 2002: 58)

Thus, a historical bloc is the union of social forces forming hegemony. Different hegemonic projects exist, representing different societal interests and struggling to form a historical bloc to achieve hegemony (Kannankulam and Georgi 2012). The recent decade has been diagnosed as affected by multiple crises (Demirovic 2013), including the economy and the environment. In the subsequent section, we will engage in a brief historic overview of the ways of coping with these crises in the global policy arena: sustainable development will be analysed as the dominant hegemonic project, in the forms of "planetary boundaries" and green growth.

Planetary boundaries and scientific inquiry

The literature on rapid biodiversity loss, also termed the sixth mass extinction, on climate change, air pollution, resource scarcity and environmental degradation is continuously growing, warning society of a "perfect storm" (e.g., Beddington 2009; Brundtland *et al.* 2012; Poppy *et al.* 2014). In the most recent attempt to quantify societal impact on nature, Rockström *et al.* (2009) posit the existence of nine planetary boundaries and associated thresholds (recent update by Steffen *et al.* 2015). They join the long-standing tradition of academic literature on boundaries regarding growth, most commonly seen to have its origins with the Club of Rome's report on the *Limits to Growth* (Meadows *et al.* 1972). Ecological economists, such as Herman Daly, have written on the steady-state economy (1991) and most recently, the notions of degrowth, a-growth and post-growth (Kerschner 2010; Kallis 2011; van den Bergh 2011) have been put forward.

Planetary boundaries, however, are not a conceptual undertaking of reconceptualizing growth. Rather, it is presented as a relatively objective, natural scientific understanding of Earth as a complex system by showing boundaries in nine planetary systems. These boundaries present "biophysical preconditions for human development" (Rockström *et al.* 2009: 474). This encompasses 11 ecological, globally aggregated boundaries: biosphere integrity (genetic and functional diversity), climate change, novel entities, stratospheric ozone depletion, atmospheric aerosol loading, ocean acidification, biochemical flows (phosphorus and nitrogen cycles), freshwater use, and land-system change. Three of those boundaries cannot be quantified (functional diversity, atmospheric aerosol loading and novel entities), eight are defined and three boundaries have already been crossed (nitrogen and phosphorus cycles and genetic diversity) (Steffen *et al.* 2015). The main message of the paper is that within these boundaries lies the safe operating space for humanity, whereas the crossing of these thresholds can lead to potentially harmful change. The update emphasizes that, while boundaries at the planetary level provide important insights, these have to be supplemented by regionally and locally specific boundaries (Steffen *et al.* 2015). However, calculating regional impact is not, as of yet, a component of the planetary boundaries concept.

What is especially interesting to see is the impact the 2009 paper had on discourse in the realm of policy making. A compilation by Galaz *et al.* (2012) in their introduction to the *Ecological Economics* special issue on *Global Environmental Governance and Planetary Boundaries* shows that the concept has influenced the UN High-Level Panel on Global Sustainability, been discussed in a meeting of religious leaders called by the Dalai Lama and spurned the set-up of a non-government organization (NGO) by the World Wildlife Fund (WWF), the Planetary Boundaries Initiative. Especially the first initiative, the UN High-Level Panel on Global Sustainability, illustrates the impact of the concept on policy making: Ban Ki-Moon is its chair and has mentioned the concept in several speeches (e.g. the speech at the Third Nobel Laureate Symposium or the speech at the Leader's Dialogue on Climate Change) and the final report includes recommendations for linking the concept with international policy (United

Nations Secretary-General's High-Level Panel on Global Sustainability 2012). Additionally, the WWF NGO on planetary boundaries submitted a Draft UN Declaration on Planetary Boundaries to the UN Rio + 20 conference. The concept thus invites the notion of global governance. In 2011, Steffen *et al.* elaborated on the impact of the planetary boundaries concept on governance:

> Ultimately, there will need to be an institution (or institutions) operating, with authority, above the level of individual countries to ensure that the planetary boundaries are respected. In effect, such an institution, acting on behalf of humanity as a whole, would be the ultimate arbiter of the myriad trade-offs that need to be managed as nations and groups of people jockey for economic and social advantage. It would, in essence, become the global referee on the planetary playing field.

The academic blogosphere[2] has been active in commenting on the impact of the planetary boundaries concept on policy. Melissa Leach began a discussion on the *Huffington Post*,[3] commenting on the move from Holocene to Anthropocene (a term strongly linked to the human impact seen in the planetary boundaries concept) by asking if "it [the Anthropocene] was welcoming us to a new geological epoch, or a dangerous new world of undisputed scientific authority and anti-democratic politics?" Scientific authority is closely associated with replacing uncertainty with manageable risks and topics such as environmental degradation or even sustainability appearing non-political. Blühdorn and Welsh (2007: 191) connect this to the shift from crises aversion to crises management – in the political arena, this shift implies that crises management becomes the operational mode with corresponding "extraordinary security measures, the suspension of democratic safeguards and the uncoupling of checks and balances".

Rayner and Heyward (2013: 132) illustrate this by defining nature as "a rhetorical resource", stating that, for example, the climate change discourse was used in the European political setting to further integration of the union. The political impact of seemingly objective scientific facts can thus be felt. This is directly related to sustainability, a term put on the political agenda through diverse political and civil society movements (Stirling 2014), turned into an umbrella term (Fischer and Hajer 1999) and now used to justify "green growth", associated with certain rhetorical strategies since "the idea of nature as the ultimate justification for our political and moral preferences seems to be so thoroughly entrenched that it is unlikely to disappear from our vocabulary any time soon" (Rayner and Heyward 2013: 143). It is within this line of thought that planetary boundaries are interpreted as non-negotiable limits. Treating them as such bears the risk of closing down debates on how to react to ecological changes in an equitable, just and democratic manner. Blühdorn and Welsh (2007) elaborate on the public's declining trust in representative democracy and political parties. They state that this leads to an understanding of "responsible" rather than "representative" governments that impose certain reforms and innovations (Blühdorn and Welsh 2007: 191). As they go on to say, "the pervasive sense of environmental crisis becomes another mean of reinforcing state authority and citizens' compliance" (Blühdorn and Welsh 2007: 191).

International relations – politics of greening?

Sustainable development has become one of the most important markers in environmental discourse. The term, originally seeking to offer a way for developing countries to develop within certain ecological limits while also achieving minimum living standards, has instead been captured by a "sustainable development historic bloc" (Newell 2008: 516). The aim of this bloc, as Newell proposes, is to steer the discussion away from the problems of market-led globalization through failing to acknowledge the connection between the logic of accumulation inherent to our current form of capitalism and the multiple crises we are experiencing globally. Blühdorn and Welsh highlight how the "state/corporate sector nexus, operating through deepening public–private partnerships, emerges as the central means of delivering sustainability" (2007: 192). In a sense, the continuing focus on economic growth within sustainable development "represents the effective subversion of any radical counter-hegemonic programme" (Blühdorn and Welsh 2007: 189). Sustainable development, however, has an increasingly negative connotation; its framing is "politically unattractive" (Jacobs 2012: 6).

The following brief historical overview and introduction to the currently prevalent notion of "green growth" aim to show that the capitalist logic of accumulation, expressed through growth, is still at the heart of current proposals for development and prosperity. Sustainable development simply succeeded in "providing the 'generative metaphor'" and provided a way to talk about ecological problems (Fischer and Hajer 1999: 2). "The key principles of consumer capitalism, i.e. infinite economic growth and wealth accumulation, which ecologists have always branded as fundamentally unsustainable, remain fully in place" (Blühdorn and Welsh 2007: 187). However, it becomes exceedingly clear that growth, especially in regard to its unequal distributional effects, has tangible social and ecological effects. These effects thus do not simply appear but are constituted and reproduced by certain policies and actors as well as material conditions. "Marketised environmental governance" (Newell 2008: 522) does not recognize that environmental problems cannot be reduced to their environmental component but that they are linked to both political and social realities that play a crucial role in creating and sustaining them. We question this project as a viable strategy for transformation since it is based on a variety of different "green" measures while "the key principles governing western practices of production, circulation, exchange and consumption remain immutable" (Blühdorn and Welsh 2007: 187).

Since the Rio +20 conference in 2012, green growth is potentially becoming the "new leading strategy in political discourse" (Brand 2012: 28). Green growth is invoked as a solution to the aforementioned social and ecological crises through measures such as "a low-carbon economy, resource efficiency, green investments, technological innovation and more recycling, green jobs, poverty eradication, and social inclusion" (Brand 2012: 29). The core, however, is the notion of growth as the harbinger of all these. Essentially, green growth is "economic growth (growth of gross domestic product or GDP) which also achieves significant environmental protection" (Jacobs 2012: 4). Green growth focuses on the compatibility of growth and environmental protection, arguing that "protecting the environment can actually yield *better* growth" (Jacobs 2012: 6). Growth, therefore, is the central tenet of economic policies put forward in the name of sustainable development.

A number of international organizations have put forward proposals centring on green growth: the European Commission (2010), OECD (2011), UNDESA (2011), UNEP (2011) and most recently an intergovernmental panel published *The New Climate Economy Report* (GCEC 2014). As an analysis conducted by Urhammer and Røpke (2013) shows, these institutions are "pro-growth" (2013: 64) and "economic growth is at the core of these proposals" (2013: 62), providing a focal point around which the debates on social and ecological crises cluster. This discourse takes place in the same policy arena – emerging "from the more mainstream and pragmatic community of environmental-economic policymakers" (Jacobs 2012: 6). In the proposals by the so-called pro-growth institutions, "the pro-growth discourse is synonymous with employment, social stability, prosperity and wellbeing" and, crucially, "does not question growth as the basic driver of the economy" (Urhammer and Røpke 2013: 68).

A brief scan of these proposals also shows that innovation is invoked as a solution with efficiency as a key ingredient. The natural environment is mainly thought of as "natural capital". This is not new; Costanza *et al.* (1997) published a paper in *Nature* proposing a value of 33 trillion US$/year for global ecosystem services and natural capital. The basis for valuation is the use of numbers for decision making. Costanza *et al.* (1997) aim to assess both market and non-market values. They conclude that, were ecosystems valued in monetary terms, price and wage structures as well as production costs would vary immensely from what they are today (Costanza *et al.* 1997: 257). Wissen and Brand (forthcoming) have recently elaborated on this, stating that financialization of nature is not a new phenomenon but seems to have become the most popular form of appropriation of natural resources. They list examples such as carbon trading or commodity trading. Another approach to the appropriation of nature is (climate) geoengineering; that is, a rather ambiguous term referring to human altering of Earth's systems (for further exploration of this, see Cairns and Stirling 2014). On the global policy agenda, however, green growth seems to be the term that, at the moment, can rally a large number of supporters.

Examples of approaches to green growth include "decoupl[ing] economic growth from the use of resources" (European Commission 2010: 4), focusing "on mutually reinforcing aspects of economic and environmental policy" (OECD 2011: 10), the need for a "technological revolution" (UNDESA 2011: vi) and the "growing recognition that achieving sustainability rests almost entirely on getting the economy right" (UNEP 2011: 17). Growth, as the main driver of equality and well-being, is not questioned. Rather, ecological, economic and social sustainability are not seen as mutually exclusive and notions claiming that there is mounting evidence that they might be are dismissed as myths (UNEP 2011). Ultimately, green growth does not, first and foremost, aim at ecological or social sustainability but the continuously smooth revving of the engine of growth: "In the long term, if climate change is not tackled, growth itself will be at risk" (GCEC 2014: 9).[4]

In many aspects, the shift from environmental discourse from "sustainability" towards "green growth" represents a further co-optng of the environmental movement by neoliberal interests (Brand and Wissen 2014; Spash 2014). Nevertheless, the concept is not unambiguous. It has become popular in a period of crises and has been linked to imaginaries of a "Green New Deal," which feature some of the more social characteristics of Fordism. In many aspects, the "green growth" discourse has been brought up by intellectuals who adhere to the paradigm of "inclusive liberalism" rather than to its conservative counterpart. Therefore, "green growth" has often been analysed as co-opting or capturing potentially more emancipatory social forces in the framework of neoliberalism. Nevertheless, its framing in a more inclusive discourse can also be seen as countering more coercive conservative projects, such as geoengineering. International negotiations over the subject might also counter tendencies towards wars over resources.

Law and Urry (2004) argue that mainstream economist discourse now widely infuses "state discourse and action". They cite wide-ranging examples, such as "unemployment, production, productivity, terms of trade, balance of trade, GDP" (Law and Urry 2004: 392) and also refer to Michel Callon's work on the influence of theories of markets in creating the realities they only claim to describe (Callon 1998). As such, scientific enquiry always interferes with reality – the goal is to engage fruitfully rather than disengage (Law 2004). One consequence, then, is that ontology takes centre stage, looking at how "what is known is also being made differently" (Law and Urry 2004: 397). The current key concern is not sustainability, but how to manage the prevailing unsustainability (Blühdorn and Welsh 2007: 192). As Blühdorn and Welsh state, "Post-democratic and neo-authoritarian tendencies are an important dimension of the politics of unsustainability" (2007: 192). We therefore argue that it is necessary to employ a political economy approach that allows for the critical and discursive analysis of existing power relations.

The role of social science in socio-ecological transformation

In his recent paper, Stirling (2014) emphasizes the role of science by employing the example of energy choices and climate change. The central issue is not technologically or physically feasible change but rather social and political barriers. Politically, vested interests in progress and modernity, epitomized first by nuclear power and currently by geoengineering, cause a power asymmetry. This gives rise to a rather conservative agenda with a focus on technological innovation and managerial, top-down transitions, which stands in the way of more radical transformations (Stirling 2014). It is here that a certain discourse gains prevalence over another and where social science plays a formative role. Within the degrowth literature, Kallis notes that crises can lead to paradigm change as "revolutionary changes, in society or science, are often punctuations after big periods of stasis or development locked in a paradigm" (Kallis 2011: 878). Using the example of scientists who research degrowth, he shows that science has the potential to "counter a false cultural story (growth as progress)" by constructing a new one.

The knowledge created in the scientific realm "can have the effect of asymmetrically emphasising particular favoured pathways at the expense of others" (Stirling 2014: 87). However, the crux of the matter is that "knowledge not only informs power, but is profoundly shaped by it" (Stirling 2014: 87). Thus, when looking at incumbents in the energy sector and their investments, they play a crucial role in steering science. Earlier in his work, Stirling (2011) proposes reflexivity and diversity as components of a multi-paradigmatic and interdisciplinary science for sustainability. He argues that different possibilities for transformations need to be discussed through "more rigorously 'plural and conditional'" (Stirling 2011: 85) approaches, where researchers also abandon the notions of objectivity and value-neutrality and position themselves as subjects of the enquiry. This is of course directly linked to increasing reflexivity in research, characterized by increasing "relations between interacting research communities", "greater humility and explicit positionality by researchers as subjects" and "deliberately nurturing plurality in observing disciplines as well as diversity in the transformative processes they inform" (Stirling 2011: 86–87).

Discussion and conclusion

In this chapter, we have explored the heuristic pre-requisites for socio-ecological transformation and provided examples from the policy arena, namely planetary boundaries and green growth. We also aimed to gain a deeper understanding of the role of social science in socio-ecological transformations. These aspects lead to different hegemonic projects of environmental discourse emerging on the top agendas of international institutions; in this realm we revisit the concept of hegemony from a Gramscian perspective. It is especially helpful in our analysis because it understands power as both consensus forming and coercive.

Invoking a perfect storm, both in the ecological and the economic realm, the current debates around climate change and environmental threats follow a very specific pattern, based on the notion that the current state of the planet is the result of humanity as an entity rather than local, political or cultural specificities (Stirling 2015). Thus, the planetary boundary discourse can be taken to support a political programme based on technological innovation, such as geoengineering, and top-down, managerial approaches, or even the exertion of control (Stirling 2015: 58–59). It is in light of this that (social) science has to not only question this representation of the system but also be reflexive and acknowledge that power asymmetries bear direct effects on the production of knowledge (Stirling 2014: 90). As such, multiple voices and viewpoints need to be heard and "science and knowledge making become integral to wider conceptions of society and democracy, and a politics of sustainability is necessarily a politics of knowledge in which our own research, engagements and communications are deeply implicated" (Leach *et al.* 2013: 88).

Wright proposes emancipatory social science as a way of conducting scientific enquiry to uncover viable utopias (Wright 2010). In his proposal, social science refers to the creation of sound scientific knowledge about institutions and other social structures. It is emancipatory in the sense that it "seeks to generate scientific knowledge relevant to the collective project of challenging various forms of human oppression" (Wright 2010: 10). Here, the focus lies on the oppression exercised by institutions and social structures, thus linking back to the coercive aspect of hegemony. The final component refers to the development of viable alternatives – a counter-hegemonic enterprise. Wright's emancipatory social science is related to methodological discussions in the social sciences (see Law 2004 and Sayer 2010), especially regarding how methodological enquiries are not value-free investigations of a reality but rather enact reality. It is here that the seemingly objective nature of the planetary boundaries concept and its rather stark influence in the policy arena come into play. Overall, we wish to highlight the importance of reflexive social science when it comes to effectively dealing with biophysical limits in the global policy scene.

Notes

1 A similar perspective is opened by Foucault's concept of *dispositive* (Foucault 1978). Compared to Gramsci, Foucault places greater emphasis on the internalization of power relations by dominated individuals (cf. Lemke 1997; Sum and Jessop 2013), while Gramsci (1971: 5ff.) offers further insights on the role of intellectuals.

2 Roger Pielke on 'Planetary Boundaries as Power Grab', available from: http://rogerpielkejr.blogspot.co.at/2013/04/planetary-boundries-as-power-grab.html, accessed on 2015-05-19.

3 Melissa Leach on 'Democracy in the Anthropocene?' (published on 28/03/2013) available from: http://www.huffingtonpost.co.uk/Melissa-Leach/democracy-in-the-anthropocene_b_2966341.html, accessed on 2015-05-19.

4 See Spash (2014) on a detailed analysis of the GCEC report.

References

Beddington, J. (2009), *Food, Energy, Water and the Climate: A Perfect Storm of Global Events?* Government Office for Science, London.

Berger, S., and Elsner, W. (2008), "European Contributions to Evolutionary Institutional Economics: The Cases 'Open-Systems Approach' (OSA) and 'Cumulative Circular Causation' (CCC)," in Hanappi, H., and Elsner, W. (eds), *Advances in Evolutionary Institutional Economics*, Edward Elgar, Cheltenham, UK.

Blühdorn, I., and Welsh, I. (2007), "Eco-Politics Beyond the Paradigm of Sustainability: A Conceptual Framework and Research Agenda," *Environmental Politics*, Vol. 16, No. 2, pp. 185–205.

Brand, U. (2012), "Green Economy: The Next Oxymoron?" *GAIA: Ecological Perspectives for Science and Society*, Vol. 21, No. 1, pp. 28–32.

Brand, U., and Wissen, M. (2014), "Financialisation of Nature as Crisis Strategy." *Journal für Entwicklungspolitik,* Vol. 30, No. 2, pp. 16–45.

Brown, D. (1991), "Thorstein Veblen Meets Eduard Bernstein: Toward an Institutionalist Theory of Mobilization Politics," *Journal of Economic Issues*, Vol. 25, No. 3, pp. 689–708.

Brundtland, G.H., Ehrlich, P., Goldemberg, J., Hansen, J., Lovins, A., Likens, G., Manabe, S., May, B., Mooney, H., Robèrt, K.-H., Salim, E., Sato, G., Solomon, S., Stern, N., Swaminathan Research Foundation, Watson, R., Barefoot College, Conservation International, International Institute for Environment and Development, and International Union for the Conservation of Nature. (2012), *Environment and Development Challenges: The Imperative to Act,* The Asahi Glass Foundation, Tokyo.

Cairns, R., and Stirling, A. (2014), "'Maintaining Planetary Systems' or 'Concentrating Global Power?' High Stakes in Contending Framings of Climate Geoengineering," *Global Environmental Change,* Vol. 28, pp. 25–38.

Callon, M. (ed.) (1998), *The Laws of the Markets,* Blackwell and the Sociological Review, Oxford.

Candeias, M. (2007), "Gramscianische Konstellationen: Hegemonie und die Durchsetzung neuer Produktions- und Lebensweisen" in Merkens, A., and Diaz, V.R. (eds), *Mit Gramsci arbeiten – Texte zur politisch-praktischen Aneignung Antonio Gramscis*, Argument, Hamburg.

Castells, M. (2009), *Communication Power*, Oxford University Press, New York.

Costanza, R., d'Arge, R., de Groot, R., Farber, S., Grasso, M., Hannon, B., Limburg, K., Naeem, S., O'Neill, R.V., Paruelo, J., Raskin, R.G., Sutton, P., and van den Belt, M. (1997), "The Value of the World's Ecosystem Services and Natural Capital," *Nature*, Vol. 387, pp. 263–260.

Daly, H.E. (1991), *Steady-State Economics*, Island Press, Washington, DC.

Demirovic, A. (2013), "Multiple Krise, autoritäre Demokratie und radikaldemokratische Erneuerung," *PROKLA,* Vol. 43, No. 2, pp. 193–215.

European Commission. (2010), *Communication from the Commission: Europe 2020, A Strategy for Smart, Sustainable and Inclusive Growth,* European Commission, Brussels.

Fischer, F. and Hajer, M. (eds) (1999), *Living with Nature: Environmental Politics as Cultural Discourse.* Oxford University Press, Oxford.

Foucault, M. (1978), *Dispositive der Macht: über Sexualität, Wissen und Wahrheit.* Merve-Verlag, Berlin.

Galaz, V., Biermann, F., Folke, C., Nilsson, M., & Olsson, P. (2012), "Global Environmental Governance and Planetary Boundaries: An Introduction," *Ecological Economics*, Vol. 81, pp. 1–3.

GCEC. (2014), "Better Growth Better Climate: The New Climate Economy Report: The Synthesis Report," in Calderon, F. *et al.* (eds), *The Global Commission on the Economy and Climate*, Washington, DC.

Georgescu-Roegen, N. (1971), *The Entropy Law and the Economic Process*, Harvard University Press, Cambridge, MA.

Gill, S. (2002), *Power and Resistance in the New World Order*, Palgrave Macmillan, Basingstoke.

Gramsci, A. (1971), *Selections from the Prison Notebooks,* edited and translated by Qu. Hoare and G. N. Smith, Lawrence & Wishart, London.

Gruchy, A.G. (1973), "Law, Politics, and Institutional Economics," *Journal of Economic Issues*, Vol. 7, No. 4, pp. 623–643.

Hobsbawm, E. (2012), *How to Change the World: Tales of Marx and Marxism*, Abacus, London.

Jacobs, M. (2012), *Green Growth: Economic Theory and Political Discourse*, Centre for Climate Change Economics and Policy Working Paper No. 108/Grantham Research

Institute on Climate Change and the Environment Working Paper No. 92, Grantham Research Institute on Climate Change and the Environment, London.

Jessop, B., and Sum, N.-L. (2013), *Towards a Cultural Political Economy*, Edward Elgar, Cheltenham, UK.

Kallis, G. (2011), "In Defence of Degrowth," *Ecological Economics*, Vol. 70, No. 5, pp. 873–880.

Kannankulam, J., and Georgi, F. (2012), "Die europäische Integration als materielle Verdichtung von Kräfteverhältnissen: Hegemonieprojekte im Kampf um das 'Staatsprojekt Europa'," *Arbeitspapiere der Forschungsgruppe Europäische Integration – Philipps-Universität Marburg 30.* http://www.uni-marburg.de/fb03/politikwissenschaft/eipoe/publikationen/publikationen/a30.pdf (accessed 10 September 2016).

Kapp, K.W. (1977), "Environment and Technology: New Frontiers for the Social and Natural Sciences," *Journal of Economic Issues*, Vol. 11, No. 3, pp. 527–540.

Kerschner, C. (2010), "Economic De-Growth Vs. Steady-State Economy," *Journal of Cleaner Production*, Vol. 18, No. 6, pp. 544–551.

Klein, P.A., and Miller, E.S. (1996), "Concepts of Value, Efficiency, and Democracy in Institutional Economics." *Journal of Economic Issues*, Vol. 30, No. 1, pp. 267–277.

Laclau, E., and Mouffe C. [1985] (2014), *Hegemony and Socialist Strategy: Towards a Radical Democratic Politics,* 2nd edn. Verso, London.

Law, J. (2004), *After Method: Mess in Social Science Research*, Routledge, London.

Law, J., and Urry, J. (2004), "Enacting the Social," *Economy and Society*, Vol. 33, No. 3, pp. 390–410.

Leach, M., Raworth, K., and Rockström, J. (2013), "Between Social and Planetary Boundaries: Navigating Pathways in the Safe and Just Space for Humanity" in ISSC/UNESCO, *World Social Science Report 2013: Changing Global Environments*, OECD Publishing and UNESCO Publishing, Paris.

Lemke, T. (1997), "Eine Kritik der Politischen Vernunft Foucaults Analyse der Modernen Gouvernementalitèat," Argument, Hamburg.

Leubolt, B. (2015), *Transformation von Ungleichheitsregimes: Gleichheitsorientierte Politik in Brasilien und Südafrika*, VS Springer, Wiesbaden.

Meadows, D. H., Meadows, D. L., and Randers, J. (1972) *The Limits to Growth*, Signet, New York.

Mouffe, C. [2000] (2009), *The Democratic Paradox,* Verso, London.

Newell, P. (2008), "The Political Economy of Global Environmental Governance," *Review of International Studies*, Vol. 34, No. 3, pp. 507–529.

OECD. (2011), *Towards Green Growth*, OECD, Paris.

Poppy, G.M., Chiotha, S., Eigenbrod, F., Harvey, C.A., Honzák, M., Hudson, M.D., Jarvis, A., Madise, N.J., Schreckenberg, K., Shackleton, C.M., Villa, F., and Dawson, T.P. (2014), "Food Security in a Perfect Storm: Using the Ecosystem Services Framework to Increase Understanding," *Philosophical Transactions of the Royal Society of London, Series B, Biological Sciences*, Vol. 369, No. 1639, 20120288.

Raworth, K. (2012), "A Safe and Just Space for Humanity: Can We Live Within the Doughnut?" Oxfam Discussion Paper, *Oxfam Policy and Practice: Climate Change and Resilience,* Vol. 8, No. 1, pp. 1–26, Oxfam, Oxford.

Rayner, S., and Heyward, C. (2013), "The Inevitability of Nature as a Rhetorial Resource," in Hastrup, K. (ed.), *Anthropology and Nature*, Routledge, London, pp. 125–147.

Rockström, J., Steffen, W., Noone, K., Persson, A., Chapin, F.S., Lambin, E.F., Lenton, T.M., Scheffer, M., Folke, C., Schellnhuber, H.J., Nykvist, B., de Wit, C.A., Hughes, T., van der Leeuw, S., Rodhe, H., Soerlin, S., Snyder, P.K., Costanza, R., Svedin,

U., Falkenmark, M., Karlberg, L., Corell, R.W., Fabry, V.J., Hansen, J., Walker, B., Liverman, D., Richardson, K., Crutzen, P., and Foley, J.A. (2009), "A Safe Operating Space for Humanity," *Nature*, Vol. 461, No. 24, pp. 472–475.

Sayer, A. (2010), *Method in Social Science,* 2nd edn. Routledge, London.

Spash, C. (2014), "Better Growth, Helping the Paris COP-out? Fallacies and Omissions of the New Climate Economy Report," *SRE-Discussion 2014/4.*

Steffen, S., Rockstrom, J., and Costanza, B. (2011), "How Defining Planetary Boundaries Can Transform Our Approach to Growth," *Solutions*, Vol. 2, No. 3. http://www.thesolutionsjournal.com/node/935 (accessed on 13.08.15).

Steffen, W., Richardson, K., Rockström, J., Cornell, S.E., Fetzer, I., Benett, E.M., Biggs, R., Carpenter, S.R., de Vries, W., de Wit, C.A., Folke, C., Gerten, D., Heinke, J., Mace, G.M., Persson, L.M., Ramanathan, V., Reyers, B., and Sörlin, S. (2015), "Planetary Boundaries: Guiding Human Development on a Changing Planet," *Science*, Vol. 347, No. 6223, pp. 736–745.

Stirling, A. (2011), "Pluralising Progress: From Integrative Transitions to Transformative Diversity," *Environmental Innovation and Societal Transitions*, Vol. 1, No. 1, pp. 82–88.

Stirling, A. (2014), "Transforming Power: Social Science and the Politics of Energy Choices," *Energy Research and Social Science,* Vol. 1, pp. 83–95.

Stirling, A. (2015), "Emancipating Transformations: From Controlling 'The Transition' to Culturing Plural Radical Progress," in Scoones, I., Leach, M., and Newell, P. (eds), *The Politics of Green Transformations,* Earthscan, London.Sum, N.L., and Jessop, B. (2013), *Towards a Cultural Political Economy: Putting Culture in its Place in Political Economy*, Edward Elgar, Cheltenham, UK.

Tool, M.R. (1977), "A Social Value Theory in Neoinstitutional Econonics," *Journal of Economic Issues*, Vol. 11, No. 4, pp. 823–846.

UNDESA. (2011), *World Economic and Social Survey 2011, The Great Green Technological Transformation,* UNDESA, New York.

UNEP. (2011), *Towards a Green Economy, Pathways to Sustainable Development and Poverty Eradication*, UNEP, Nairobi.

United Nations Secretary-General's High-Level Panel on Global Sustainability. (2012), *Resilient People, Resilient Planet: A Future Worth Choosing,* United Nations, New York.

Urhammer, E., and Røpke, I. (2013), "Macroeconomic Narratives in a World of Crises: An Analysis of Stories about Solving the System Crisis," *Ecological Economics*, Vol. 96, pp. 62–70.

van den Bergh, J.C.J.M. (2011), "Environment Versus Growth: A Criticism of 'Degrowth' and a Plea for 'A-Growth'," *Ecological Economics*, Vol. 70, No. 5, pp. 881–890.

Veblen, T. (1898), "Why is Economics Not an Evolutionary Science?" *The Quarterly Journal of Economics*, Vol. 12.

Wissen, M., and Brand, U. (forthcoming), "Financialization of Nature as Crisis Strategy," *Journal für Entwicklungspolitik.*

Wright, E.O. (2010), *Envisioning Real Utopias*, Verso, London.

Part II

Crisis in Greece and Cyprus

9 The crisis in Greece

A story in pictures

Christis Hassapis, Nikolaos Skourias and Panos Xidonas

Introduction

It is a fact now. The "Mediterranean diet" is not working any more. And it's been more than half a decade, since Southern Europe embarked on a harsh diet and a rigorous fitness regimen. Of course, the main protagonist here is Greece, whose outlook now seems more impaired than ever.

There is no doubt that the situation in the "country of sun" is so sarcastic. Once upon a time some betrayers had been signing Memoranda, making people terrified of "a life without the euro." One day some heroes overthrew them. They signed a new Memorandum and "saved" the country from the "calamity" without the euro. Well, let's see how this all began. Unarguably, the agreement reached by the Greek government in August 2015, after negotiations of six whole months, is finally considered to be much worse than the one which could have been reached if the government had not negotiated at all. But what is the final conclusion? Instead of "annulling" the Memorandum by means of a new law and an article (as they were saying), ultimately, Greece asked for a new Memorandum, maybe the worst of all the previous ones.

Unfortunately, Greece is the country where pensions are being cut in order for early retirements to be financed. Greece is the country where, according to the current rates of taxation, in a company with four partners and an annual profitability of 500 kEUR, the total revenue for each one of them is just 12.5 kEUR, namely an income probably much lower than the annual earnings of a public servant. Hence, instead of the promotion of private initiatives and of entrepreneurial risk-taking reward, the ideas of pursuing tax avoidance and of throwing oneself on the public-sector bandwagon in any way are being spread. Greece is the country where the public sector is the "ultimate sacred cow." The country where 1.5 million Greeks are unemployed and 250,000 have already emigrated. One could wonder: how many of these were public servants?

Greece is the country which received loans of EUR 650 billion, net subsidies of EUR 300 billion and interest-free investment subsidies of EUR 25 billion since 1981. However, despite all these, some groups of people fervently wish to go back to the drachma. Their argument is that such a choice could improve the competitiveness of the domestic market. This is another big myth. In 1980 the drachma–dollar exchange rate was determined at $1 to GRD 43. In 2000, this exchange rate was closing at $1 to GRD 309. In other words, within 20 years the drachma had lost critical value on the basis of its relationship to the dollar. Apart from that, during these 20 years the amount of exports had only marginally been doubled, namely from $5 billion to $10 billion. Furthermore, the trade deficit – from $6 billion in 1980 – approached $19 billion in 2000. Thus, it is manifestly concluded that the depreciation of the drachma was not able, in any case, to increase the competitiveness of the Greek economy.

As the Great Recession, begun in the USA in 2007–2009, spread to Europe, the flow of funds lent from the European core countries to the peripheral countries, such as Greece, began to dry up. Reports in 2009 of Greek fiscal mismanagement and deception increased borrowing costs. The combination meant Greece could no longer borrow to finance its trade and budget deficits, thus in order to become more competitive, Greek wages fell nearly 20% from 2010 to 2014, as a form of deflation. This resulted in a severe overall recession; a significant reduction in income and gross domestic product (GDP) and a huge rise in the debt-to-GDP ratio. Unemployment has risen to nearly 28%, from below 10% in 2003. The Greek government debt crisis was the first of five sovereign debt crises in the Eurozone. Triggers included the turmoil of the Great Recession, structural weaknesses in the Greek economy and a sudden crisis in confidence among lenders. In late 2009, fears developed about Greece's ability to meet its debt obligations, due to revelations that previous data on government debt levels and deficits had been misreported by the Greek government. This led to a crisis of confidence, indicated by a widening of bond yield spreads and the cost of risk insurance on credit default swaps compared to the other Eurozone countries.

In this chapter, we explore a series of crucial parameters that directly affected and triggered the Greek crisis. These factors include issues such as the underlying *fiscal* consolidation, the adopted austerity measures, the aggressive contraction and external imbalances of the Greek economy, as well as the "lethal" twin deficits. Moreover, we comment on the viability of the Greek debt synthesis, the role of the European Central Bank (ECB), the "slaughter" of the labor force and the sacrifices made to achieve competitiveness. Finally, we also investigate the Greek business environment, the behavior of the markets and the permanent "wound" of deflation.

The whole story

The fiscal impact

Since the signing of the first Memorandum in 2010, Greece's fiscal performance has significantly improved. The fiscal adjustment that has been achieved has resulted in a significant narrowing of the underlying deficits (Figure 9.1).

The general government deficit fell by €30.5 billion in 2015 compared to 2009, the same time that the primary balance shrunk by €25.5 billion, 12.0 and 10.9 percentage points lower, respectively. Greece is expected to record a headline deficit of 3.2% in 2015 and a surplus of 0.7% of GDP excluding interest paid.

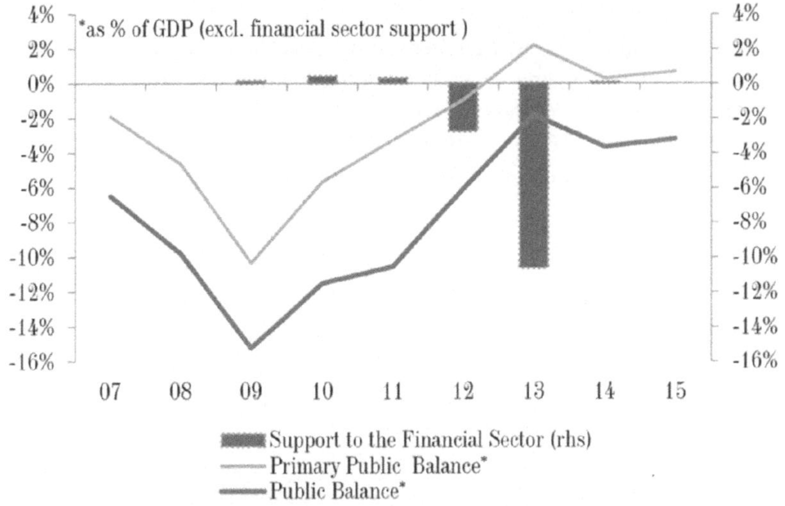

Figure 9.1 Fiscal consolidation

The dead-end austerity measures

Over the last 5 years, a series of spending cuts and measures to increase revenue have been implemented amounting to 36.7% of GDP or €72.6 billion, as part of the effort to trim past years' excessive deficits. The austerity measures were bound to impact economic activity, with real GDP losses estimated to be around €55.9 billion or 25.7% of GDP (Figure 9.2).

The adverse mix of fiscal consolidation initiatives that were mainly focused on increasing revenue, and much less on spending cuts, amplified the underlying recessionary impact. Unfortunately, austerity measures were not accompanied by an ambitious set of structural reforms that could have increased potential output, thus, strengthening economic fundamentals, investment, and other components of aggregate demand, and partially offsetting the contraction in economic activity. At the same time, the lack of competitiveness did not allow the external sector to take over from domestic demand that was plunging under the weight of internal devaluation.

Obviously, the recession has limited the positive achievements in public finances, as the astonishing improvement in cyclically adjusted public balance readings showed, as a far less severe economic contraction would have contributed in a faster and less painful fiscal adjustment, thus, softening the vicious circle of recession and austerity.

The aggressive contraction of the Greek economy

Fiscal consolidation and internal adjustment (devaluation) threw Greece into a destructive recessionary spiral, from which it managed to escape in 2014, after 5 years of negative economic growth rates and a widening output gap. During 2014 the Greek economy experienced a positive growth rate of 0.7% for the first time in 6 years (Figure 9.3).

Greece's economy proved resilient in the first three quarters of 2015 despite the introduction of the emergency bank holiday, capital controls, and heightened uncertainty related to prolonged negotiations with the troika (the EU, International Monetary Fund and ECB). Fortunately, the rising concerns, as economic and business sentiment plummeted following the bank holiday and the imposition

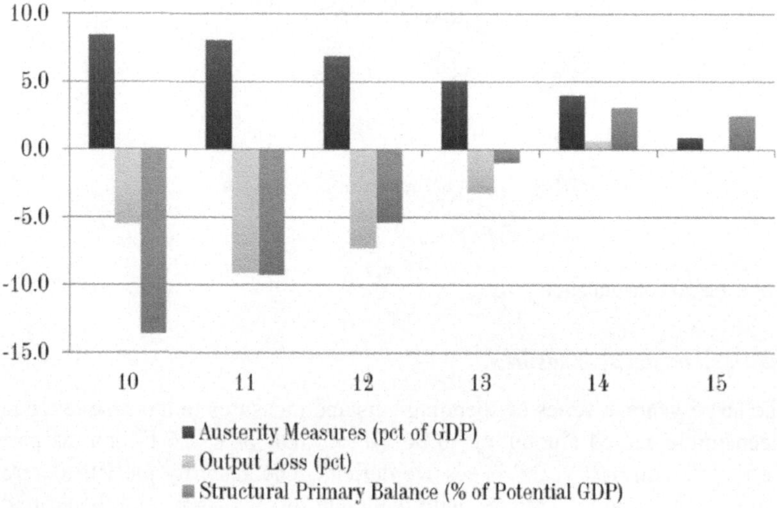

Figure 9.2 Economic and fiscal impacts of the austerity measures

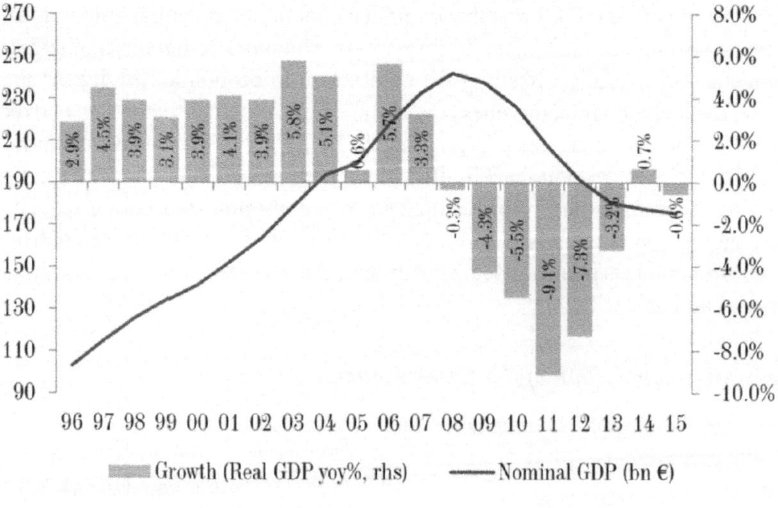

Figure 9.3 Real GDP contraction

of capital controls, have not materialized. Private consumption was stronger than expected, due to the fall in the rate of unemployment and negative saving rates, at the same time that households chose to spend their deposits to avoid potential deposit haircuts. The external sector contributed as well to the better than forecasted economic performance, as trade deficits of goods shrunk due to a leap in exports excluding oil as well as the global crude oil rout, while the tourism sector continued to perform exceptionally well during the autumn, following another solid summer.

As a result, estimated economic growth has been revised upwards, but Greece did not avoid returning back to the contraction zone. Real GDP dropped 0.6% compared to government and European Commission last forecast for 0.0%. Despite a slightly weaker performance, the economy fared relatively well given the two general elections in the space of just 7 months, a referendum between, a bank holiday and capital controls since July, declining much less than had been anticipated only a few months before. Nominal GDP fell as well in 2015 for the seventh straight year to €175.5 billion, 26.1% lower than 2009, as deflationary pressures lingered. Looking into 2016, economic activity is expected to contract by 0.7% as the negative carry-over from 2015 and the faltering domestic demand will likely weigh during the first semester; however, the swift completion of the bailout plan's first review and a stable political arena should help the economy to rebound in the second semester of the year.

External imbalances, the permanent illness

Significant progress has been achieved in resolving external imbalances, with the current account deficit having been almost eliminated, the dependence on capital inflows reduced, as, for the 1st time in recent years, Greece recorded a surplus in 2015, 0.3% compared to a 12.4% deficit in 2009. At the same time, the trade deficit (goods and services) shrank to 0.1% of GDP, while in 2009 it stood a 9.1% (Figure 9.4).

The improvement in the external balance is largely due to: (a) the reduction in the balance of trade, which is mostly attributed to the recession and the plunge in crude oil prices, and, very recently, due to the capital controls that have restricted imports; (b) the significant improvement in the balance of services account, due to the recovery in tourism and tourist receipts; (c) the higher transfers from the EU and refunds of profits, as well as coupon payments from Greek government bonds held by the Eurosystem (ECB and other European central banks); and (d) the reduction in the income balance, due to the dip of costs for servicing the public debt to non-residents, as opposed to gains in competitiveness and export growth. The economy, however, is finally and steadily reaching equilibrium and is slowly transitioning towards an "open economy" development model, as consumer spending and imports fall.

The twin deficits

The unprecedented fiscal adjustment that has been implemented in conjunction with the stabilization of the external sector makes Greece a much less vulnerable economy, despite the fragile nature of recent achievements, as they cannot be characterized as viable yet (Figure 9.5). Together, the twin deficits are approaching 2.9% of GDP, a 24.6 percentage points improvement in just 6 years.

What is owned and where

The composition of the Greek public debt has significantly been altered following public-sector involvement and the buy-back that took place in March

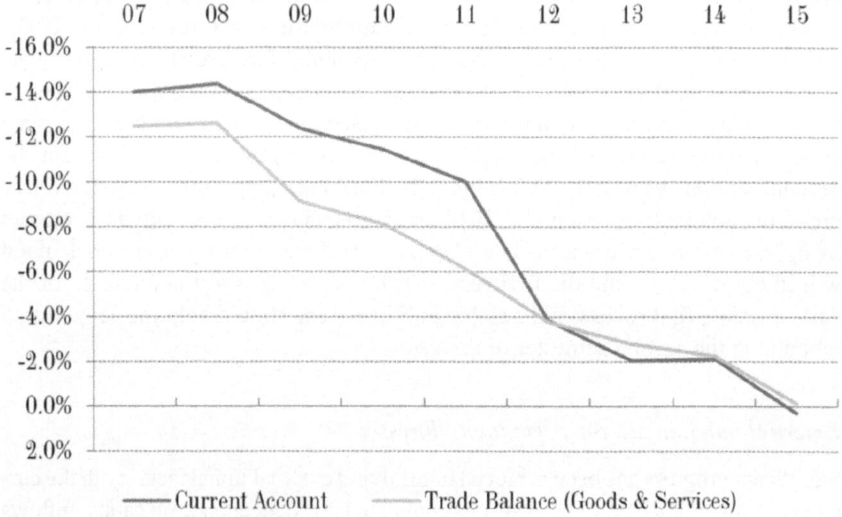

Figure 9.4 External imbalances

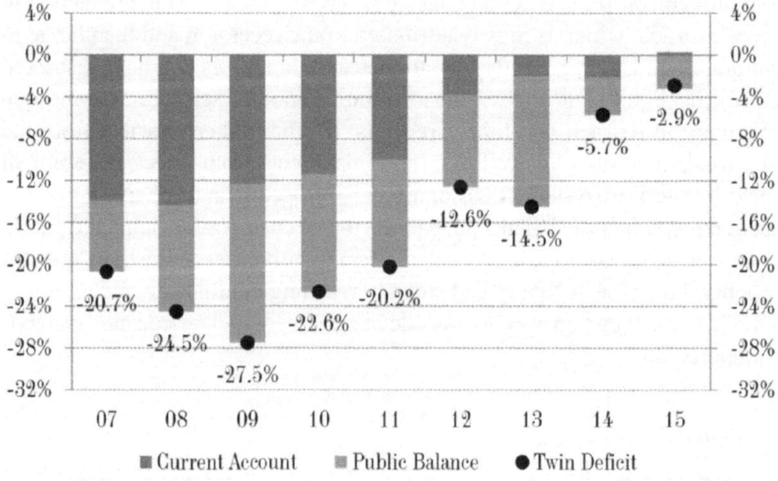

Figure 9.5 Twin deficits

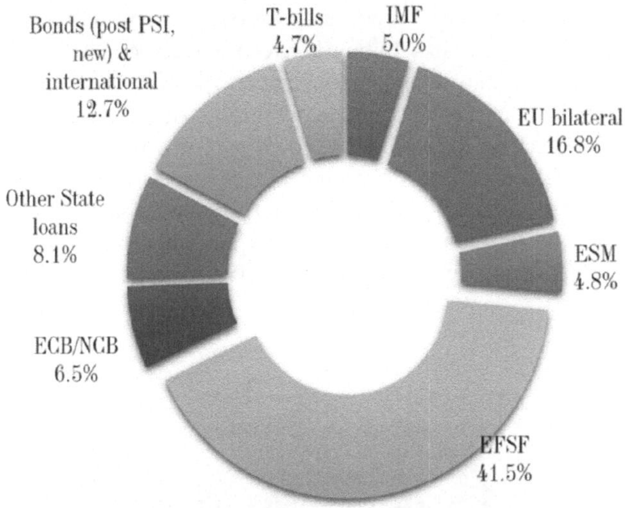

Figure 9.6 Composition of Greek debt. IMF, International Monetary Fund; EU, European Union; ESM, European Stability Mechanism; EFSF, European Financial Stability Facility; ECB, European Central Bank; NCB, National Central Bank; PSI, private-sector involvement; T-bills, Treasury bills

(€100 billion) and December 2012 that led to a €100 billion and €30 billion cut, respectively. As of September 2015, the public sector held 82.6% of total debt (Figure 9.6). It is worth noting that the main characteristics of the debt, controlled by the public sector, are its long maturity and its low interest.

The Greek debt in absolute and relational values

In both absolute and relative terms, the Greek debt is approximately €316.5 billion in 2015 (180.3% of GDP), up by €16.8 billion or 54.2 percentage points since 2009 (Figure 9.7). Many consider the debt as being relatively high and at unsustainable levels. General government deficits, despite their major downsizing, continue to create new financing needs and increase the debt in absolute terms.

At the same time, the continuous fall in nominal GDP raises the ratio of debt to GDP. Interest payments, the support towards pension and social security funds, combined with the recapitalization of the banking sector, are the main reasons for the observed deterioration, and, in short, have wrecked the benefits of the private-sector involvement and the 2012 debt repurchase.

The ECB funding role

The highly adverse operating environment, characterized by the deep and prolonged economic contraction coupled with increased uncertainty, has eroded the banking sector's asset quality, due to the sizeable increase in non-performing loans and exposures (35.8% and 46.6% according to third-quarter results release), and weighted on profitability and funding, and, as a consequence, on credit expansion. Accelerating deposit outflows (€43.4 billion between November 2014 and July 2015), amid rising uncertainty and increasing concerns on a possible haircut and a risk of Grexit weighed on the domestic banking sector's health. As of December 2015, private-sector deposits reached €123.4 billion, down by €50.8 billion and €114.4 billion compared to December 2011 and September 2009, respectively (Figure 9.8).

Although credit growth remained in negative territory during the same time, due to the necessary deleveraging, the ratio of loans to deposits jumped to 165.6%, leading to a dramatic deterioration of liquidity conditions, as well as an increase in ECB-related

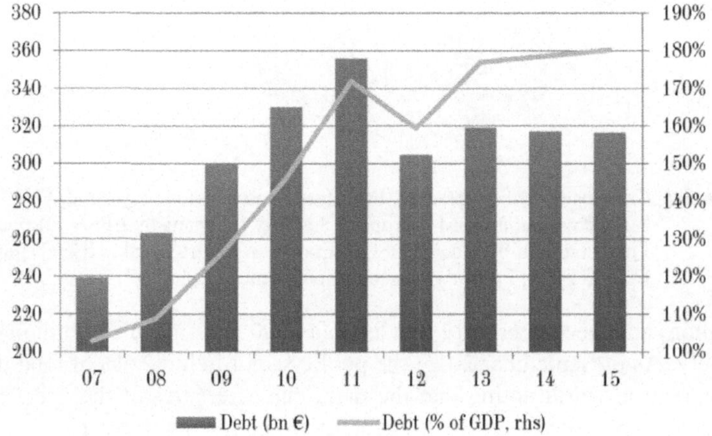

Figure 9.7 Greek debt in absolute and relative terms

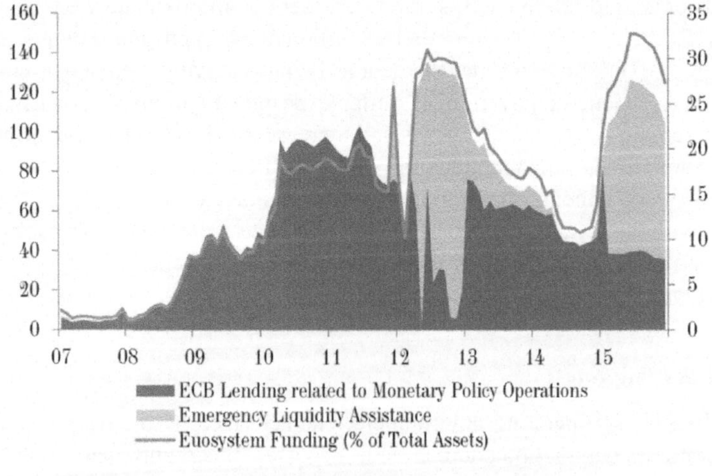

Figure 9.8 Dependence of the Greek banking system on ECB funding

financing dependence. ECB funding resulting from the continuing gap between loans and deposits, as well as the exclusion of Greek banks from the interbank market, took off at €113.4 billion (29.5% of assets), compared to €50 billion (10% of assets) before the Greek debt crisis, and €5 billion (1.5% of assets) before the global financial crisis. The completion of the third recapitalization in 3 years, €14.4 billion (€8.3 billion in 2014 and €28.8 billion in 2013), coupled with the restructuring of bad loans, as well as anticipated deposit inflows is expected to contribute to a gradual return to normality.

The "slaughter" of the labor force

The surge in unemployment over 25.0%, at socially unacceptable levels, as a result of the severe recession, has created a vicious cycle, where the decline in economic activity and rise in economic uncertainty destroyed jobs, at the same time that higher unemployment, falling wages and a higher tax burden reduced disposable income, and, as a consequence, exacerbated the underlying recessionary forces (Figure 9.9).

However, the gradual normalization of the economic situation, since the middle of 2013, as is evident from of the rebound in job creation in the private sector over the last 3 years, helped to abate unemployment to 24.6% in November 2015, despite the imposition of bank capital controls and the economy recession's in the second semester increase, after having peaked at 27.9% in September 2013. At the same time, we are seeing some recovery in retail sales and industrial production, and, as a result, in economic expansion.

The sacrifices of competitiveness

The competitiveness losses suffered in the aftermath of Greece's Economic and Monetary Union (EMU) entry have been fully recouped, as the downward

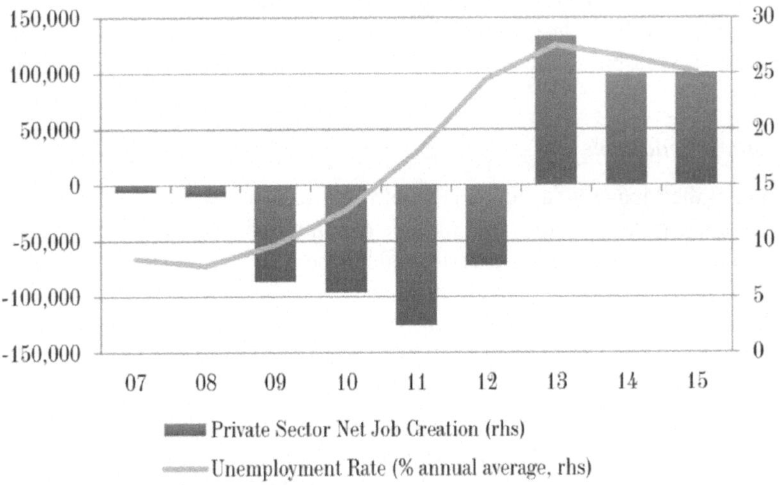

Figure 9.9 Labor market conditions

Figure 9.10 Cost competitiveness

adjustment in nominal unit labor costs continues, albeit at a slower pace. Wages had dropped by 22.87%, on average, in the third quarter of 2015 relative to their high recorded in the first quarter of 2010, as a result of the decline in nominal wages, the decrease in the minimum wage, the high rate of unemployment and the liberalization of the employment market (Figure 9.10).

They are now beginning to show their first signs of stabilization. By contrast, price competitiveness has not followed to the same extent, and this should be mainly attributed to the stickiness of non-tradable sector prices. More specifically, competitiveness based on unit labor costs has increased by 37.41% over the 2010–2015 period, according to ECB data, while competitiveness based on consumer prices has risen by just 16.12%, but still remains 2.11% lower versus the fourth quarter of 2001.

The business conditions

The target of the Memoranda, beyond that of fiscal adjustment, was to improve the competitiveness of the economy and reshape the underlying business environment in order to make it more growth-friendly and business-supportive and to offset the recession and deflationary impact of the fiscal consolidation and internal devaluation policies implemented in order to correct the Greek economy's main imbalances.

Structural reforms were supposed to strengthen economic fundamentals, investment, and other components of aggregate demand and to counteract recession and deflation. The structural reforms envisaged were so far implemented on a limited scale, due to internal political resistance. Even those that have been implemented to some extent have not been able to significantly change things for the better. According to World Bank data from the survey "ease of doing business," although the ranking of the country has improved, the distance from best has widened (Figure 9.11). Also, the political upheaval of 2015 and the emergence of the radical left government delayed the strenuous efforts of the country to modernize.

The overall competitiveness score

Even today, after 5 years of crisis and Memoranda implementation and despite any successes achieved in the areas of labor costs and business environment, the country's overall competitiveness, as measured by the World Economic Forum, remains poor (Figure 9.12); as a consequence, the country is not able to attract foreign investors and support domestic entrepreneurship.

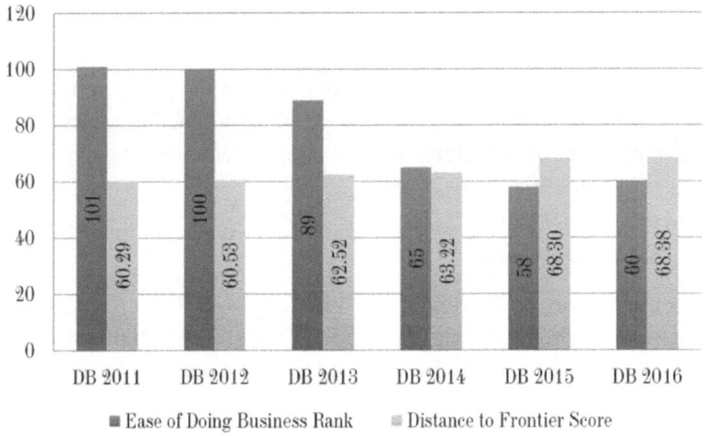

Figure 9.11 Business environment

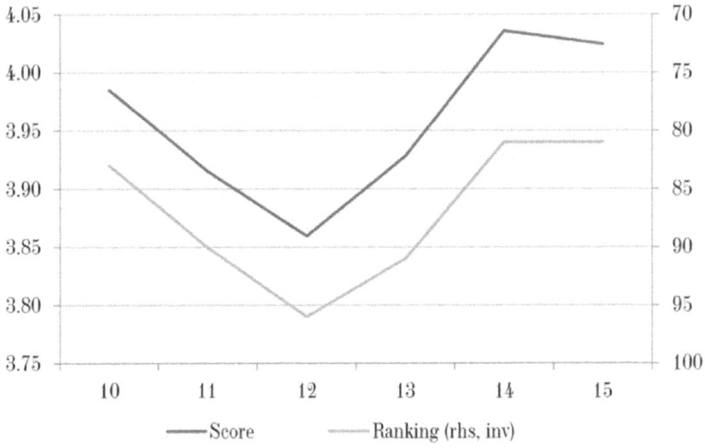

Figure 9.12 Total competitiveness

This, along with on-going internal devaluation, is the most important reason for the Greek economy's entrapment in a continuous recession.

What the markets say

Following EMU membership, Greek 10-year bond spreads over Bund stood at very low levels that did not reflect their inherent risk; they jumped from around 30 basis points in 2009 to 3,000 basis points at the height of the debt crisis in the summer of 2011, just before the private-sector involvement implementation, and since then have gradually declined along with the normalization of the economic and political situation. The lowest levels were achieved from March to August 2014, when yields were below 500 basis points (479.9 on average), for the first time since March 2010, as positive expectations regarding the Greek "success story" strengthened and the country was able, for the first time since 2010, to tap credit markets (Figure 9.13).

Since then, yields have reversed their downward trend and climbed by over 700 basis points at the end of 2015, having previously touched a high of 1,500 after the announcement of the referendum, the implementation of capital controls and the revival of fears of a likely Grexit.

The Greek stock market crash

Major Greek assets were negatively affected by the Greek debt crisis. Especially, equities and real estate are among the biggest losers. Their cumulative losses, from October 2019 to December 2015, approach 73.3% and 39.3%, respectively.

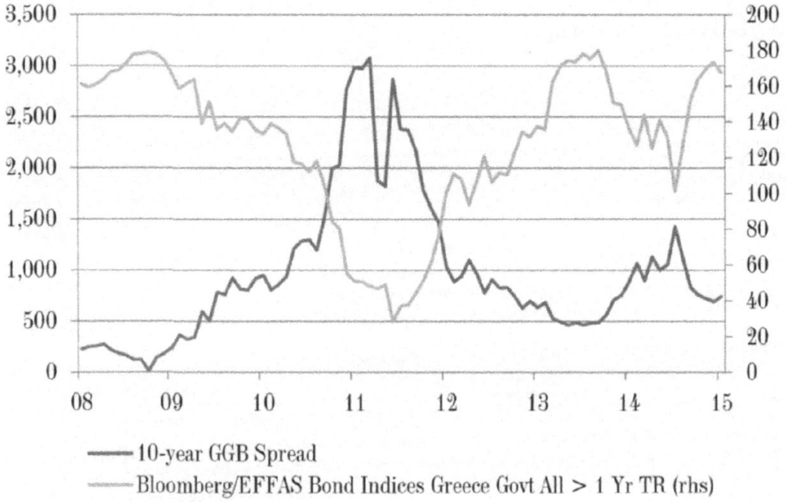

Figure 9.13 Spread and Greek government bond (GGB) prices. EFFAS, European Federation of Financial Analysts Societies

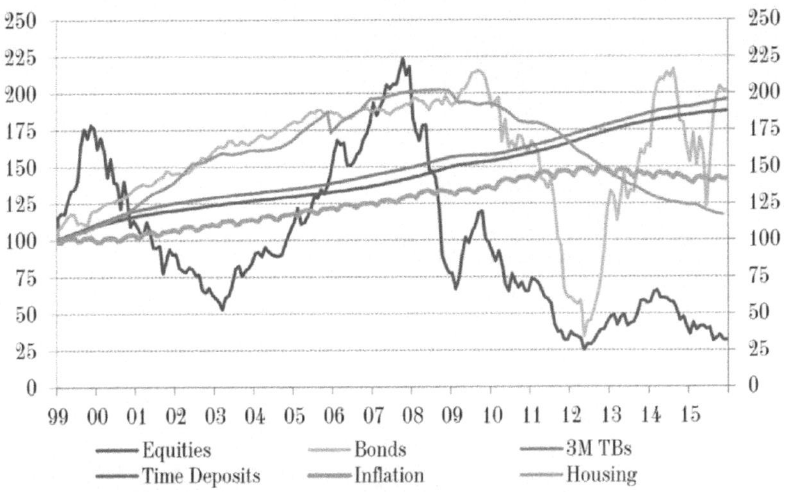

Figure 9.14 Total returns of major Greek asset classes

By contrast, government bonds recorded limited losses of just 5.8%, despite debt restructuring in March 2012, which resulted in a 53.5% haircut in nominal values (Figure 9.14).

Cash and Treasury bills were the only asset classes that provided capital protection. Despite the liquidity problems of the "bankrupted" domestic banking system that have led to four capital injections, deposits surprisingly managed to avoid a haircut from a potential bail-in.

The wound of deflation

Consumer prices drifted in negative territory during the 2011–2014 period, due to the decrease in demand, as a result of the shrinking disposable income and the subsequent economic recession. The decline, however, was not strong enough to offer support to economic activity. The decline in prices was relatively moderate, given the significant contraction in economic activity.

In December, inflation was positive for the first time in almost 3 years, as the latest VAT hikes gave a boost to prices, but inflation at constant tax rates remained negative for the 37th month in a row. The Harmonized Index of Consumer Prices inflation turned out negative in 2015 (–1.1% on an average annual rate of change basis), for the third straight year, since the effect of lower oil prices and soft demand outweighed the increase in VAT rates (Figure 9.15). Deflation should, however, ease further in 2016 in line with the anticipated economic recovery. Inflation is forecast by the government and the European Commission to turn positive in 2016 and to converge steadily towards Eurozone average.

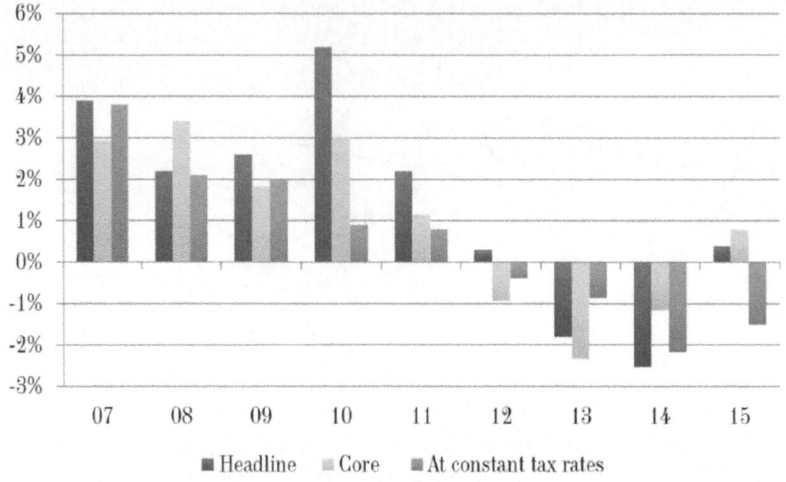

Figure 9.15 Harmonized consumer prices and deflationary pressures

Conclusions

In this chapter, we have investigated a series of crucial issues that directly affected and triggered the Greek crisis: factors such as the underlying fiscal consolidation, the adopted austerity measures, the aggressive contraction and external imbalances of the Greek economy, the twin deficits, the competitiveness, and deflation.

There is no doubt that the 2012 Greek debt exchange was a milestone event in the euro area debt crisis. It generated an agony of contagion and was viewed as a threat to the euro currency. Although it achieved historically unprecedented debt relief, it was "too little, too late" in terms of restoring Greece's debt sustainability. On this basis, there was an escalated debate, as to whether debt restructuring should have taken place sooner, when Greece's adjustment program was agreed to in May 2010; perhaps a deep up-front haircut would have been seen as unnecessary and deeply dangerous. But delaying the restructuring beyond mid-2011, when it became clear that Greece's debt was unsustainable, was unjustified.

Initial fears that Greek debt restructuring would pose a serious threat to the euro area's financial stability proved to be unrealistic. And finally, the Greek experience is likely to remain unique in the history of debt restructuring; however, some lessons can be learned from its specific features, mainly the political ones.

"Lies had been told that felt ashamed of themselves, since no shame had the mouths that had been telling them," once wrote Menelaos Lountemis, a famous Greek *littérateur*. And this dictum became, unfortunately, the rule for the majority of the political personnel in Greece in recent years. On the other hand, the strong proponents of the drachma, without even having to present a comprehensive alternative plan, focus only on the *impasse* of the exit from the euro. They never said what kind of education they wanted for Greece, what kind of democracy and what kind of state. At the end of the day, the single solution for Greece is the following: a united national coalition, the composition of creative forces and the isolation of extreme political wings.

References

All the figures in this chapter have been exclusively designed, developed, and processed by the authors, based on qualitative and quantitative data from organizations and institutions such as Elstat, Greek Ministry of Finance, Bank of Greece, Iniochos Advisory Services, ECB, World Bank, World Economic Forum, and Bloomberg.

10 Structural reform–growth nexus

An examination over time – the importance of Eastern Europe

Andreas Assiotis

Introduction

Understanding what drives economic growth across countries has been a very important among academic researchers and policy makers alike. Early literature points out that human capital, physical infrastructure, macroeconomic indicators such as inflation, investment, government spending and trade matter for growth. In recent decades, however, the focus has been shifted towards structural reform and its impact on economic growth. In the quest for higher economic growth, various structural reform agendas have been designed and implemented over time. The efforts to establish a structural reform–growth nexus have been made for a long time with not much progress towards reaching a satisfactory answer. Although there may be several possible driving forces for economic growth, sound structural reform plays an important role in economic growth.

Several studies (see, e.g. Levine, 1997; Chinn and Ito, 2006; Braun and Raddatz, 2007) report a positive association between structural reform and economic growth. More recently, Prati *et al.* (2013) investigated the impact of real (trade, agriculture and networks) and financial (domestic finance, banking, securities and capital account) sector reforms upon growth. Their findings suggest that both real and financial-sector reforms are positively associated with growth to a varying degree across countries. The positive heterogeneous effects across different kinds of reforms have been attributed to the level of constraints on executive power and to its distance from the technological frontier. Other empirical findings also suggest a positive association between trade and domestic financial reforms and growth. However, these studies fail to examine whether the impact of these reforms differs over time and across regions. These studies also have not considered whether these reforms are influenced by existing institutions in the country.[1]

In this paper, we explore whether the impact of different reforms upon growth varies across regions. Often, individual countries behave differently, so the effects of such reforms may be substantially different across world regions such as Asia, Africa, Latin America or Europe. Hence, we intend to check whether the results of previous studies (particularly Prati *et al.*, 2013) are primarily driven by the segmentation of the countries, and explore inherent reasons as to why some reforms are more relevant and effective in one region than others. The logic behind this argument is that not all kinds of reforms would influence growth in the same way.

For instance, real-sector reforms might be more pro-growth in region A rather than financial-sector reforms or vice versa. What drives these structural reforms? The rationale of this point is that usually reforms come in packages and perhaps political reforms are inducing these structural reforms. Finally we examine the extent to which those reforms are influenced by the institutions that exist in the economy. The importance of the last exploration stems from the fact that reforms of any kind would have a positive and significant impact in countries with good institutions (Butkiewicz and Yanikkaya, 2006).

Although empirical research has not yet established a conclusive relationship between various reforms and economic performance, economic theory suggests that structural reforms promote growth by removing obstacles in trade and commerce, thereby increasing economic growth. Babecky and Campos (2011) providee an extensive survey on the effects of structural reforms and economic growth. They collected a data set covering more than 500 estimates of the effect of reforms on growth from more than 40 empirical studies and reported that the direction of the effect of structural reforms on economic performance and its statistical significance depends on whether the contemporaneous or cumulative impact is considered. They present evidence that the long-run effect on growth is substantially larger than that of the short-term effect. They document that reforms have no immediate impact, but do have a positive effect with some time lag. The result was derived by separating the results of 40 studies according to their long-term and short-term nature.

While much has yet to be explored about the impact of various reforms on growth, some insights from the existing literature are helpful to mention. Christiansen *et al.* (2013) examined the relationship between economic performance and three groups of economic reforms: domestic finance, trade and capital account liberalization. They found that only domestic financial and trade reforms are robustly associated with economic growth but did not find any systematic positive relationship between capital account liberalization and economic growth. This paper further examined the interactive effect of reforms and the quality of political institutions and reported that sufficiently developed property rights may be a necessary condition for reforms to be effective and to stimulate economic performance.[2]

A variety of explanations have been offered on the effect of capital account reforms on growth. Klein and Oliver (2008) documented that developed countries with more open capital accounts experience higher economic growth, but they did not find any such relationship in the case of developing countries. Another strand of literature (see, e.g. McKinnon, 1973; Chinn and Ito, 2006; Tressel and Detragiache, 2008) provides strong evidence that greater financial liberalization is associated with higher subsequent economic growth and economic efficiency. They argue that financial repression in developing countries hinders an efficient allocation of capital and that financial liberalization would boost financial development and growth. These studies also point out the need for sufficiently developed institutions for any kind of reforms to function well.

A large number of empirical studies have often relied on a *de facto* measure of structural reform to proxy for liberalization and structural reforms, such as openness to international trade for trade reforms, the ratio of number of telephone lines to population for network reforms, population covered by electricity for electricity markets, financial development for financial-sector reforms. While *de facto* measures are important and useful indicators of success, they do not capture the direct effect of structural reforms on economic growth, since they are the outcome measure that is influenced by a variety of macroeconomic conditions beyond the reform considered (Christiansen *et al.* 2013).

In this study we exploit a newly developed database of *de jure* indicators of structural reform in both real and financial sectors of the economy for both industrialized and developing countries (see Appendix I for full description of structural reform indices). The new dataset has several advantages over past studies – proxy and binary variables have been used to represent various structural reforms. Our dataset is much more refined and direct to represent structural reforms of economy. More importantly, we exclusively focus on *de jure* indicators of structural reforms. These capture respectively three and two comprehensive structural reform measures of real and financial sectors of the economy. The three indices of structural reform of real sector of the economy are: (1) reduction of public intervention in the agricultural market; (2) the degree of liberalization in the telecommunication and electricity market; and (3) the extent of openness to international trade. The indicators of structural reforms in the financial sector comprise liberalization in the domestic financial sector and two additional sub-indices that capture banking and security market; the final indicators refer to external capital account liberalization. Given the nature of the dataset it is important to empirically test the different hypotheses on the relationship between structural reforms and growth. The existing literature has not explored the short- and long-run effects of such reforms on economic growth and their underlying causes across the world. We intend to bridge the gap in the literature.

The objective of most empirical work is to establish which variables (or reforms) have more or less impact on economic growth and the underlying reasons why a given variable is more or less robustly related to economic growth. For instance, the relationship between trade liberalization and economic growth is somewhat unclear (see, e.g. Sachs and Warner 1995; Dollar and Kraay 2004; Wacziarg and Welch 2008). A consensus appears to be emerging in the importance of institutional quality and initial conditions as the main factors in decreasing and increasing the effect of reforms on economic growth.

Institutions, reforms and growth

The debate on whether institutional quality matters for economic growth is gaining new momentum among economists. Financial crises and poor economic growth have stressed that well-functioning institutions are paramount to the goal of achieving higher economic growth. Several studies have examined the impact of institutions and policies (or reforms) on economic growth. Their findings support that good institutions create an environment that promotes economic activity, and is an incentive to investment and thereby economic growth; bad institutions retard growth (see, e.g. Butkiewicz and Yanikkaya, 2006; Eicher and Schreiber,

2010). Institutions refer to "the rules of the game". North (1981) defines institutions as "humanly devised constraints that shape human interactions".

The existing literature often uses "institutional measures" with different lables. For example, Hall and Jones (1999) use social infrastructure to refer to institutions. Rodrik et al. (2004) simply prefer institutions. Acemoglu (2005) evaluates institutions divided into "contracting institutions" and "property rights institutions," while Persson (2004) uses "growth promoting policies" or "structural policies." On the other hand, Hall *et al.* (2010) use data on "risk of expropriation" as a measure of institutional quality. All of these terms are used to refer to identical or very similar fundamental data (specifically International Country Risk Guide measures of property rights protection and/or openness) (Eicher and Schreiber, 2010).

Although these institutional characteristics, such as democracies and rule of law, are important, their interaction does not often become conducive to growth (Assiotis and Sylwester, 2010). Conventional wisdom says that the quality of institutions affects the efficacy of reforms. Economic reforms do not work as expected; they depend on compatibility with the institutions that exist in the economy (Carlin, 2010). Countries with better institutions – more secure property rights, and less distortionary policies – will invest more in physical and human capital, and will use these factors more efficiently to achieve a greater level of income (North, 1981; Rodrik, 1999).

The growth literature has documented empirical evidence on the role of institutions and the mechanism by which institutions affect growth. For instance, Hall *et al.* (2010) developed a growth model where they found that increases in physical and human capital led to output growth in countries with good institutions. Countries with bad institutions result in negative growth rates because they claim that addition to the capital stock tends to be employed in rent seeking and other socially unproductive activities.

The significance of good institutions can be clearly viewed by the analysis of African countries' stagnant progress in economic development versus some Asian countries' fast economic growth in the past half-century. Sub-Saharan African countries increased their investment in schooling more than any region since 1960, and yet these countries could not come out of poverty, while Asian "tigers" such as South Korea and Taiwan had smaller increases in education level but flourished economically (Easterly, 2001). The stark reality of this difference is that Asian countries had the required institutions while African countries lacked the institutional foundations to support the investment in physical and human capital. Another example could be the former Soviet Union countries. Transition in former Soviet bloc countries has been slower and much more costly than policy makers and economists initially anticipated. The slow growth in these countries can often be attributed to the neglect of the role of institutions in the initial analysis and design of the reforms (Carlin, 2010). The differential performances in transition countries have been closely linked to differences in institutions across countries (Eicher and Schreiber, 2010).

The impact of reforms on growth requires an empirical evaluation with respect to the quality of institutions. Empirical analysis of the impacts of each institutional type on growth has found that maintenance of the rule of law enhances growth

(Butkiewicz and Yanikkaya, 2006). However, these analyses have not examined how the reforms are influenced by institutional type. In addition to investigating the long- and short-run effects of reforms on growth, this chapter intends to disentangle the indirect effect of institutional characteristics on structural reforms.

The rest of the chapter is organized as follow. First, the data and methodology are described, followed by presentation of the empirical results, and in the final section we draw our conclusion.

Empirical methodology

The data

We employ annual data for 185 countries during the period 1960 to 2006. Annual real gross domestic product (GDP) per capita growth (Growth) and the natural log of real GDP per capita (GDP) are taken from the Penn World Tables, version 6.3. The data are adjusted for purchasing power parity. We consider the following regions: sub-Saharan Africa (SSA), South Asia (SASIA),[3] East and Southeast Asia (ESEA), Eastern Europe and Central Asia (EECA), the New World countries of Latin America and the Caribbean (NEW), and, in the final group, the countries of Western Europe as well as the "neo-Europes" of Australia, Canada, New Zealand and the USA (EUR).

The reform variables are taken from Prati *et al.* (2013). We consider two types of reform: real-sector reforms and financial-sector reforms. For real-sector reforms we exploit the trade, agriculture, current account restrictions and network variables compiled by Prati *et al.* (2013). On the other hand, for financial-sector reforms we utilize their domestic finance, banking, securities, and capital account liberalization (resident and non-resident) variables. (See Prati *et al.* (2013), for a more detailed description of the reform variables.)

Empirical model

Following Prati *et al.* (2013), we exploit fixed-effects specification, in which we allow the effects of the different reforms to vary over time. We use annual data to best pinpoint the timing of the reforms. Country and time-fixed effects are included to capture time-invariant country characteristics and global events, respectively.

The model

$$\text{Growth}_{i,t} \equiv \ln\text{GDP}_{i,t} - \ln\text{GDP}_{i,t-1} = \alpha_0 + \alpha_1 \ln(\text{GDP})_{i,t-1} + \sum \rho_j * (\text{Region})_j * (\text{Reform})_{i,t-1} + \eta_i + \delta_t + \varepsilon_{i,t} \quad (1)$$

Equation (1) presents the baseline specification, where i,t denote country and time, respectively. Growth is the growth rate of real GDP per capita adjusted for purchasing power parity. Country and year fixed effects are denoted by η_i and δ_t. Region_j

equals one for region j, and zero otherwise and the summation in equation (1) is taken over the eight regions listed in the previous subsection. Finally, ε denotes the error term where E $(\varepsilon_{it}) = 0$ for all i and t. $(\text{Reform})_{i,t-1}$ denotes a 1-year lag of each indicator of structural reforms. As in Prati *et al.*, we compute clustered standard errors to allow for the possibility of spatial correlation across countries.

A potential concern of the above specification deals with the inclusion of the dependent variable in the right-hand side. In other words, we allow for lagged income as it becomes standard in the growth regressions. To lessen this concern we follow the proposition of Nickell (1981), where he shows that biases from the inclusion of lagged dependent variables on the right-hand side are small when the time dimension goes to infinity. Judson and Owen (1999) report that biases on these right-hand side variables are less than 3% when using more than 20 periods. We have over 20 years of data for most of our countries. Roodman (2007) also suggests using fixed-effects estimators with "large T" panels.

Estimation and results

Baseline specification

Among real-sector reforms, according to Prati *et al.*, liberalization of the current account and of the agriculture sector is clearly associated with growth acceleration, with the indices improving about 3 years before the up-break and continuing on an upward trend afterwards. Conversely, growth decelerations are associated with a tariff-based trade liberalization index below the country average and with deteriorating indices of current account liberalization and agriculture. Among financial-sector reforms, liberalization of the domestic financial sector and of the capital account are both associated with growth accelerations. The banking component of the domestic financial-sector index starts improving about 2 years before an up-break. As in the case of most real-sector indices, growth decelerations are associated with a downward trend of all financial indices, which tends to begin around the time of occurrence of the down-break and markedly continues afterwards.

Based on the baseline specification, with the exception of reforms in the electricity and telecommunications markets (network), the coefficient estimates of all the remaining indices of structural reforms are positive and statistically significant at conventional levels. As it concerns reforms of the real sectors of the economy, the coefficient estimate for the current account has the largest magnitude and is statistically significant at 1% . The coefficients of international trade and agricultural market reforms have a smaller magnitude and are statistically significant at 10% and 5%, respectively.

The overall indicator of reforms of the domestic financial market (the composite index of six financial-sector sub-indices) shows the largest positive coefficient magnitude and is also precisely estimated. Reforms of the banking and security sectors also show positive and statistically significant coefficient estimates, with the coefficient magnitude of the second variable being smaller than the first one.

The coefficient estimates of the three indices of the external capital account openness are also positive and statistically significant, even though smaller in magnitude and less precisely estimated than the ones pertaining to the domestic financial sector. It may be surprising that the electricity and telecommunications markets do not show a positive association with growth, but as subsequent robustness analysis shows, this result is driven by the fact that network reforms started much later than other reforms.

To gauge the size of the estimated correlation between structural reforms and increase in per capita income, we focus on long-term multipliers which take into account the different dynamics of each reform and make their association with growth comparable across the different kinds of reform. Specifically, a full liberalization of the current account, which corresponds to a discrete jump of its index from the minimum of zero to the maximum of 1, is associated with an estimated increase of output per capita by almost 65% in the long run. As mentioned above, the largest estimated coefficient refers to reform of the domestic financial market: a discrete jump of this indicator from zero would more than double output per capita in the long run.

Conclusions

This chapter has examined whether real and financial reforms over the last three decades have been associated with higher growth, and whether there has been a differential growth response due to a country's institutional environment. Underpinning the empirical analysis is a significant data collection effort that involves the compilation of indicators of structural reforms for a large sample of developing and developed countries over the past three decades. Not only is the resulting dataset unique in its country and time coverage, but it is also much broader in terms of the sectorial coverage of reforms, as long as it includes indicators of liberalization in domestic product markets, international trade, several indicators of liberalization of the domestic financial sector and measures of capital account liberalization.

Table 10.1 reports the results when exploiting specification (1). It becomes apparent that both sets of reform are most relevant for the EECA region. While all levels of reform are statistically significant, the greater magnitude seems to appear through reforms related to domestic finance and banking. Our results show that the results obtained by Prati *et al.* are mainly driven by the Eastern Europe and Central Asia region. However, real-sector reforms are closely collated with the Pacific region, while financial-sector reforms are more closely correlated with East and Southeast Asia. This is not to say that reforms in other regions are in less need; but perhaps, the regions mentioned above could benefit more greatly from these kinds of reform. Additionally, these results provide a good foundation in order to further examine the reasons behind these findings. For example, are reforms needed more where existing regimes are absent? Or do reforms need to take place because existing regimes are too inefficienct? We leave this for future research.

Table 10.1 Panel data regressions (annual). Dependent variable is the natural log of the per capita income (purchasing power parity: PPP)

	Real-sector reforms				*Financial-sector reforms*					
Estimation method	*TR*	*CUR*	*AG*	*NW*	*DF*	*BK*	*SM*	*CAP*	*CAPRES*	*CAPNONRES*
REFORM * SSA	0.015	0.026	–0.010	–0.030	0.034	0.021	0.018	0.003	0.008	–0.005
	(0.020)	(0.015)*	(0.011)	(0.032)	(0.019)*	(0.020)	(0.010)*	(0.013)	(0.012)	(0.012)
REFORM * SASIA	–0.005	0.008	–0.030	–0.006	0.038	0.026	0.012	0.013	0.017	0.000
	(0.007)	(0.012)	(0.009)***	(0.011)	(0.020)*	(0.020)	(0.012)	(0.011)	(0.009)*	(0.011)
REFORM * ESEA	0.032	0.045	–0.003	0.002	0.079	0.064	0.031	0.039	0.026	0.027
	(0.031)	(0.016)***	(0.007)	(0.015)	(0.021)***	(0.022)***	(0.008)***	(0.022)*	(0.022)	(0.014)*
REFORM * EECA	0.077	0.078	0.092	0.063	0.185	0.158	0.119	0.074	0.041	0.084
	(0.029)***	(0.035)**	(0.034)***	(0.017)***	(0.064)***	(0.065)**	(0.019)***	(0.026)***	(0.013)***	(0.034)**
REFORM * NEW	0.005	0.025	0.006	–0.009	0.021	0.013	–0.005	0.016	0.011	0.013
	(0.014)	(0.011)**	(0.008)	(0.011)	(0.015)	(0.013)	(0.014)	(0.012)	(0.010)	(0.012)
REFORM * PAC	–0.120	–0.114		0.159				–0.068	–0.055	–0.049
	(0.013)***	(0.019)***		(0.011)***				(0.010)***	(0.009)***	(0.009)***
REFORM * MENA	0.062	0.034	0.014	0.005	0.046	0.036	0.017	0.013	0.015	0.003
	(0.016)***	(0.022)	(0.016)	(0.018)	(0.020)**	(0.020)*	(0.012)	(0.018)	(0.011)	(0.023)
REFORM * EUR	0.008	0.029	–0.001	–0.007	0.040	0.027	0.023	0.026	0.016	0.026
	(0.012)	(0.013)**	(0.004)	(0.009)	(0.013)***	(0.012)**	(0.007)***	(0.013)**	(0.010)	(0.013)**
lnGDP ($t-1$)	–0.050	–0.052	–0.038	–0.047	–0.059	–0.056	–0.056	–0.053	–0.049	–0.053
	(0.007)***	(0.009)***	(0.007)***	(0.008)***	(0.011)***	(0.011)***	(0.009)***	(0.009)***	(0.009)***	(0.009)***
Observations	3,418	3,530	3,390	3,796	2,653	2,653	2,653	3530	3556	3530
R-squared (within)	0.198	0.143	0.190	0.156	0.233	0.224	0.221	0.141	0.138	0.141

Notes: Robust standard errors clustered at country-level parentheses. All specifications are estimated by ordinary least squares (OLS) and include country and year fixed effects.

Annual data over 1973–2006. Gross domestic product in real terms and PPP adjusted.

TR, trade; CUR, current account restrictions; AG, agriculture; NW, networks and telecom; DF, domestic financial liberalization; BK, banking; SM, securities; CAP, capital; CAPRES, capital (resident); CAPNONRES, capital (non-resident); SSA, sub-Saharan Africa; SASIA, South Asia; ESEA, East and Southeast Asia; EECA, Eastern Europe and Central Asia; NEW, New World countries of Latin America and the Caribbean; PAC, Pacific region; MENA, Middle East and North Africa; EUR, the countries of Western Europe as well as the "neo-Europes" of Australia, Canada, New Zealand and the USA.

*significant at 10%; **significant at 5%; ***significant at 1%.

Appendix I

Reform indices	*Description*
Real indices	
Trade openness	Average tariff rates, with missing values extrapolated using implicit weighted tariff rates. Index normalized to be between zero and unity: zero means the tariff rates are 60% or higher, while unity means the tariff rates are zero
Current-account restrictions	The index represents the sum of two sub-components, dealing with restrictions on trade in visibles, as well as in invisibles (financial and other services). It distinguishes between restrictions on residents (receipts for exports) and on non-residents (payments for imports)
Agriculture	Given that developing countries constitute most of our sample, the degree of regulation in agriculture, which continues to account for a large part of many of these economies, is an essential aspect of product market competition. Index aims to capture intervention in the market for the main agricultural export commodity in each country. Each country–year pair is assigned one of four degrees of intervention: (i) maximum (public monopoly or monopsony in production, transportation, or marketing); (ii) high (administered prices); (iii) moderate (public ownership in relevant producers, concession requirements); and (iv) no intervention
Financial indices	
Capital account openness: aggregate	Qualitative indicators of restrictions on financial credits and personal capital transactions of residents and financial credits to non-residents, as well as the use of multiple exchange rates. Index coded from zero (fully repressed) to three (fully liberalized)
Capital account openness: residents (non-residents) only	Measures the extent to which residents (non-residents) are free from legal restrictions to move capital into and out of a country
Domestic financial liberalization	The index of domestic financial liberalization is an average of five sub-indices: (i) interest rate controls, such as floors or ceilings; (ii) credit controls, such as directed credit, and subsidized lending; (iii) competition restrictions, such as limits on branches and entry barriers in the banking sector, including licensing requirements or limits on foreign banks; (iv) the degree of state ownership; and (v) the quality of banking supervision and regulation, including power of independence of bank supervisors, adoption of a Basel I capital adequacy ratio, and framework for bank inspections
Product markets	
Telecom and electricity industries	Simple average of the electricity and telecom markets sub-indices, which are constructed, in turn, from scores along three dimensions. For electricity: (i) the degree of unbundling of generation, transmission, and distribution; (ii) whether a regulator other than government has been established; and (iii) whether the wholesale market has been liberalized. For telecom: (i) the degree of competition in local services; (ii) whether a regulator other than government has been established; and (iii) the degree of liberalization of interconnection changes

Notes

1 Eicher and Schreiber (2010) investigate the short-run effects of structural policies on growth by utilizing an 11-year panel for 26 transition countries. They construct structural policy indices of price liberalization, foreign exchange/trade liberalization, small/large-scale privatization, enterprise reform, competition policy reform, banking sector reform and reform of non-banking financial institutions.

2 Christiansen *et al.* (2013) tried to examine the interactive effects of different types of economic reforms and the quality of political institutions (property rights), but their measures of reforms are different from the ones we have used in this study.

3 For SASIA we have only four countries in our sample. Thus, we do not present the results for this region, although they are available upon request.

References

Acemoglu, Daron. (2005). "Unbundling institutions," *Journal of Political Economy,* 113, pp. 949–995.

Assiotis, Andreas, and Sylwester, Kevin. (2010). "Do good institutions lower the benefit of democratization?," *Southern Illinois University Carbondale, Working Paper.*

Babecky, Jan, and Campos, Nauro F. (2011). "Does reform work? An econometric survey of the reform-growth puzzle," *Journal of Comparative Economics,* 39, pp. 140–158.

Braun, Matias, and Raddatz, Claudio. (2007). "Trade liberalization, capital account liberalization and the real effects of financial development," *Journal of International Money and Finance*, 26, pp. 730–761.

Butkiewicz, James L., and Yanikkaya, Halit. (2006). "Institutional quality and economic growth: maintenance of the rule of law or democratic institutions, or both?" *Economic Modelling*, 23, pp. 648–661.

Carlin, Wendy. (2010). "Institutions and economic reforms," *Review of Economics and Institutions*, 1(1). Retrieved from http://www.rei.unipg.it/rei/article/view/2 (accessed September 11, 2016).

Chinn, Menzie, and Hiro, Ito. (2006). "What matters for financial development? Capital controls, institutions, and interactions," *Journal of Development Economics,* 61, pp. 163–192.

Christiansen, L., Schindler, M., and Tressel, T. (2013). "Growth and structural reforms: A new assessment," *Journal of International Economics*, 89(2), pp. 347–356.

Dollar, David, and Kraay, Aart. (2004). "Trade, growth, and poverty," *The Economic Journal*, 114, pp. 22–49.

Easterly, William. (2001). "Can institutions resolve ethnic conflict?" *Economic Development and Cultural Change*, 49, pp. 687–706.

Eicher, Theo S., and Schreiber, Till. (2010). "Structural policies and growth: time series evidence from a natural experiment," *Journal of Development Economics,* 91, pp. 169–179.

Hall, Robert E., and Jones, Charles I. (1999). "Why do some countries produce so much more output per worker than others?" *Quarterly Journal of Economics,* 114, pp. 83–116.

Hall, Joshua C., Sobel, Rusell S., and Crowley, George R. (2010). "Institutions, capital, and growth," *Southern Economic Journal,* 77, pp. 385–405.

Judson, Ruth A., and Owen, Ann L. (1999). "Estimating dynamic panel data models: a guide for macroeconomists," *Economics Letters*, 65, pp. 9–15.

Klein, Michael W., and Oliver, Giovanni P. (2008). "Capital account liberalization, financial depth, and economic growth," *Journal of International Money and Finance,* 27, pp. 861–875.

Levine, Ross. (1997). "Financial development and economic growth: views and agendas." *Journal of Economic Literature,* 35, pp. 688–726.McKinnon, Ronald I. (1973). *Money and Capital in Economic Development,* Washington, D.C.: Brookings Institution.

Nickell, Stephen. (1981). "Biases in dynamic models with fixed effects," *Econometrica,* 49, pp. 1417–1426.

North, Douglass C. (1981). *Structure and Change in Economic History*. New York: W.W. Norton.

Persson, Torsten. (2004). "Consequences of constitutions," *Journal of the European Economic Association,* 2, pp. 139–161.

Prati, Allesandro, Gaetano Onorato, Massimiliano, and Papageorgiou, Chris (2012). "Which reforms work and under what institutional environment? Evidence from a new dataset on structural reforms," *Review of Economics and Statistics,* 95 (3), 946–968.

Rodrik, Dani. (1999). "Where did all the growth go?" *Journal of Economic Growth*, 4, pp. 385–412.

Rodrik, Dani, Subramanian, Arvind, and Trebbi, Francesco. (2004). "Institutions rule: the primacy of institutions over geography and integration in economic development," *Journal of Economic Growth,* 9, pp. 131–165.

Roodman, David. (2007). "The anarchy of numbers: aid, development, and cross-country empirics," *The World Bank Economic Review*, 21, pp. 255–277.

Sachs, Jeffrey D., and Warner, Andrew. (1995). "Economic reform and the process of global integration," *Brookings Papers on Economic Activity*, 1, pp. 1–95.

Tressel, Thierry, and Detragiache, Enrica. (2008). "Do financial sector reforms lead to financial development? Evidence from a new dataset," *IMF Working Paper*1–42.

Wacziarg, R., and Welch, K. (2008). "Trade liberalization and growth: new evidence," *The World Bank Economic Review*, 22, pp. 187–231.

11 The vicious cycle of Cyprus's economic crisis

Stavros Tombazos

During the last decades there was remarkable economic growth in Cyprus, albeit based on a model of capitalist accumulation with an expiration date. The growth model which prevailed was the source of considerable social inequalities, ecologically problematic, structurally unbalanced and, as proven now by reality, especially sensitive to developments in other economies. We shall review it, giving emphasis to the most recent period before the crisis.

The 'Achilles heel' of this model of development was the 'hypertrophic' banking sector, which had extended unreasonably in the international market, and resulted in Cyprus not being able to withstand the prolonged consequences of the Greek crisis. The latter dragged Cyprus, mainly through the collapse of the Cypriot banks, into the biggest crisis after the Turkish invasion in 1974.

The banking crisis soon turned into a crisis of public debt, inaugurating thus the era of the Memorandum.

The management of the crisis by the Cypriot government and the troika (the EU, International Monetary Fund and European Central Bank) led the country into recession without solving the banking crisis.

The Cypriot model of development and the accession of Cyprus to the EU

The economy of Cyprus is an economy of services. The latter represent 81% of gross added value; at the same time industry, construction and agriculture represent just 9%, 8% and 2% respectively (Figure 11.1).

The Cypriot economy is a very open economy, importing mainly goods and exporting services (Figure 11.2). In 2011, services to businesses accounted for 31% of export revenues. These are services to 'offshore' companies, which have now been renamed as 'foreign' companies. The latter settled in Cyprus after the destruction of Lebanon in the 1970s.

Taxation policy in Cyprus has been and continues to be particularly favourable for those businesses. Corporate tax rate increased from 10% to 12.5% due to the Memorandum imposed on Cyprus, but still remains the lowest in the euro area. It is only in Ireland that corporate tax is also 12.5%.

Since the accession of Cyprus to the EU in 2004, until the global crisis, the balance of trade in Cyprus presented a growing deficit. This deficit rose from 1.2% of

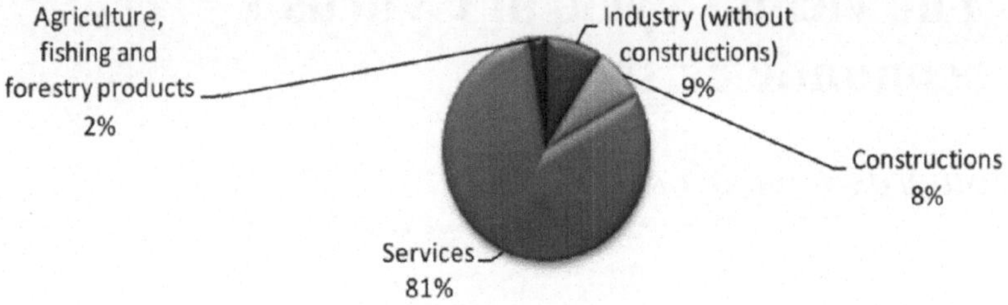

Figure 11.1 Structure of gross added value, 16.3 billion euros in 2011

Source: AMECO (Annual Macro-Economic database of European Commission): http://ec.europa.eu/economy_finance/ameco/user/serie/SelectSerie.cfm

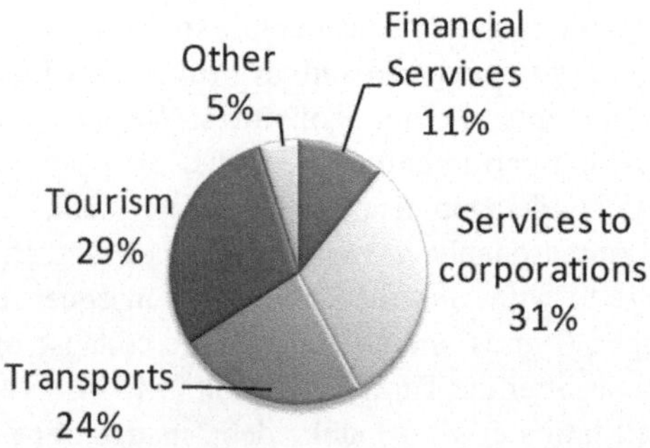

Figure 11.2 Income from exports of services, 6,262 billion euros in 2011

Source: Natixis (2013)

gross domestic product (GDP) in 2003 to 11.1% in 2008.[1] Since then, however, the trade balance has shown significant improvement. As shown in Figure 11.3, in 2013 it turned into a surplus. Of course, this positive development was mainly due to the contraction of imports, which is the reality in other southern European countries too.

As in other countries of southern Europe,[2] the upward trend in trade deficit in Cyprus before the global crisis was not due to an 'autonomous' increase in salaries. Since the accession of Cyprus to the EU, labour productivity had been increasing faster than real wages, a fact that was reflected in a reduction of the real unit labour cost (Figure 11.4).

During the period between the accession of Cyprus to the EU and the global crisis (2004–2008) there was a significant increase in imports, much more significant than in exports. The rise of the euro exchange rate played a key role in the price competitiveness of Cypriot products. Despite the fact that Cyprus adopted the euro in 2008, the exchange rate of the Cypriot pound against the dollar and other national currencies fluctuated along with the euro exchange rate: the Central Bank of Cyprus had a policy of absolute parity of the Cyprus pound with the euro.

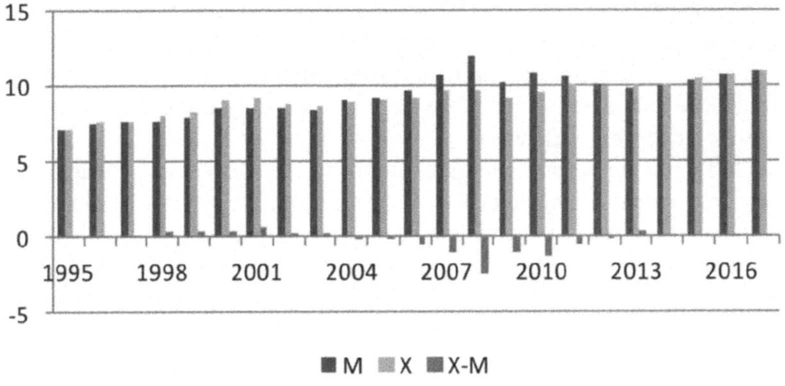

Figure 11.3 Imports, exports and balance of goods and services in billion euros (current prices), 1995–2017

X, exports, M, imports, X – M, balance of goods and services

Source: AMECO (Annual Macro-Economic database of European Commission): http://ec.europa.eu/economy_finance/ameco/user/serie/SelectSerie.cfm

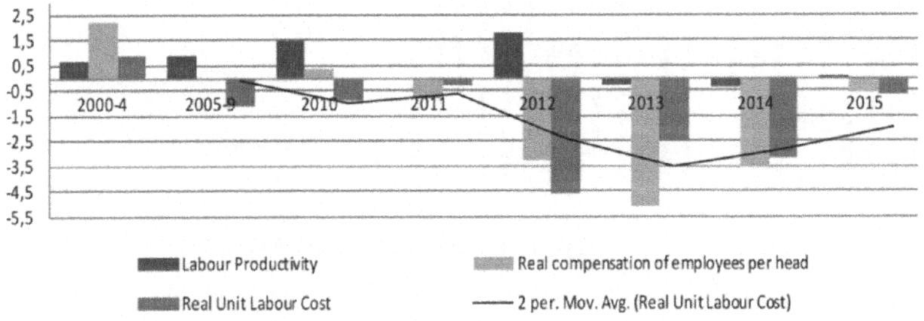

Figure 11.4 Annual growth rates of productivity, wages and unit labour costs, 2000–2015

Source: *European Economy, Statistical Annex*, Winter 2014

During the 2000s, the price of Cypriot exports to 36 developed countries, expressed in dollars, increased significantly: 15% between 2001 and 2009. It declined, however, with the fall of the euro exchange rate during the period 2010–2012, by 7.5%.[3] As with other countries of southern Europe, Cyprus's deeper cause for the reduced price competitiveness of exports and the growth of trade deficit that followed is the German wage policy. Stagnation of real wages in Germany during the 2000s, which resulted in the increase of its trade surpluses, led to the appreciation of the euro.[4]

During the 2000s until the downturn of 2009, real GDP growth in Cyprus was considerable, especially between 2004 and 2008 (Figure 11.5). The GDP in 2008 was larger than in 2003 by 23.5%.

During this period, private consumption and construction contributed decisively to GDP growth. Between 2000 and 2008, gross fixed capital formation in residential construction almost doubled. It increased from 0.7 billion euros in 2000 to 1.3 billion euros in 2008.[5] Today, much of the housing built during this period, particularly in tourist areas, remains vacant because of reduced internal and external demand. And of course, the large construction companies are unable to service their debts to local banks.

Since 2004, private consumption grew more rapidly than average wages. Of course, the gap created between the two decreased significantly during the recession of 2009 and continued to decline until today (Figure 11.6).

The economic growth of the 2000s, especially after joining the EU, was based on shaky foundations: a building industry highly sensitive to fluctuations in the foreign market and on private consumption growth, which deviated considerably from growth in wages.

The accession to the EU, the linking of the Cyprus pound to the euro and the prospect of euro adoption made the growing trade deficit less threatening.

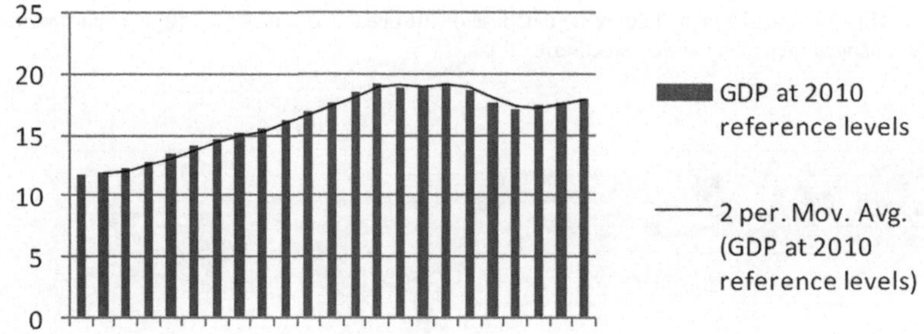

Figure 11.5 The volume of GDP of Cyprus in billion euros, 1995–2017

Source: AMECO (Annual Macro-Economic database of European Commission): http://ec.europa.eu/economy_finance/ameco/user/serie/SelectSerie.cfm

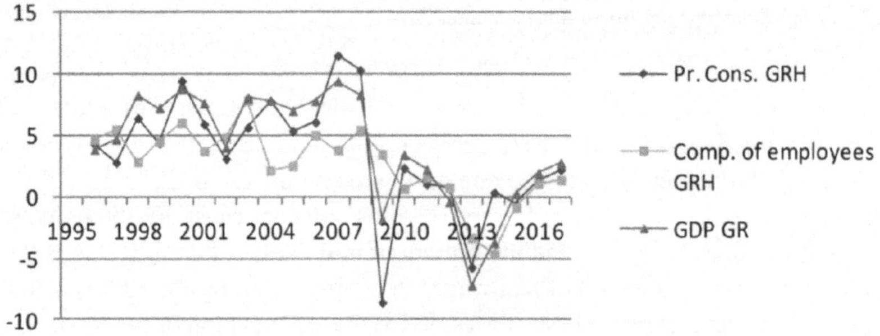

Figure 11.6 Percentage increase in per capita private consumption (Pr. Cons.), per capita compensation of employees and GDP (based on nominal values), 1996–2017. GRH, growth rate per head

Source: AMECO (Annual Macro-Economic database of European Commission): http://ec.europa.eu/economy_finance/ameco/user/serie/SelectSerie.cfm

Table 11.1 Deposits (in millions) in Cypriot banks and cooperative institutions

Date	*Domestic residents*	*Other euro area residents*	*Rest of world residents*	*Total*	*Annual growth rates of total*
Dec. 2007	32,294.2	1,390.4	18,829.4	52,514.0	26.2
Dec. 2008	39,461.8	1,090.6	15,456.8	56,009.3	6.4
Dec. 2009	41,011.6	1,290.7	15,852.7	58,009.3	4.4
Dec. 2010	45,379.3	4,035.3	20,525.2	69,939.7	18.2
Dec. 2011	43,746.9	5,355.4	20,194.2	69,297.6	–2.2
Dec. 2012	43,316.8	3,887.6	21,518.0	70,157.4	1.7
Dec. 2013	32,743.0	2,253.1	11,767.4	47,004.2	–22.3
Dec. 2014	32,282.6	1,957.8	11,884.0	46,124.4	–1.9
Dec. 2015	32,882.4	2,731.2	10,354.7	45,968.3	–0.3

Source: Central Bank of Cyprus, Monetary and Financial Statistics: http://www.centralbank.gov.cy/nqcontent.cfm?a_id=9837&lang=en

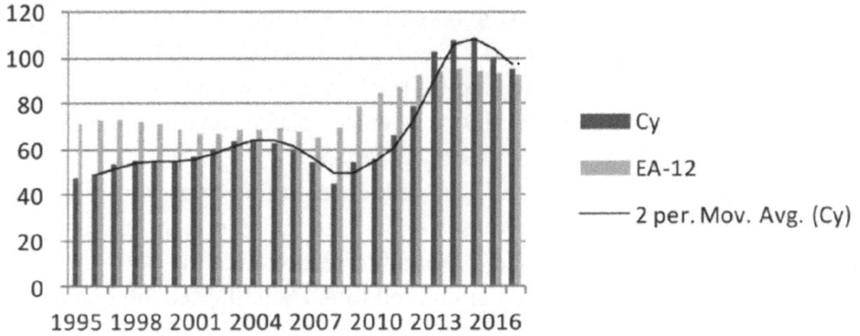

Figure 11.7 Government debt in Cyprus (Cy.) and the euro area (12 countries: EA-12) as a percentage of GDP, 1995–2017. 2 per. Mov. Avg. (Cy.), two-period moving average (country)

Source: AMECO (Annual Macro-Economic database of European Commission): http://ec.europa.eu/economy_finance/ameco/user/serie/SelectSerie.cfm

The 'markets' supplied the banking system with ample liquidity, thus creating a hypertrophic banking system, a credit 'bubble' and highly risky banking investments.

As shown in Table 11.1, total deposits in commercial banks and cooperative institutions continued to rise even during the first years of the global crisis (2008–2011). At an early stage, 2010–2011, Cyprus seemed to benefit from the Greek crisis through the transfer of deposits from Greece to Cyprus. This fact is confirmed by the increase in deposits in the category of 'other euro area residents'.

As in the case of Spain and, even more so, Ireland (unlike Greece), sovereign debt in Cyprus had never been particularly high compared with average debt in the euro area. In 2009 and 2010, the public debt of Cyprus still ranged under 60% of GDP, while in the euro area it was 79.2% in 2009 and 85.9% in 2010 (Figure 11.7).

Cypriot banks, recession in Greece and Cyprus Memorandum

The real 'Achilles heel' of the economy of Cyprus was its banking system, particularly because of its large exposure to the risks of the deep and prolonged recession in Greece.

The assets of the Cypriot banking system, including the branches of the Cypriot banks abroad, and the subsidiaries of foreign banks in Cyprus, approached 900% of GDP in 2010. By comparison, the corresponding figure in the euro area was limited to less than 350% of GDP in 2009. Even if the activities of the Cypriot banks abroad were not taken into consideration, the assets of the banking system in Cyprus would still be seven times greater than the GDP.[6]

The percentage of non-performing loans increased rapidly in 2011, in particular through the branches of Cypriot banks in Greece. In the third quarter of 2012, the percentage of non-performing loans in Greece rose to 17.3% for the Bank of Cyprus and to 32% for the Popular Bank.

In addition, the restructuring of the Greek public debt through 'the contribution of the private sector' (private-sector involvement) cost the Cypriot banks about 4.5 billion euros in 2012, equivalent to 25% of Cyprus's GDP (18.7 billion euros in 2012). Amid the global crisis, the Cypriot banks were engaging in speculative investments by buying securities of billions of euros related to Greek public debt in the secondary market (mainly from German banks).

These developments led to a significant reduction in the index core tier one. At the Bank of Cyprus this index decreased to 5.1% in the second quarter of 2012 from 8.1% in 2010. In July 2012, the state had to recapitalize the Popular Bank with 1.8 billion euros. Its index core tier one fell to 4.4% in the second quarter of 2012 – 9% is required.

Also, in 2011, the profitability of the Cypriot banks, which had been decreasing from the beginning of the global crisis, turned to negative, while the market value of bank shares vanished.[7]

The banking crisis quickly turned into a sovereign debt crisis, not only because the state decided to recapitalize the banking system but also because financing the public deficit through the markets had already become increasingly difficult and expensive, despite the fact that Cyprus's debt remained lower than the EU average. The successive downgrades of the Cypriot banks and the state itself by the international rating agencies discouraged the markets from lending to the state of Cyprus.

The necessity for recapitalizing the banking system and the shift of this burden on to the shoulders of the taxpayer was essentially the last straw that led to the exclusion of the Cypriot state from the international markets. In 2012 the sale of short-term public debt securities in the local market was not enough to finance the budget deficit and the state had to resort to interstate borrowing. It borrowed 2.5 billion euros from Russia.

The major problems of the banking system rendered the need to find resources for their management imperative. The negotiations with the troika led to a first Memorandum, which included a series of austerity measures, very similar to those applied in Greece and other southern European countries as a prerequisite for a loan of 17.5 billion euros.

However, while the Cypriot government began implementing the austerity measures, the EU refrained from formally adopting the Memorandum before the presidential elections in Cyprus, which were held in February 2013. The EU preferred to renegotiate the Memorandum again with the government of the Right, whose victory was expected. The new Memorandum, which has been agreed and put in force since then, is fundamentally different from all other Memoranda that have been implemented in other countries of southern Europe.

The final Memorandum[8] smashed the development model of the economy from one day to the next. The final Memorandum differs from the first in several respects, but what makes it extremely groundbreaking, not only in relation to the first Memorandum but also in relation to all others being implemented in other countries of southern Europe, is the fact that it destroyed confidence in the private banking system of Cyprus, confidence that cannot easily be regained. It provided for the 'rescue' of the banking system through the 'method' of bail-in, i.e. with funds from shareholders, creditors and depositors of banks, and not through external recapitalization (bail-out).

The bail-in of the banks aimed to reduce the bail-out amount needed for the Cypriot economy from 17.5 billion euros, provided in the first Memorandum, to 10 billion euros, provided in the final one. Of course, these 10 billion euros of troika loan will be released if and when Cyprus implements the austerity measures agreed in a strict and timely manner: privatization of the profitable public companies and ports, wage and pension cuts in the public and private sector, reduction of public deficit mainly through contraction of public spending and minimal increases in taxes related to capital and wealth, introduction of regulations providing for very flexible arrangements in the labour market, raising of the retirement age and restructuring of the banking sector.

The bank restructuring undertaken in Cyprus was certainly incompatible with the existing institutional framework of the EU. It required a strict control of capital flow both within Cyprus (transfer of funds from one bank to another, for example) as well as abroad. In the case of Cyprus, however, the EU not only allowed for the control of capital movement but, by imposing an immediate contraction of the banking sector, forced the Cypriot authorities to adopt it.

Cyprus' economy and management of the troika

Despite the extreme management measures imposed by the troika in the banking system in Cyprus, the crisis cannot be considered to be 'under control'. Deposits in the Cypriot banking system (including cooperatives) continued to decline in 2013, despite strict restrictions on the outflow of deposits: Since the end of December 2012 until the end of December 2013, they decreased by 22.3% (Table 11.1, a reduction which of course includes the bail-in). Since then they have been relatively stable.

Table 11.2 Non-performing loans (NPL, in millions, local operations) in Cypriot banks and cooperative institutions

Date	*Total facilities*	*NPL*	*NPL (% of total facilities*	*GDP (end of respective year)*	*NPL (% of GDP)*
30/6/2013	68,627,300	24,105,915	30.59	18,064,620	133.44
30/9/2013	64,713,867	26,006,059	37.25		
31/12/2013	62,725,662	26,848,178	41.46	18,064,620	148.62
31/3/2014	61,241,284	27,672,232	43.84		
30/6/2014	59,638,432	28,098,255	46.40		
30/9/2014	57,970,405	28,228,436	48.47		
30/11/2014	56,809,089	27,802,434	49.69	17,393,680	159.84
31/1/2015	60,387,565	27,803,371	46.04		
30/4/2015	59,284,565	27,754,302	46.81		
31/7/2015	57,784,473	27,390,896	47.40		
31/10/2015	57,116,396	27,428,600	48.20		
30/11/2015	59,469,480	27,388,602	46.05	17,781,040	154.03

Source: Central Bank of Cyprus, Aggregate Cyprus Banking Sector Data, http://www.centralbank.gov.cy/nqcontent.cfm?a_id=13029&lang=en

But the most important problem is the large increase in non-performing loans, despite the fact that a significant number of loans were restructured (Table 11.2).

In November 2015, non-performing loans were 46% of total loans and 154% of GDP. Such a figure would be mathematically impossible in many European countries, as their total private debt as a proportion of GDP is less than 154%.

The perpetuating crisis of the financial system is certainly not unrelated to the austerity policies and their aftermath: reduction in the primary deficit, great recession in 2013, reduction of wages in the public and private sectors and rising unemployment.

It is difficult to achieve reduction of public deficit through reductions in state expenditure, without great social costs at a time during which state expenditures (including interest) as a percentage of GDP were and still are significantly less than the average for the EA-12 (despite the fact that the interest on the public debt as a percentage of GDP of the latter is much lower than that of Cyprus, because of the lower debt rate). On the other hand, it is very difficult to imagine the current government increasing corporate tax. There is no doubt it will call upon the dependence of the economy on foreign companies. However, since consumer taxes have already been increased, it would be difficult for the government to turn in this direction without serious social consequences. With these data at hand we anticipate further reductions in salaries of state employees, who, moreover, have been the scapegoat for the dominant ideology during the last years. Such a development, however, would have a negative impact not only on the growth rate of the economy, but also on non-performing loans.

The unemployment rate in Cyprus has been over time much lower than in the EA-12. But it has been increasing rapidly in recent years. From 3.8% at the beginning of the global crisis in 2008, it increased to 15.6% in 2015,[9] while youth unemployment reached 40%[10] in 2014.

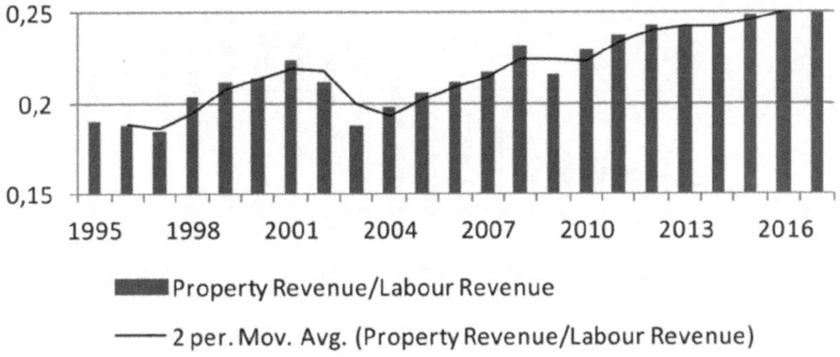

Figure 11.8 Property revenue/labour revenue. 2 per. Mov. Avg. (Cy.), two-period moving average (country)

Source: AMECO (Annual Macro-Economic database of European Commission): http://ec.europa.eu/economy_finance/ameco/user/serie/SelectSerie.cfm

Notes:

1. Property revenue = gross operating surplus adjusted for imputed compensation of self-employed
2. Labour revenue = compensation of self-employed (gross operating surplus – gross operating surplus adjusted) + wages

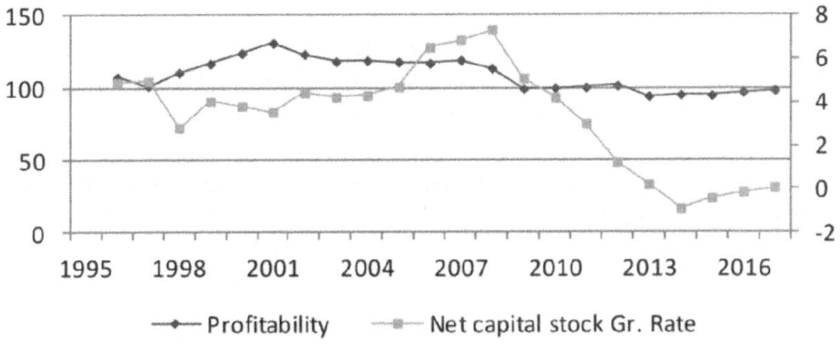

Figure 11.9 Net return on net capital stock (profitability, 2010 = 100) and net capital stock growth rate (Gr. Rate)

Source: AMECO (Annual Macro-Economic database of European Commission): http://ec.europa.eu/economy_finance/ameco/user/serie/SelectSerie.cfm

While wages have been drastically reduced during the last years, this is not the case with corporate profits. The cost of the crisis is mainly paid by wage labour since, for as long as the crisis lasts, the ratio of property revenue to labour revenue depicts a significant increase, as shown in Figure 11.8.

The ratio of property revenue/labour revenue, which has been rising steadily since 2009, in 2015 reached its highest point since 1995. It is for this reason that the rate of profit on fixed capital has been relatively stable since 2009 (Figure 11.9).

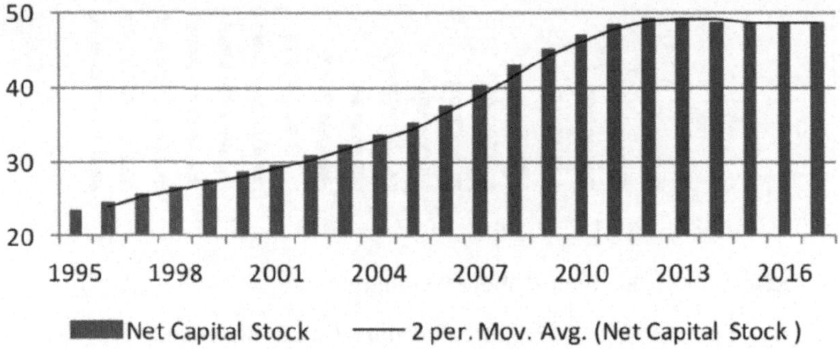

Figure 11.10 Volume of fixed capital in Cyprus, 1995–2017 (in 2005 market prices). 2 per. Mov. Avg. (Cy.), two-period moving average (country)

Source: AMECO (Annual Macro-Economic database of European Commission): http://ec.europa.eu/economy_finance/ameco/user/serie/SelectSerie.cfm

Retaining the profit rate at high levels is not conducive to economic growth, because the decline in unit labour cost does not lead to a corresponding decline in commodity prices, but mainly to an increase in the rate of exploitation of labour power. The international competitiveness of Cypriot products does not increase and therefore potential growth through exports is not in sight.

The prolonged downturn of the economy, combined with the absence of a medium-term state policy for restructuring the production capacity of the country, reduces investment opportunities that promise high profit rate. The result of this situation is the growing deviation between the rate of accumulation of fixed capital and the profit rate (Figure 11.9), and the reduction in the volume of fixed capital since 2013 (Figure 11.10).

Conclusions

1 The Cyprus crisis manifested as a crisis of the financial sector, which developed out of proportion and created a financial bubble. The link of the Cyprus pound to the euro and the adoption of the euro in 2008 are directly related to the inflated financial sector and the creation of the bubble.
2 The Cyprus crisis can be regarded as a product of the crisis in the euro area that was introduced in Cyprus mainly through the prolonged recession in Greece.
3 The management of the crisis in 2013 by the Cypriot government and the troika has not as yet resolved the crisis in the banking system, but has plunged the country into recession. This creates a vicious circle, where the crisis in the financial sector fuels the recession in the real economy, and vice versa.
4 The inflexibility of the profit rate does not allow the increase of price competitiveness for Cypriot products. Social gains are sacrificed, for the moment at least, on the altar of profit and not competitiveness.[11]

5 Under these circumstances it is difficult to argue that a new bail-out of the banking system through public money will not be necessary. There is a strong possibility that public debt will follow a course opposite to the optimistic predictions of the European Commission.

Notes

1 For a detailed analysis of the current account and the reasons for the significant deviation of the trade balance, see Central Bank of Cyprus (2013).
2 See Husson (2013).
3 See INEK-PEO (2012).
4 See Tombazos (2011).
5 See INEK-PEO (2012).
6 See Stephanou (2011).
7 See INEK-PEO (2012).
8 See Memorandum of Understanding on Specific Economic Policy Conditionality.
9 *European Economy, Statistical Annex* (2015).
10 IMF (2014).
11 See also INEK-PEO (2013).

References

Central Bank of Cyprus, (2013). *Annual Report 2012*, Nicosia, Central Bank of Cyprus.

European Economy, Statistical Annex, (2015, autumn). http://ec.europa.eu/economy_finance/publications/eeip/2015-sa-autumn_en.htm (accessed 11 September 2016).

Husson Michel, (2013). "Économie politique du système euro," in *Social Studies.* Annual trilingual Social Research Review, No. 2–3. Alexandria, Athens.

IMF, (2014, April). *Country Report, No 14/92, on Cyprus*, http://www.imf.org/external/pubs/ft/scr/2014/cr1492.pdf (accessed 11 September 2016).

INEK-PEO, (2012). *Report on the Economy and Employment 2012*, Nicosia, INEK-PEO.

INEK-PEO, (2013). *Report on the Economy and Employment 2013*, Nicosia, INEK-PEO.

Memorandum of Understanding on Specific Economic Policy Conditionality, http://www.mof.gov.cy/mof/mof.nsf/final%20MOUf.pdf (accessed 11 September 2016).

Natixis, (2013) *Flash Economics. Economic Research*, March 29, 2013-No. 245, p. 5, *Cyprus: The Bail-in/out and its Implications*, https://www.research.natixis.com/GlobalResearchWeb/Main/GlobalResearch/DownloadDocument/Si2f5S4Q3SqqlvGshyWwWg%3D%3D (accessed 21 September 2016).

Stephanou Constantinos, (2011). "Big Banks in Small Countries: The Case of Cyprus," *Cyprus Economic Policy Review*, Vol. 5, No. 1.

Tombazos Stavros, (2011). "Centrifugal Tendencies in the Euro Area," *Journal of Contemporary European Studies*, Vol. 19, No. 1, 33–46.

12 Government response to the Eurozone crisis

The cases of Greece and Cyprus

Savvas Katsikides and Georgia Yiangou

Introduction

Historically, Greece is no stranger to financial hardship. So far, the state has defaulted on its arrears six times, with the more recent default taking place in the summer of 2015. Strangely enough, Greeks owe the founding of their country at most part to loans obtained by British banks during the war of Independence against the Ottoman oppressors. Yet in 1826, due to mismanagement of the aforementioned loans and the ongoing civil war, the Greeks failed to pay the tranches due. The Great Powers (Britain, France and Russia) intervened in the war for the Greeks, eventually crushing the Ottoman armada at Navarino in 1827. The aftermath of the battle was the creation of the tiny Greek state. In reality, the Great Powers were merely bailing out the Greeks to facilitate the smooth repayment of the revolutionary loans.

This historical incident highlights not just the volatile financial history of Greece but also the perils of relying heavily on foreign debt. What is striking is that, since independence, Greece has suffered a repeated pattern of debt traps, conditionality clauses and enforced Memoranda (Reinhart and Trebesch 2015, p. 5). The recent default just proves how difficult it is to handle foreign directives in order to bring about necessary changes to enduring and inflexible socio-economic and political structures that stand in the way. After a series of failed negotiations, Greece has agreed to its third bailout agreement with the troika (the EU, International Monetary Fund (IMF) and European Central Bank), which adds more debt to the existing amount and imposes harsher directives and control measures for its implementation.

In this chapter we examine the chronicle of the Greek debt crisis to shed light on Greek political reasoning and response. For this purpose, it is necessary to outline the events that culminated in the introduction of the first Memorandum of understanding and the subsequent political apprehensiveness. Special attention is stressed on the mentality of the political elite and its overt unwillingness to take measures when the crisis unfolded. Due to the ongoing nature of the crisis, it is difficult to extract credible conclusions on its outcome as Greece has recently agreed to put a third bailout deal into effect.

The story before the flashpoint

The only time Greece experienced sustainable economic growth was between 1950 and 1973. This particular period was dubbed the “Greek economic miracle”, as

Greece was able to score the second best growth rate in the world and attract foreign investors. Sadly, the positive trend came to an end in the 1980s. During this decade, the Greek economy fell back despite becoming a member of the European Community. The most striking figure was the sharp climb of the debt to GDP ratio: between 1981 and 1993 Greek debt rose from 28% to 111%. According to Kouretas and Vlamis (2010, p. 394), the intention of the socialist government was to promote consumption and improve Greek living standards. This rapid change in fiscal mentality would eventually lead the Greek economy into an impasse. The prospect of joining the European Monetary Union and implied compliance with the Maastricht Criteria would bring about some fiscal improvements. It was later revealed that the unusually high performance of the economy was due to the Greek government's concealment of the real debt and deficit figures. This deceptive craftiness would later be dubbed as "Greek statistics" (Smith 2015). Suspicions among European authorities emerged and so EUROSTAT – the official statistical institution of the EU – conducted an inquiry into the fiscal statistics previously handed out by the Greek government. The findings shocked the European authorities: Greece was never eligible to join the euro. Despite losing credibility and trust, the Greek government shamelessly continued to provide false data to the EU until 2009.

With the deficit rising to 15.4% and the debt accumulating to 298 billion euros, the government resigned amid accusations of "abandoning ship in the middle of a tempest". The next prime minister rose to power with vague promises of increasing wages. Despite inheriting a dire economy, the government failed to take fiscal consolidation measures. Instead, it distributed subsidies and wage benefits to the workers and pensioners. Throughout the developing crisis, Greece's creditworthiness suffered greatly, with multiple downgrades by international credit rating agencies mainly due to insufficient efforts to contain the fiscal downward spiral. Simultaneously, Greek risk premiums (spreads) began to widen. The latest development prompted the government to apply for fiscal assistance from the EU and the IMF. The application was accompanied by the government's commitment to implement a series of austerity measures. Specifically, Greece requested 80 billion euros from the Eurozone member states and the European Central Bank (loan facility agreement) and 30 billion from the IMF (stand-by arrangement). The final contract between Greece and the lenders would later be dubbed as Memorandum of understanding.

First bailout agreement

One of the most critical demands of the troika was the need to curb public expenditure. Greek political parties have traditionally exploited public money to appoint supporters in governmental positions and provide cronies with lucrative benefits. Over time, this took a toll on the budget and it was one of the most significant reasons for the economic deadlock. When Greece had its own currency, the government used devaluation to subsidize its populist policies. As a consequence, debt, inflation and budget deficits soared through the 1980s, making it really hard for Greece to recover. Euro membership brought about hopes for recovery and so Greece was motivated to improve its fiscal performance. Despite brave attempts, the convergence criteria were unreachable, leading Greek authorities to engage in the infamous data manipulation scandal. It is important to mention that, after

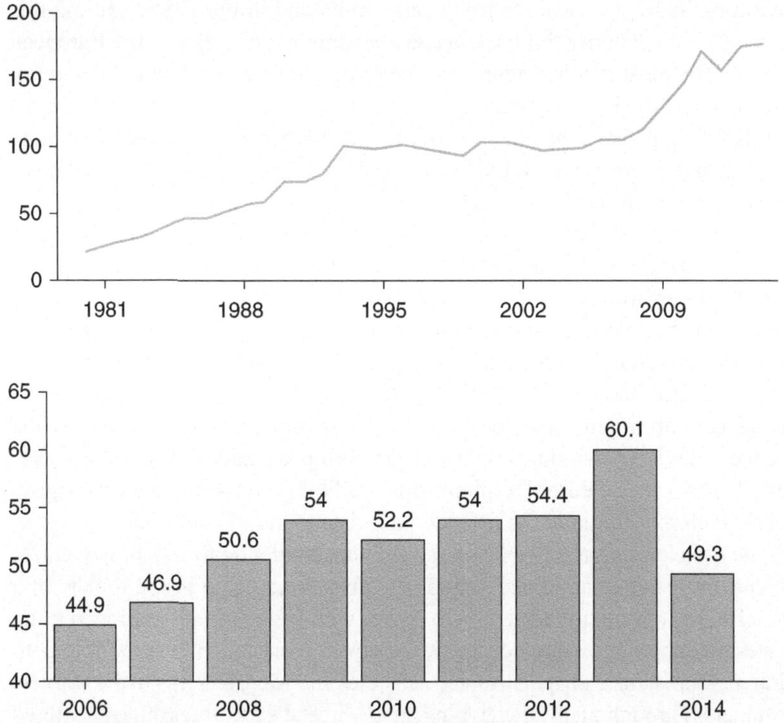

Figure 12.1 Greece government debt and spending
Source: Eurostat (2016)

introducing the euro, Greece gained access to "easy money" with low interest rates, backed by a world reserve currency and low inflation risk. This facilitated the continuation of spending borrowed money to serve populist tactics. Thus, public debt climbed massively in 2009, way above the threshold of 100% to GDP ratio. To make matters worse, government outlays amassed to more than 50% of the revenue (Figure 12.1).

With figures soaring and social unrest fermenting, immediate action was required. The government announced a starting package of measures such as salary freeze and subsidy cuts. However, the powerful trade unions of the public sector reacted vigorously against the measures, paralysing the state with strikes. As time went by, the possibility of missing the next payment was apparent, so a new set of measures was mandatory. The government agreed to more cuts on benefits of the wider public sector, as well as increases in VAT, import and fuel tax. The measures were welcomed with discontent and more strikes ensued. With no tangible improvement to the fiscal indicators, the government was forced to announce the introduction of the Memorandum. This time the plan included more taxes, tariffs and some cuts to the benefits of civil servants and pensioners.

Furthermore, the layoff limits were extended, the minimum wage was reduced and the retirement age of female workers was increased to 65. As a result, strikes turned into protests, human casualties and continuous social unrest.

Even though the Memorandum was approved by the enraged Greek parliament, some legal technicalities emerged in relation to the constitutionality of its provisions. More specifically, disagreements were expressed on the authorization of the Minister of Finance to engage in agreements on behalf of the Greek state without the explicit ratification of the parliament. Here, the problem lies in the agreement and its bitter stipulations because it did not go through the parliament directly. As for the Memorandum, it was deemed constitutionally sound but some of its provisions were condemned. Among the most alarming disputes were the prohibition of unilateral arbitration in case of labour disputes, the reductions in benefits of the armed forces and pensioners and the zero-deficit clause of social security funds (later changed to sustainability rule). Based on this decision, the Greek government was compelled to reimburse pensioners with over 3 billion euros. For the first time the Greek government decided to lift the existing protectionism of certain privileged occupations of the private economy. These were the cases of liberalizing restricted professions like truck and taxi driving, lifting *cabotage* restrictions on cruise vessels, reducing the positions of curators and cutting the salaries of mass transportation employees.

The consequences of the approved measures manifested on the real economy. The levels of inflation and unemployment increased considerably. Small and medium-sized enterprises were greatly affected and many were forced to shut down their operations, as their profits shrank dramatically. So far, government-owned enterprises (DEKO) were enjoying privileges that were about to come to an end, based on the requirements of the Memorandum. Their legal status changed to allow contracts with trial periods and the possibility of termination without compensation, as well as ceilings on mixed income and slight reduction of benefits. By the end of 2010, the debt climbed to 142.8% of the GDP, the budget deficit rose to 10.5%, unemployment reached 16.2% and the real economy contracted about 4.5%. As a result, growing societal and political dissatisfaction let to the formation of movements whose members refused to pay fees. One of these anti-austerity movements was labelled *Aganaktismenoi* (Indignants). Inspired by a similar movement in Spain (*Indignados*), it encompassed people of all ages who were fed up with the continuous decline of the economy. It later became evident that the economy deviated significantly from the original goals and so parliament was called to vote on a new set of interim measures. This time parliament agreed to create a privatization board which would facilitate the selling of public assets with the goal of retrieving 50 billion euros. Despite the deterioration of the real economy, more taxes were put into force together with added contributions to the social security funds.

Debt restructuring and second bailout agreement

The poor performance of the Greek economy alarmed the EU, which sought to protect Greece from financial speculators. For this purpose, a new loan agreement was proposed at the 2011 European summit. Based on the agreement, 109 billion euros would derive from the EU and the IMF and 43 billion euros would come from private investors and government bonds. Another measure that was agreed upon was the lengthening of bond maturity for up to 30 years. Immediately after this decision, international rating agencies Moody's and Fitch preemptively downgraded Greece to the status of orderly default. Several countries expressed explicit concern about participating in a new loan arrangement. Specifically, Finland demanded collateral through a bilateral agreement. Soon other member states followed suit and demanded similar contracts. In the end, Germany had to step in to invalidate the bilateral agreement. The deplorable state of the economy forced the troika to threaten not to approve the sixth tranche of the loan and so a new series of measures were issued. These measures included new temporary taxes, budget cuts, pension reductions and the liberalizing of all so-called "closed professions". Greece also experienced its first bank nationalization that emerged during the crisis and requested the assistance of the European Financial Stability Facility.

Greece's orderly default was followed by the infamous debt-restructuring deal. Inspired by the Latin American Brady bond deal of 1989, this project essentially destroyed the sovereign bonds of the private sector (private-sector involvement or PSI) by reducing their value to just 35 billion euros. It went down as the biggest debt-restructuring regime ever experienced. More significantly, it set a negative precedent for becoming the first of its kind in the European Union, despite previous claims on its impossibility (Zettelmeyer *et al.* 2013). Convincing a significant amount of creditors to act in accordance with the rules of the PSI restructuring was not an easy task. European authorities needed to overcome the burden of having to deal with individual sovereign bondholders and multiple litigation procedures. Previously, sovereign bondholders could negotiate the terms of their agreements individually and within various legal contexts, retaining the right to decline a new rule or a deal. This created a collective action problem for the negotiators, as the bondholders engaged in free riding. The proposed remedy was to implement a retroactive collective action clause that would force the private bondholders to comply with the proposed offer (Boudreau 2012). For this reason, the Greek government passed new legislation on February 2012 – the Greek Bondholder Law – that would constrict the flexibility of the non-complying bondholders if a third of the creditors came to a consensus. The overwhelming majority of private bondholders participated in the PSI deal and accepted the exchange of the old bonds with new ones, losing most face value in the process, as the new bonds were worth only 47 cents. PSI participation peaked as high as 85.8% of the private bondholders, approaching the initial expectations of 90%. The progress of the Greek economy would be permanently monitored for the careful implementation of reforms and the Greek banks affected by the haircut would be recapitalized. The project was finalized in March 2012 and affected 206 billion bonds in total. It should be noted that the International Swaps and Derivatives Association was placed under scrutiny for refusing to evaluate Greece as defaulted. Eventually, the credit default swaps were triggered, but the liabilities involved were insignificant, amounting to just 3.2 billion dollars (Darrow and Hans 2012).

Once the process of the debt-restructuring PSI agreement was completed, the EU was able to proceed with the new economic adjustment programme. While the PSI deal was taking place, the Greek prime minister revealed his plans to hold a referendum on the impending loan arrangement. His aim was to force the party dissidents and the opposition to provide their support. His decision caused political commotion and prompted some of his MPs to condemn his motives. In addition, the cost of the Greek and other European bond yields rose notably. Angered by the irresponsible behaviour of the Greek prime minister, European leaders urged for the repeal of the referendum and threatened to withhold the forthcoming tranche of the rescue package. At the same time, the President of the European Commission, Manuel Barroso, expressed his willingness to support a new coalition government with the opposition party New Democracy. It was evident that the European partners were wary of a potential spillover of the crisis to the rest of the Eurozone. Ultimately, the referendum was prevented after several MPs of the ruling party stressed the advantages of the euro for the Greek economy and a new coalition government was formed.

In February 2012, the government ratified the second Memorandum. Its provisions would put additional stress on the already distressed state of the economy. The most outstanding demands were the reduction of the basic salary by between 22% and 35%, the destruction of 150,000 public service positions, the abolition of the permanent job status for state-controlled enterprises, the liberalization of 20 professions, the cancellation of tax exemption, further cutbacks on pensions and benefits, and increase in the cost of public transportation. These measures would take a further toll on the already bleeding economy. The government eventually collapsed and new elections were announced. This time the political landscape would change for good; the coalition parties lost a significant portion of their clientele, to the point that no government was able to form. After many weeks of desperate attempts to regulate the political scene, a new coalition government emerged with Antonis Samaras as Prime Minister. Soon after, negotiations with the troika resumed and the interim Framework of Fiscal Strategy was agreed. According to this development, Greece committed to taking fiscal measures that would yield 19 billion euros. As a result, more taxes were levied and several benefits were modified. Among the most notorious reaction to the new fiscal framework were the proposed strikes of the public school teachers during the examination period, which prompted the government to impose requisitions. The government collapsed in December 2014, after repeated attempts to elect the president of the republic were blocked by the opposition.

Third bailout agreement

In the beginning of 2015, Alexis Tsipras became the new prime minister, promising to put an end to the austerity measures and the Memorandum. The leader of the far left political party Syriza formed an odd coalition with ANEL, the far-right-wing populist party headed by Panayiotis Kamenos. Thus began a series of unfortunate events for Greece. The first was the refusal to negotiate with the troika, an event that was marked by the incredible standoff of the finance minister Yianis Varoufakis and Jeroen Dijsselbloem. Troika was renamed "Institutions" and was blocked from inspecting Greek finances, as had previously been agreed. The fiasco of the new government continued for about 6 months, during which Greece suffered permanent damage. Previous positive signs of the economy emerging from the deadlock (growth was estimated at 3% as well as a timid primary surplus) gave way to uncertainty and loss of confidence. Government employees who had been fired and compensated were reinstated. Refugees and illegal immigrants flooded the islands, demanding safe passage to northern Europe after the minister of migration closed down the refugee camps and opened the borders. In an act of despair, Tsipras looted portions of the security funds and withheld EU farming subsidies. Moreover, the government employed the strategy of brinkmanship with its European partners and the IMF. This act disrupted the flow of much-needed cash and analysts began to worry that Greek would not survive the forthcoming months. The tranche of 7.2 billion euros was never sent because the evaluation was never carried out. To make matters worse, Varoufakis infuriated the IMF when he chose to pay 750 million euros by tapping the IMF holdings account.

The final strike came when Greece, starved of cash, missed the ensuing tranche of 1.55 million euros to the IMF. Once again, Greece broke another record, as it became the first developed country to default on the IMF. Therefore, Tsipras had to renegotiate a new bailout agreement with Europe to find a way through the fiscal impasse. The proposed bailout scheme would provide 29 billion euros for the next 2.5 years. Dissatisfied with the offer, Tsipras placed the decision in the hands of the Greek people by declaring a referendum. The ballot, which contained the draft proposal (preliminary debt sustainability analysis) and the pending provisions of the second Memorandum, asked for approval or disapproval of the total rescue package. Tsipras himself urged the people to vote against his own proposed deal.

The decision to conduct a referendum caused panic and led to bank runs. With reserves running low, the government finally shut down the banks for more than 2 weeks and imposed capital controls. The recently recapitalized banks suffered extensively from massive cash outflows and demanded extensive emergency liquidity assistance. Due to the imposition of capital controls, the entire economy stalled; the manufacturing and retail sectors experienced shortages of material, online purchases froze, imports were limited and businesses demanded to be paid in cash. Tsipras eventually won the battle of the referendum, with 62% of the people voting yes.

The outcome of the referendum brought about a chain of events. First, financial minister Varoufakis ruptured relations with Tsipras and was replaced by Euclid Tsakalotos. The next move was to restart negotiations in order to produce a new bailout agreement. The third Memorandum was finalized in mid-July. The ruling party, Syriza, did not welcome the impending agreement, as this would cause an about-face on many electoral promises and so many MPs abstained or voted against it. The new deal was ratified with the help of the opposition. Unable to maintain a majority in parliament, Tsipras dissolved the government and declared new elections. Syriza ultimately won and formed a new government after striking out the dissidents.

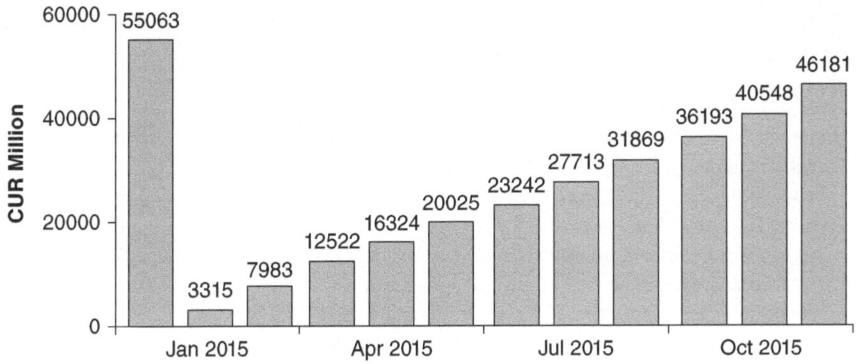

Figure 12.2 Greece fiscal expenditure

Source: Eurostat (2016)

Recently, Harvard has declared Tsipras's negotiation strategy as the worst in 2015. According to Shonk (2016), when the Greek leader asked for new financial assistance, he employed "brinkmanship with benefactors", angering the creditors and ending up with a terrible deal. The Syriza experiment has been an awakening for both the Greek people and their European partners. For most of the course of the crisis, the voters have fallen victims to populist declarations and vague promises of ending austerity and making Greece proud again. This is the biggest problem in Greek society: a mentality which seeks evanescent gains at the expense of others characterized by immaturity and inflexibility. The adoption of the third and most painful Memorandum is the legacy of constant mockery and hypocrisy of Tsipras towards his people and his European counterparts. When Tsipras realized there was no other source of income available to fund his expensive socialist promises other than the troika, he folded. Once again, Greek politicians have shown that they cannot be trusted on serious matters, as they never hesitate to gamble the future and prosperity of their citizens. Not only has the new deal placed stringent controls on the execution of the directives, but it has also evaporated all illusions of debt write-off and reduced the influence of the drachma lobby.

As expected, the cost of bad negotiation and political incompetence will be assigned to the tax payers. While most Greeks have complained about severe budget cuts and layoffs, the real economy is contracting. Many companies chose to escape paying advance corporate income tax of 26% by outsourcing their businesses to neighbouring Bulgaria or Cyprus due to the comparatively favourable rates. Apart from corporate tax, other tax increases include income (46%), VAT (23%) and social security tax (42%). Apart from capital flight, overtaxing facilitated the departure of skilled and educated manpower and encouraged the growth of the shadow economy or "black market". Just like the previous Memoranda, the recipe of tax dodging will only sink the economy even deeper into despair, exacerbate social effervescence and possibly lead to another doomed bailout agreement. To our surprise, the bailout creditors have sanctioned these policies despite their lack of effectiveness. As Salsman remarks, "most people focus on the economics, while assiduously ignoring the ethics (or lack) of it" (2012).

References

Boudreau, M.A. (2012). Restructuring sovereign debt under local law: are retrofit collective action clauses expropriatory? *Harvard Business Law Online*, 164. Available from: http://www.hblr.org/2012/05/retrofit-collective-action-clauses/ [accessed 2 January 2016].

Darrow, P.V. and Hans, R.F. (2012). A Greek Odyssey: Greece's sovereign debt restructuring and its impact on holders of Greek bonds. *DLA PIPER*. Available from: https://www.dlapiper.com/en/europe/insights/publications/2012/03/a-greek-odyssey-greeces-sovereign-debt-restructu__/ [accessed 5 January 2016].

Eurostat. (2016). *Greece government debt to GDP*. Available from: www.tradingeconomics.com/greece/government-debt-to-gdp [accessed 17 September 2016].

Kouretas, G. P. and Vlamis, P. (2010). The Greek crisis: causes and implications. *Panoeconomicus*, 4, 391–404.

Reinhart, C. and Trebesch, C. (2015). The pitfalls of external dependence: Greece 1829–2015. *NBER* Working Paper 21664. Available from: http://www.nber.org/papers/w21664 [accessed 2 January 2016].

Salsman, R. (2012). Greece's disgraceful debt default – and calls to "euthanize" bondholders. *Forbes Online*. Available from: http://www.forbes.com/sites/richardsalsman/2012/03/20/greeces-disgraceful-debt-default-and-calls-to-euthanize-bondholders/#2715e4857a0b2db584633fe7 [accessed 3 January 2016].

Shonk, K. (2016). Top 10 worst negotiations tactics of 2015. *Harvard Law School Daily Blog*. Available from: http://www.pon.harvard.edu/daily/negotiation-skills-daily/top-10-worst-negotiation-tactics-of-2015/ [accessed 11 January 2016].

Smith, Y. (2015). Lies, damned lies and Greek statistics. *Naked Capitalism*. Available from: http://www.nakedcapitalism.com/2015/07/lies-damned-lies-and-greek-statistics.html [accessed 2 January 2016].

Zettelmeyer, J., Trebesch, C., and Gulati, M. (2013). The Greek debt restructuring: an autopsy. *Peterson Institute of International Economics.* Working Paper 13-8. Available from: http://iie.com/publications/wp/wp13-8.pdf [accessed 2 January 2016].

13 Manufacturing consent or informing the public?

A review of recent research on how international mainstream media covered the Greek crisis

Lia-Paschalia Spyridou and Pavlos Koktsidis

Introduction

In a mediatized world the media plays a pivotal role in the formation of an informed citizenry able to comprehend, analyze, and act upon important issues concerning both the private and the public domain. During crises the public becomes even more dependent on the media for news that may be vital for survival and for important messages from public and private authorities (Graber, 1980). More specifically, people "look to the media for information, explanations and interpretations" (Graber, 1980, p. 228). Given the uncertainty and complexity of economic developments during the severe financial crisis that erupted in 2008 and soon spread in Europe (Mylonas, 2012; Tracy, 2012), it becomes clear that the media has played a decisive role in terms of how the public perceives the situation and judges policy options since in this case first-hand experience proves inadequate. Reasonably enough, it can be argued that the current financial crisis is different to a certain degree compared to previous ones, among other reasons due to the powerful role of mediated communication and information in portraying and explaining the complex economic, political, and social factors responsible for both creating and solving the crisis (Chakravartty and Schiller, 2010).

When representing economic crises, the media plays a profound role in setting the parameters of meaningful debate about them, a subject that raises important questions in terms of how meaning and perceptions are constructed. Therefore, how the media frames a crisis event, the causes mentioned, the actors responsible, and the remedies proposed tends to influence public impressions and understanding of the situation. Following agenda-setting and framing theories, the most salient issues and frames in media coverage exert substantial influence on the shaping of public opinion (Norris, 2000; Scheufele and Tewksbury, 2007).

Against this background, the present chapter is structured as follows. First, drawing upon the concept of mediatization and frame building, we provide a comprehensive account of the field of journalism and its dependencies which tend to directly affect journalistic output. Second, the chapter reviews the relevant literature on why the financial press failed to timely and rightly warn people of the imminent financial crisis, thus abdicating its public responsibility to investigate wrong-doing. Third, we focus on Greece and analyze how the legacy media of the country framed the causes and potential solutions of the crisis. The findings are discussed in conjunction with relevant literature explaining the origins and characteristics of the Greek financial crisis and the remedies needed to help the country exit the crisis.

Quiring and Weber (2012) argue that, at times of crises, media coverage can have two major repercussions. First, it can become exceptionally influential as a source of information and judgment for the public. Second, in case the legitimacy of economic policy is questioned, (favorable) media coverage should be a crucial precondition for gaining legitimacy for economic policy, by placing an independent stamp of approval on the actors' policy. This chapter designates a third case: media coverage can systematically align with the interests of specific political and economic actors, and thus misinform the public by adhering to erroneous attributions and solutions of the crisis in an effort not only to clear the corrupted political system responsible for the crisis and but also to sustain the status quo. Furthermore, in countries that undergo a severely poor and prolonged financial situation, news reporting of the crisis may have a direct performative impact on both policy and societal reaction. It is argued that biased and de-contextualized reporting of the crisis in Greece not only undermined specific policy reforms, but contributed to increased cynicism and mistrust towards institutions along with a tremendous sense of helplessness (Chryssochoou et al., 2013), a detrimental effect for the democratic process.

Mediatization and frame building

Ideally a news media system suitable for a democracy ought to provide its audience with the vital resources for processes of information gathering, deliberation, and analysis that enable citizens to participate in political life and democracy to function (Fenton, 2015). "News is a social resource. A source of knowledge, a source of power, news is a window on the world" (Tuchman, 1978: 217). But, as Dahlgren (2009) argues, the media "are a prerequisite – although by no means a guarantee – for shaping the democratic character of society" (p. 2). Journalism scholars have critiqued news in many ways, but a central thread of criticism involves questions around truth and accuracy.

Profound changes in public communication since the 1990s have amplified such concerns, which tend to fall under the concept of "mediatization," a term used to refer to the problematic dependencies, constraints, and exaggerations of (mass) media as a result of its technological, semiotic, and economic characteristics (Schulz, 2004). Strömback (2008) views the "mediatization of politics" as a four-dimensional process. First, the media operates as the most important or dominant source of information on politics and society. Second, the media depends on political institutions in terms of how they are regulated. Third, media content is governed by media logic[1] (as opposed to political logic) which emphasizes the need for profits and power. Finally, political actors tend to be governed by the media logic themselves in an effort to gain visibility and media support. Although variances might occur across time and place, the "mediatization" of politics is difficult to dispute, signaling a development towards increasing media influence being exerted over people's perceptions and over political institutions, respectively.

Under neoliberal conditions described as free-market policies (Chomsky, 1999), the political power of giant mass media corporations (Crouch, 2015; Fenton, 2015) tends to amplify the growing influence exerted by the media over political processes (Hjarvard, 2008), and reasonably enough, raises long discussions on the interactions between media, politics, the public, and democracy in contemporary times. At the core of such discussions lies the notion of communication power, succinctly described by Altheide (2013) as "the ability to define a situation" (p. 224), and therefore influence social order, social reality, and social change. The notion of social reality construction through mediated communication, the latter used as important means of creating society-wide resonance for specific constructions and definitions of reality, is not new. Critical media studies have long ago viewed communication technologies as pervasive and potent ideological media that tend to construct reality rather than reflect it (Tuchman, 1978; Gurevitch et al. 1982; Herman and Chomsky, 1992; Schudson, 2003).

Having explained the dialectical and increasing process of influence occurring between the media, political actors, and political parties, the issue of how the media covers and frames stories reasonably comes to the fore. In his well-known book *Is Anyone Responsible*?, Iyengar (1991) demonstrates that news media frames issues in specific ways emphasizing specific aspects and attributes. It is argued that news media can frame questions of responsibility, which in turn leads the audience to determine the causes and solutions for social problems. Framing is a process which involves message construction, presentation, and interpretation, and has effects on the audience's cognitive, affective, and behavioral responses (Scheufele and Tewksbury, 2007). The significance of framing lies in the fact that it can affect both individuals and society at large. An individual-level consequence may result in altered attitudes after exposure to certain frames. On the societal level, frames can affect processes such as political socialization and collective actions (De Vreese, 2005). Regarding the 2008 financial crisis in particular, Boomgaarden et al. (2011) found that media exposure strongly affected expectations regarding the future development of the national economic situation, while being largely unrelated to personal economic expectations. Furthermore, the study showed that media dependency increases the magnitude of the media effect.

Many studies of news framing have explored how the media represents certain issues, for instance poverty (Iyengar, 1990; Kensicky, 2004), immigration (Cheng et al., 2014; Milioni et al., 2015), protests (Gitlin, 1980; Spyridou, 2015), and more recently, the economic crisis that began in 2008 (Schranz and Eisenegger, 2011; Mylonas, 2012; Titley, 2012; Tracy, 2012; Doudaki et al., 2016). However, left largely unexplored is the question of what makes the media frame an issue in a certain way. Scheufele (1999) introduced the notion of frame building, referring to the factors and processes that influence the creation or modification of frames applied by journalists. Scheufele argued that a "key question is what kinds of organizational or structural factors of the media system, or which individual characteristics of journalists can impact the framing of news content" (1999, p. 115).

Following the medialization thesis, it may well be argued that the frame-building process is influenced by the complex and dynamic interaction among journalists, media institutions, and other political actors. The outcome of the frame-building process, namely the creation of news stories, actually reflects such close and dialectical relationships.

Reporting the economic crisis

The global financial crisis has given rise to a range of critical questions regarding the capacity of journalism to map and represent complex financial issues and developments, echoing journalism's normative role in sustaining a functioning democratic society (Berry, 2013). Reviewing the relevant literature, most scholars and financial journalists agree that the business press never conveyed a real sense of alarm until institutions and countries began to collapse. The causes are to be found in the professional culture of journalism, the dominant practices and routines of mainstream journalism, the lack of training in business and finance, the commercial pressures faced by news organizations, and last but not least, to the fact "that most business journalists were enjoying the upward spiral as much as the investment bankers and analysts whom they counted among their best contacts and lunch companions. [So], why spoil the party?" (Fraser, 2009: 80). As a result, many media outlets lacked the independence and critical judgment needed to investigate the financialization of the economic system and warn of serious excesses and, sometimes, criminal conduct (Schechter, 2009). Let us elaborate on each.

Commercial pressures on news production and profit-driven journalism is certainly not a new thing. Journalism's dependence on corporate advertising and subsidy has been a major obstacle in revealing information that would jeopardize the reputation and work of the financial sector (Schechter, 2009; Tambini, 2010). Not only did substantial advertising revenue come from banks, credit card companies, and real-estate advertising, but there was also fear of lawsuits from businesses eager to silence or suppress "bad press" in an era when so many wealthy companies had invested in sophisticated public relations. Within that climate, journalists tried really hard to be careful and avoid negativity, argues Usher (2012), while Schechter (2009) draws a more painful conclusion: "We had gone from telling to selling" (p. 21).

Besides the economic shortcomings in the conduct of journalism, many financial reporters did not ask really difficult questions simply because they are not knowledgable in finance and could not comprehend the imminent dangers posed by high-risk investments, cheap credit, and accumulating private and public debt (Fraser, 2009; Hope, 2010; Schifferes and Coulter, 2012). Along with inadequate training, and lack of resources as a result of serious cuts in costly investigations (Schechter, 2009), journalists became too dependent on experts, banking and corporate sources (Starkman, 2009; Tambini, 2010; Davis, 2011, Mercille, 2013; Rafter, 2014), who used public relations consultants and press offices to deliberately suppress information flows and control inconvenient information (Manning, 2013). The problematic sourcing of news, commonly associated with the use of elite and minimal sources, seems to have been exacerbated in the case of financial reporting as journalists came too close to their sources and thus too uncritical of their sayings and arguments (Stiglitz, 2011; Thompson, 2013).

During news production, journalists engage in routines and recurrent practices to meet deadlines and follow competition. Business reporting in particular is driven by competitive pressure for scoops (Fraser, 2009). The accelerating news cycle of the web era and the appearance of multiple blogs claiming scoops and specialized investment information culminated in increased work pressures leaving little time for off-diary features, analysis, and "big picture" reflections on larger trends (Fraser, 2009; Hope, 2010). Additionally, the standardized "socialization" of journalists in the realm of mainstream journalism calls for "a conformity of production and selection" (Harrison, 2000: 112–113, in Harcup, 2015). When a journalist steps outside the "norm," namely "outside the range of official debate to provide alternative perspectives or to raise issues those in power prefer not to discuss, this is no longer professional" (McChesney, 2002: 17). Therefore, it has been rather difficult for financial reporters to take up the role of the "alarmist," or the "doom and gloomer" at a time of "growth and success stories" (Fraser, 2009; Schechter, 2009).

Finally, besides organizational and professional constraints, ideological pressures promoting a neoliberal *modus operandi* have also obscured the truth. The financial press not only avoided asking difficult questions, but overall has been responsible for promulgating financialization as the epitome of growth and success, paying less attention to the consequences of sheer deregulation on the economic and political process (Knowles et al., 2015). This observation coincides with Mercille's (2013) study; Mercille analyzed the role of the media in sustaining Ireland's housing bubble during the "Celtic Tiger" years. The findings confirm arguments based on the political economy of the media perspective: news organisations are part of and share similar interests and views with the political and corporate establishment. Therefore, the media not only made little mention of the shortcomings of the financial sector's activities in Ireland, but also tried to refute claims of any wrong-doing. In short, due to economic dependencies, organizational and professional constraints, as well as ideological choices, the media failed to properly inform the public through balanced and independent reporting; rather it overtly supported the status quo to the detriment of the populace.

Contextualizing the Greek crisis: what had gone wrong?

Having answered the question of why the media failed to timely and rightly report on the imminent financial crisis, and before moving on to investigate how the Greek media covered the unfolding crisis, it would be useful to take a closer look at the Greek problems and particularities that actually led to the country's economic collapse.

What started in 2007 as a mortgage crisis in the USA soon spread in the form of a global financial crisis. Initially, Greece appeared to be protected from the economic fallout (Monastiriotis, 2011). Underneath this façade, however, there were important structural constraints that soon exposed Greece to an unprecedented fiscal crisis. Reviewing the relevant literature, Greece's financial problems can be broadly attributed, first to the country's structural pathogeneses, and second to the unsustainable growth model pursued for more than 40 years. Unsurprisingly, both sources of problems are closely related to the corrupted and clientilistic political system that governed the country since 1974 (Featherstone, 2008, 2011; Lyrintzis, 2011; Ladi, 2014; Baldwin and Giavazzi, 2015).

Pillar I: Structural pathogeneses

Featherstone (2008, 2011) provides a succinct and accurate account of the country's endemic weaknesses and systemic underpinnings preventing the much-delayed structural reforms. First, the tradition of state-driven development. The state exercised disproportionate influence over the economy, through extensive regulation, protectionist measures, transfers, and subsidies. Moreover, these instruments were applied in a particularistic manner, with the state subject to pervasive "rent-seeking" behavior and favoring certain sectors and interests (Sotiropoulos, 2004 in Featherstone, 2008, p. 11). Yet, whilst the state was omnipresent, it was also fundamentally weak; its weakness stemmed primarily from the fact that its potent influence was intimately related to a clientele system, which it has been precisely intended to serve (Tsoukalis, 1997 in Featherstone, 2008, p. 11). Second, there was poor intragovernmental coordination and lack of skills, leading to low efficiency and waste of resources (Featherstone, 2011). Third, alongside Greece's chronic inability to control its public expenditure, it was blatantly unable to generate sufficient revenues in line with countries elsewhere in Europe (Featherstone, 2011; Monastiriotis, 2011). Revenue-wise, Greece significantly underperformed relative to the European average, with tax revenues as a share of gross domestic product (GDP) being about 7 percentage points lower (around 32%) and declining since the early 2000s (Servera and Moschovis, 2008 in Monastiriotis, 2011, p. 49). Fourth, weak tax collection mechanisms and pervasive corruption are deep-rooted problems that have systematically contributed to a weak and unregulated economy (Matsaganis and Flevotomou, 2010; Featherstone, 2011; Monastiriotis, 2011). Surprisingly, corruption in Greece has also legal roots. The report of Transparency International Greece (2013) (www.transparency.gr) notes that, although Greece has many laws in place to fight corruption, in many cases other laws effectively condone it. Finally, the problems of the Greek economy are to be found in the systemic problems of the European Monetary Union design, which created a structural asymmetry within the Eurozone, and resulted in real currency appreciation and continuous loss of competitiveness in the European south (Habermas, 2013).

Moreover, special attention needs to be paid to Greece's systematic failure to reform several sectors. As argued by Monastiriotis and Antoniades (2009), persistent reform failures and a continuum of half-way reforms have characterized much of the country's recent history. Bureaucratic clientelism and political immaturity are found to determine the failure to achieve or complete reforms in several public administration practices and operations, such as the social insurance/pensions reform which was attempted in 2001 and in 2007 (Tinios, 2010) or the information communication and technology implementations in the Taxation Information System (TAXIS) (Prasopoulou, 2011). More radical economic and social reforms, such as fiscal adjustment to the EU goals, had systematically failed. Greece has been accumulating public deficits for years, and this has been "a choice of governments, rather than the unfortunate result of macroeconomic conditions turning out less favorably than expected" (Kaplanoglou and Rapanos, 2011). Monastiriotis and Antoniadis (2009) argue that, instead of identifying "vested interests" and "reform resistance" (i.e., actors that block reforms), one should seek to understand the specific pathologies leading to the "highly problematic" reform record of the country. First, politicians/policy makers appear to have pre-set agendas and not to engage in a systematic way with expert advice, independent or commissioned. Second, even in cases where a consultation processes with experts takes place, the resulting policies are often in disagreement with the expert advice. The third factor is the continuing dominance and ill-perceived antagonism between the two main political parties that ruled the country since the fall of the junta in 1974. The two political parties (PASOK and Nea Dimokratia) were able to penetrate and control almost all areas of public life, including organized interests, civil service, local and regional authorities, and the universities. In the same way they have determined the development of the private sector through links of dependency from the party/state mechanisms in order to secure loans, business licenses, and lucrative deals (Lyrintzis, 2011). "*Partitocrazia*" and "bureaucratic clientelism" are terms accurately describing the functioning of the Greek political system. The two parties had access and controlled the state mechanisms to secure the power position of specific persons or groups. Accordingly, public administration was trapped in a perpetual cycle of failed reforms and mismanagement (Lyrintzis, 2011; Ladi, 2014). Despite prevailing discourse, the size of the Greek public sector was always close to the European average. It was the way it functioned that caused significant problems.

Pillar II: Greece's unviable growth model

Growth performance of the Greek economy had little to do with a dynamic capitalist economy. Growth primarily relied on the twin pillars of state borrowing and EU transfers. State and EU structural funds were filtered down and distributed by the state. The Greek economy was largely based on overconsumption, ever-increasing debt levels, and a capital accumulation process divorced from the real economy, albeit Greek public spending was among average EU spending, Greece consumed more than it could produce (92.9% of GDP went to consumption, whereas the EU average was 80.7% in the period 1993–2009) (Hellenic Foundation for European and Foreign Policy (ELIAMEP), 2015).

Raising government spending during the 1980s and 1990s was not a new recipe for artificial growth. After the fall of dictatorship in Greece, the deficit and public debt never stopped growing, but in reality, Greece never had a growth rate so high that it could help repay in part the debt that the country's governments were creating. Increases in public expenditure relied on loans, which had tripled the public debt by 2009. Additionally, increased expenditure caused a high inflation rate that demotivated investments, and later, when the state borrowed from international markets, this demand caused an increase in loan rates. From 1991 to 2007, the Greek economy raced at a higher average growth performance rate compared to the EU average (3.1%, whilst the EU average was estimated at 2.2%) (ELIAMEP, 2015). Deficit remained high in the period from 2001 to 2009 while government spending had been steadily increasing. Indicatively, increases in state expenditures rose from 45.4% in 2001 to 54.5% by 2009, corresponding to a drastic deficit increase (from 4.5% of GDP in 2001 to a staggering 15.6% of GDP by 2009 (ELIAMEP,2015). What is more impressive, though, is that increases in public expenditure were not associated with an increase in wealth production. Since the accession of Greece to the Eurozone, Greek product prices were noticeably increased over those of its main trading partners. With relatively high prices, and without the capacity to devaluate its currency, Greece faced a competitiveness downturn. In short, heavy reliance on consumption-driven growth based on imported goods coupled with the gradual loss of competitiveness resulted in current trade balances showing an increasing deficit. The country had virtually ceased to produce. The fact that Greece imported more than it exported has impacted heavily on deficit production in the country's trade account balance and, in this case, resorted to external borrowing to finance the shortfall. In other words, trade deficits were covered mainly by state borrowing. Naturally this approach led to a vicious circle in which the state was constantly borrowing. The loans went to the consumer, increasing the demand for imported goods (Galenianos, 2015). This increased the trade deficit which in turn was covered by more loans. When borrowing was dramatically reduced the economy collapsed.

The accession to the euro eliminated macroeconomic strategies for currency devaluation and made reforms to improve productivity the only way to recover competitiveness. However, raising productivity, which would facilitate the repayment of foreign debt, did not materialize, at least not to the extent anticipated. This resulted in further loss of competitiveness and growing dependence on continuing capital inflows. The governments of Greece, by contrast, took advantage of the favorable credit conditions to increase their lending, causing even greater reduction in national savings. This reinforced the need to borrow from abroad and further increased the current account deficit, exacerbating economic weaknesses. Hence, the so-called growth model, which was based on increased consumption and low competitiveness, had inevitably become dependent on increased government borrowing which in turn raised public debt to unsustainable levels. Indicatively, from 1993 onwards, public debt was drastically starting to increase, and by 2009 public debt ultimately reached 129% of GDP (that is, about 300 billion euros) (ELIAMEP, 2015).

In a nutshell, the global financial crisis revealed the Greek economy's chronically distorted growth and structural deficiencies; namely, Greece's consumption-driven and borrowing-dependent growth model coupled with the country's inefficient, corrupt, and heavily bureaucratized economy and public administration.

Bailout coverage: how the legacy media covered the crisis in Greece

Having contextualized the roots of the Greek financial crisis, the next question of interest to the chapter is how mainstream media in Greece covered the unfolding crisis. This chapter uses data retrieved and adapted from a study conducted by Doudaki, Boubouka, Spyridou and Tzalavras (2016). The original study collected data from the online editions of *Ta Nea* and *Kathimerini*, two daily newspapers with the highest circulation in the country. Notwithstanding the growing appearance of web-only and alternative media heralding a shift in the allocation and management of symbolic power, mainstream media still plays a significant role in both framing and providing visibility during crisis conditions (Cammaerts et al., 2013; Zeri, 2014). The study focused on three periods[2] marked by important political developments associated with the bailout mechanisms. A total of 576 news items were analyzed. In particular, this section explores how legacy media in Greece presented the causes of the crisis and the solutions to overcome it during the first two bailouts (2010–2012).

What were the origins of the crisis?

The findings (Table 13.1) indicate that press coverage blatantly failed to identify the real causes of the financial crisis. Instead, the results of the real causes (such as public debt and excessive deficit) are presented as the origins of the problem whereas the real generating factors, namely Greece's mismanagement, tax evasion, lack of competitiveness, and the governance of the country by a corrupt and clientilistic political system favoring specific actors and business, were hardly mentioned in the relevant coverage. As time went by and the crisis deepened due to the implementation of extensive austerity measures, such as salary and repetitive pension cuts, growing unemployment, deregulation of the labor market,[3] increasing instances of non-paid employees in the private sector[4]), the media engaged in progressive decreasing coverage related to the causes of the crisis; this pattern peaked in the second and third period. The latter finding may well be associated with the electoral collapse of the two major political parties and the ascent of SYRIZA. SYRIZA increased its electoral power from 4.59% in 2009 to 16.79% in 2012, whereas the aggregate electoral power of PASOK and New Democracy was reduced from 77.43% in 2009 to 32.03% in 2012.[5]

Table 13.1 manifests a pattern of "non-attribution" which permeates the findings in general. The country was faced with a remarkable crisis, which was obviously multidimensional and complex, but according to the media it seemed to have developed in a vacuum. News coverage not only abstained from any kind of explanatory journalism abdicating its informational role, but quite tellingly resorted to misinformation when masking the perennial pathogeneses and liabilities of the political system which nurtured a non-sustainable economic model.

What should the solutions to the crisis be?

In March 2010 and at various stages subsequently, the Greek governments adopted a series of austerity measures aiming at reducing its excessive budget deficit to

Table 13.1 The causes of the crisis

Causes mentioned	*Period A*		*Period B*		*Period C*	
	April 16, 2010–May 10, 2010		*October 20, 2011–February 19, 2012*		*April 29, 2012–June 24, 2012*	
	*n = 192**		*n = 192*		*n = 192*	
	n	*%*	*n*	*%*	*n*	*%*
Public debt	40	20.8	49	25,5	16	8.3
Excessive deficit	38	19.8	23	12,0	25	13.0
Banking system/ capitalism	34	17.7	2	1,0	1	0.5
Greece's mismanagement	21	10.9	2	1,0	0	0
Unbalanced system in Eurozone	11	5.7	3	1.6	1	0.5
Corrupt political system	6	3.1	1	0.5	1	0.5
Tax evasion	4	2.1	1	0.5	4	2.1
Greece's reluctance/ unwillingness/inability to follow the agreed terms/to reform	4	2.1	2	1.0	3	1.6
Lack of punishment	3	1.6	1	0.5	0	0
Lack of competitiveness	3	1.6	7	3.6	3	1.6
Privileged social/ professional groups	2	1.0	1	0.5	1	0.5
Extensive public sector	2	1.0	3	1.6	1	0.5
Clientelism	1	0.5	1	0.5	0	0
Lazy Greeks	1	0.5	0	0	0	0
High salaries and pensions	0	0	3	1.6	0	0
Established elites and interests	0	0	3	1.6	2	1.0

Source: The data in Table 13.1 are retrieved and adapted from Doudaki et al. (2016).

*Table 13.1 contains the aggregates of the two newspapers for each period. Ninety-six news items were used for each newspaper.

below the 3% threshold (from 15.4% in 2009) (Christodoulakis, 2014). The path to recovery for the Greek economy had to follow a harsh austerity program focusing almost exclusively on budget curtails, while other options of increasing revenue (i.e., privatizations, inducements for economic activity to create growth, combat of tax evasion, structural reforms to reduce expenditure) were practically ignored (Monastiriotis, 2011), leading to deep recession amounting to 23% and record-type unemployment amounting to 27.5% in 2013 (ELIAMEP, 2015). A public deficit reduction policy through fiscal discipline, though necessary and desirable, does not render an economy competitive by itself, and thus fiscal discipline alone cannot translate into economic development. In addition, exclusive preoccupation with fiscal imbalances has distracted policymakers from other more important reforms, associated with the country's particularities, which if resolved would prove more suitable for helping Greece to emerge out of the crisis (Galenianos, 2015).

Considering the aforementioned problems and limitations of the Greek situation, one would reasonably argue that, along with major steps to rationalize its public expenditures, Greece would need to engage in thorough structural reforms as well as enhance its productive capacity in an attempt to revamp its economy. According to the press (Table 13.2), the solutions claimed necessary revolve around cuts of salaries and pensions, the deregulation of the labor market, layoffs in the public sector, and tax increases. This neoliberal austerity package is consistently projected as the suitable solution throughout the study. However, these "unpopular" solutions are progressively undermentioned, especially in the third period, when the country gets into election mode. Interestingly enough, the solutions proposed are inconsistent with the real origins of the crisis, yet correspond to the need to eliminate the public debt and deficit. However this goal was strongly undermined by the deep recession caused by extreme and one-sided austerity. As a result, public debt as a percentage of GDP had snowballed from 126.7% in 2009 to 159.4% in 2012, and eventually reached the dramatic percent of 178.6 in 2014.[6] At the same time other structural reforms, such as the need to combat tax evasion or speed up the judicial system, were left out of the picture.

During the second and third period, journalists, instead of exercising their watchdog role and warning of the wrong remedies implemented, again avoided putting up a different solutions-related discourse and insisted on the same propositions, yet in a less emphatic manner as the manifestations of austerity were affecting a growing number of citizens. The press uncritically followed the political developments and the political actors' discourse. Amid growing concern regarding the country's non-

Table 13.2 Solutions mentioned

Solutions mentioned	*Period A:*		*Period B:*		*Period C:*	
	April 16, 2010–May 10, 2010		*October 20, 2011–February 19, 2012*		*April 29, 2012–June 24, 2012*	
	n = 192		*n = 192*		*n = 192*	
	n	*%*	*n*	*%*	*n*	*%*
Cut salaries/pensions	33	17.2	44	22.9	11	5.7
Increase competitiveness via flexible labor conditions/deregulate closed professions	32	16.7	31	16.1	4	2.1
Lay off civil servants	13	6.8	24	12.5	2	1.0
Increase taxes	12	6.3	7	3.6	4	2.1
Privatizations	10	5.2	9	4.7	8	4.2
Combat tax evasion	9	4.7	6	3.1	3	1.6
Haircut	8	4.2	67	34.9	6	3.1
Limit social welfare	5	2.6	15	7.8	0	0
Clean up political system	5	2.6	0	0	1	0.5
Dispense justice	5	2.6	0	0	4	2.1
Extension of bailout/funding	1	0.5	4	2.1	16	8.3

Source: The data in Table 13.2 are retrieved and adapted from Doudaki et al. (2016).

sustainable debt (International Monetary Fund, 2015), the haircut solution gained prominence in the relevant coverage. At the same time, the idea of further limiting social welfare appeared in the solution-related discourse to further support the one-sided austerity dogma. During the third period, solution discourse diminished greatly; the country was in election mode and the need to protect the political system proved critical as the threat of SYRIZA (a left-wing party) gaining parliamentary power was possible. The focus this shifted to the extension of the bailout agreement, which by no means comprised a measure to heal the inherent problems of the Greek economy. It seemed that the political actors were trying to buy time, and the media was providing it by bringing this solution forward.

The role of the media: manipulating public opinion

Six years down the line Greece is still in economic, political, and social turmoil. The country has systematically been accused of reluctance to implement the structural reforms required for fiscal consolidation and debt sustainability. In fact this is a recurrent theme in the debate of why Greece has failed to exit the crisis, whilst Portugal and Ireland seem to be on the right track. However, evidence suggests that Greece has engaged in extensive structural reforms; in fact the country was a frontrunner in structural reforms during the crisis years 2007–2014 (OECD, 2015). But Greek reforms had three negative and interrelated features: they were badly sequenced, emphasised fiscal performance rather than more generalized structural reforms, and were implemented by short-sighted political parties which sought to sustain the political status quo although the country has been on the verge of economic and social collapse.

Certainly the austerity dogma aiming to generate surpluses and thus secure debt sustainability was not a Greek idea, but rather an "obsession" of the country's creditors. On the other hand, the political parties share great responsibility for both creating the crisis as well as not dealing with it in an efficient and just manner. This chapter has shown that in the mismanagement of the country before and during the crisis, the political parties have had an important ally: the Press. The media attempts to legitimise its increasing political involvement with reference to democratic expectations of providing adequate and reliable information as well as monitoring the state, and protecting citizens from potential abuses of its power. On the other hand, though, the media operates under conditions of "immunity" as it is hard for the media to "sanction" itself in case of bad performance. This institutional contradiction poses a serious challenge to democracy:

> While the political parties are accountable for their policies to the electorate, no constitution foresees that the media be accountable for their actions. Absence of accountability can imply serious risks for democracy, because it violates the classic rule of balances of power in the democratic game, making the media (the fourth branch of government) an influential and uncontrollable force that is protected from the sanction of popular will.
>
> (Mazzoleni and Schultz, 1999: 248)

As shown earlier, the media failed to timely and rightly inform people of the imminent global financial crisis. And when the crisis hit Greece hard, the legacy media chose to fully support the policies implemented although there were clear signs that the remedy used had significant flaws, as it blatantly underestimated the adverse effects that extensive fiscal correction might have on growth (Christodoulakis, 2014). The media promoted erroneous attributions of the crisis which in reality were the outcome of the country's chronic mismanagement (i.e., public deficit and debt). By suggesting no endemic causes and weaknesses, the media followed a detached, no-real-solution coverage which promoted the austerity dogma while concealing its economic and social ramifications. In doing so, the press protected the political system and its pathogeneses. Exhibiting no sense of accountability, journalists contributed to a knowledge gap between what the public knows, what it wants to know, and what it needs to know so that citizens keep abreast of current developments and thereby are in a position to hold the political and financial system to account.

An obvious question to be raised is why did the legacy media in Greece fully support the memoranda policies (Pleios, 2013) and took the blame off the political system? The answer lies in the chronic tension between commercialism and democratic journalism that not only hinders the watchdog role of the press, but often contributes to corruption and propaganda (McChesney and Nichols, 2010). The case of Greece represents a typical example of the polarised pluralistic model in the typology put forward by Hallin and Mancini (2004). A prominent feature of the Greek media system is the strong ties and interdependences between media and the political system. "Greek newspapers have always been political instruments above all, rooted culturally in passionate ideological divisions, and often tied to the state and/or parties, which have provided financial subsidies, help with distribution, and other forms of assistance" (Hallin and Mancini, 2004: 98). Most media organizations are owned by industrialists with interests in shipping, travel, construction, telecommunication, and oil industries that have a long tradition of being used as means of pressure on politicians (Hallin and Papathanassopoulos, 2002). This pressure is useful when fighting for government contracts due to the structure of the Greek economy, in which the state plays a much larger role than in developed capitalist countries and so many important decisions affecting entrepreneurs rest in the hands of politicians (Papathanassopoulos, 2001). Freelance journalist Nikolas Leontopoulos comments on the close relationship between Greek media owners and the political and financial centers of power. "They didn't care so much to earn money out of their media businesses; they cared more about winning state contracts."[7] The interplay between the political system and the media has resulted in great interventionism regarding journalistic output, which in turn diminished journalistic autonomy and nurtured a weak professional culture on the part of journalists. Exposure of wrong-doings has been selective as the dominant journalistic culture was very cautious about reporting that could embarrass state officials (Papathanassopoulos, 2007). Nikos Xydakis, columnist in the daily newspaper *Kathimerini*, explains: "A big part of the media is controlled by construction moguls and oligarchs. They reproduce the talk, talk,

talk of politicians. This is not journalism, it is everyday propaganda."[8] In general, Greek journalism has always represented (and still does) and defended the interests of the parties to which is linked (Papathanassopoulos, 2001: 519).

The ongoing economic crisis has wiped out both public works and advertising, putting media organizations in an ultimately poor situation. The oversized media sector (Poggioli, 2013) is faced with shrinking advertising revenue[9] (Pleios, 2013) and large bank loans (Smyrnaios, 2013). Consequently news media has become more vulnerable to political and business pressures. Massive layoffs[10] (Poggioli, 2013), huge salary cuts (Smyrnaios, 2013), and precarious labour (Spyridou et al. 2013) have undermined further the autonomy and accountability levels of the already weak watchdog culture of Greek journalists.

Concluding remarks

Drawing upon the notion of mediatization and the frame-building perspective which emphasize the dialectical and dynamic relationship between news organizations, political and economic actors, this chapter has sought to demonstrate the role of journalism in policy formation. Notwithstanding the normative obligations of journalism for explanatory and contextual journalism (Fink and Schudson, 2013), along with evidence suggesting an increasing demand for financial journalism (Reuters Institute Digital News Report, 2013), the media, due to organizational, professional, economic, and ideological constraints, has failed to contextualize and interpret the political and economic developments, and therefore provide an objective critique of what was going on before and during the crisis. This is a worrying trend and one that runs in the opposite direction to the general efforts to democratize governance (Isakhan and Slaughter, 2014). For deep structural reforms to succeed, a sense of justice and collectiveness is necessary, and the media performs an important role in that direction. When covering the crisis, however, the media appeared disconnected from the broader economic and political conditions that led to the crisis, nurturing a sense of mistrust towards the political system. More importantly, the media supported the policies implemented even when those were inappropriate, thus eliminating the most fundamental role of the press: to watch out for wrong-doings and abuse of power. Problematic coverage therefore not only undermined specific policy reforms, but contributed to increased cynicism and mistrust towards institutions along with a tremendous sense of fear and frustration (Chryssochoou et al., 2013), a detrimental effect for the democratic process. Unsurprisingly, after six years of austerity, impoverishment, and a shattered economy, Greece seems to be struggling with public perceptions on the necessity for and scope of the requested reforms (Featherstone, 2015).

Notes

1 "Media logic" refers to specific news values, story-telling techniques, and organizational routines aiming primarily at maximizing audience share (see Altheide and

Snow, 1979) or, depending on the media system and the degree of political parallelism, serving political interests and nurturing ties between the media and the political parties (Hallin and Mancini, 2004).

2 Period A: April 16, 2010–May 10, 2010. On 23 April 2010, the Greek Prime Minister, Giorgos Papandreou, appealed for a bailout intervention by the troika (EU/European Central Bank/International Monetary Fund), since the Greek economy was in intensive care and the measures taken the previous months to avoid its collapse had not proven successful. Within this context, the activation of the agreed "rescue" package of €110bn was presented as inevitable for the salvation of the country's economy.

Period B: October 20, 2011–February 19, 2012. Amid great recession, poor fiscal performance, and social discomfort, a second bailout program was agreed between the Greek government and the troika. Greece would receive €130bn of bailout loans and 53.5% "haircut" of its debt to the private sector. As a result of simmering governmental instability, the Greek Prime Minister resigned and the technocrat and former vice-president of the European Central Bank, Loukas Papademos was appointed to lead the country to elections.

Period C: April 29, 2012–June 24, 2012. Following negotiations with the troika, the Greek government voted for more austerity measures, while unemployment rose to 22.6% and recession hit another record of 6.5% in the first quarter of 2012 (after being reduced by 6.9% in 2011). The government survived the voting procedure yet with serious damage, as 43 MPs decided to vote against the party line or abstain from voting. Amid severe governmental instability the Prime Minister resigned and Loukas Papademos is chosen to lead the country in elections. No party managed to form a government on May 6th, so a second round took place in June. The results of the second election confirmed that a new party map was formed. The traditional political parties of PASOK and New Democracy lost more than 60% of their voting power, SYRIZA – a coalition of left, radical left, and green groups – got 16.6% (from 4.6% in 2009) and Golden Dawn – an extreme right-wing party – attracted 6.92% of voters (from 0.29% in 2009). In the end New Democracy, PASOK, and Democratic Left formed a coalition government.

3 Featherstone (2015).

4 Source: Report by GSEE cited in: http://www.imerisia.gr/article.asp?catid=26516&subid=2&pubid=113187834.

5 In May 2012 New Democracy was voted by 18.85% of the electorate and PASOK was voted by 13.18%. In October 2009 the two parties had received 33.49% and 43.94% of the votes respectively (source: Hellenic Parliament, http://www.hellenicparliament.gr/Vouli-ton-Ellinon/To-Politevma/Ekloges/Eklogika-apotelesmata-New/#ID).

6 Source: Eurostat, http://ec.europa.eu/eurostat/tgm/table.do?tab=table&init=1&language=en&pcode=teina225&plugin=1.

7 Source: Poggioli (2013).

8 Source: Poggioli (2013).

9 It is estimated that between 2009 and 2012 advertising revenue diminished by 30% (source: Pleios, 2013).

10 It is estimated that during 2009–2013 4,000 media workers lost their jobs (source: Poggioli, 2013).

References

Altheide, D. (2013). Media Logic, Social Control, and Fear, *Communication Theory*, 23: 223–238.

Altheide, D. L. and Snow, R. P. (1979). *Media Logic*. Beverly Hills: Sage Publications.

Baldwin, R. and Giavazzi, F. (eds.) (2015). *The Eurozone Crisis: A Consensus View of the Causes and a Few Possible Solutions*. London: Centre for Economic Policy Research.

Berry, M. (2013). The Today Programme and the Banking Crisis, *Journalism*, 14(2): 253–270.

Boomgaarden, H.G., van Spanje, J., Vliegenthart, R. and de Vreese, C.H. (2011). Covering the Crisis: Media Coverage of the Economic Crisis and Citizens' Economic Expectations, *Acta Politica*, 46(4): 353–379.

Cammaerts, B., Mattoni, A. and McCurdy, P. (eds.) (2013). *Mediation and Protest Movements*. Bristol: Intellect e-Journals.

Chakravartty, P. and Schiller, D. (2010). Neoliberal Newspeak and Digital Capitalism in Crisis, *International Journal of Communication*, 4: 670–692.

Cheng, L., Igartua, J., Palacios, E., Acosta, T. and Palito, S. (2014). Framing Immigration News in Spanish Regional Press, *International Migration*, 52(6): 197–215.

Chomsky, N. (1999). *Profit Over People: Neoliberalism and Global Order*. New York: Seven Stories Press.

Christodoulakis, N. (2014). From Grexit to Growth: On Fiscal Multipliers and How to End Recession in Greece, *National Institute Economic Review*, 224(1): 66–76.

Chryssochoou, X., Papastamou, S. and Prodromitis, G. (2013). Facing the Economic Crisis in Greece: The Effects of Grievances, Real and Perceived Vulnerability, and Emotions Towards the Crisis on Reactions to Austerity Measure, *Journal of Social Science Education*, 12(1): 41–49.

Crouch, C. (2015). The March Towards Post-Democracy, Ten Years On, *The Political Quarterly*, 87(1): 71–75.

Dahlgren, P. (2009). *Media and Political Engagement: Citizens, Communication, Democracy*. Cambridge: Cambridge University Press.

Davis, A. (2011). News of the Financial Sector: Reporting on the City or to it?, *Open Democracy*, 31 May 2011, http://www.opendemocracy.net/print/59797 (accessed 11 September 2016).

De Vreese, C. (2005). News Framing: Theory and Typology, *Information Design Journal + Document Design*, 13(1): 51–62.

Doudaki, V., Boubouka, A., Spyridou, L.-P. and Tzalavras, C. (2016). Dependency, (Non)liability and Austerity News Frames of Bailout Greece, *European Journal of Communication*, 31(4): 426–445.

Featherstone, K. (2008). *Varieties of Capitalism' and the Greek Case: Explaining the Constraints on Domestic Reform*, GreeSE Paper No 11, Hellenic Observatory Papers on Greece and Southeast Europe, London: LSE.

Featherstone, K. (2011). The Greek Sovereign Debt Crisis and EMU: A Failing State in a Skewed Regime, *Journal of Common Market Studies*, 49(2): 193–217.

Featherstone, K. (2015). External Conditionality and the Debt Crisis: The 'Troika' and Public Administration Reform in Greece, *Journal of European Public Policy*, 22(3): 295–314.

Fenton, N. (2015). Post-Democracy, Press, Politics and Power, *The Political Quarterly* 87(1): 81–85.

Fink, K. and Schudson, M. (2013). The Rise of Contextual Journalism, 1950s–2000s, *Journalism*, doi:10.1177/1464884913479015

Fraser, M. (2009). Five Reasons for Crash Blindness, *British Journalism Review*, 20(4): 78–83.

Galenianos, M. (2015). The Greek Crisis: Origins and Implications. ELIAMEP Hellenic Foundation for European and Foreign Policy Crisis Observatory Research Paper No 16 /2015.

Gitlin, T. (1980). *The Whole World is Watching: Mass Media in the Making and Unmaking of the New Left*. Berkeley: University of California Press.

Graber, D.A. (1980). *Mass Media and American Politics*. Washington, D.C.: Congressional Quarterly Press, pp. 225–241.

Gurevitch, M., Bennett, T., Curran, J. and Woollacott, J. (eds.) (1982). *Culture, Society and the Media*. London: Methuen.

Habermas, J. (2013). Democracy, Solidarity and the European Crisis, May 7, 2013, http://www.pro-europa.eu/index.php/en/at-issue/european-identity/11-j%C3%BCrgen-habermas-democracy,-solidarity-and-the-european-crisis (accessed 21 September 2016).

Hallin, C.D. and Mancini, P. (2004). *Comparing Media Systems: Three Models of Media and Politics,* Cambridge: Cambridge University Press.

Hallin, C. and Papathanassopoulos, S. (2002). Political Clientelism and the Media: Southern Europe and Latin America in Comparative Perspective, *Media Culture Society*, 24(2): 175–195.

Harcup, T. (2015). *Journalism: Principles and Practice*, 3rd edition. London: Sage.

Hellenic Foundation for European and Foreign Policy (ELIAMEP). (2015). Crisis Observatory Database, http://crisisobs.gr/en/database/ (accessed 11 September 2016).

Herman, E. and Chomsky, N. (1992). *Manufacturing Consent: The Political Economy of the Mass Media*. New York: Pantheon.

Hjarvard, S. (2008). The Mediatization of Society, *Nordicom Review*, 29(2): 105–134.

Hope, W. (2010). Time, Communication, and Financial Collapse, *International Journal of Communication*, 4: 649–669.

International Monetary Fund (IMF). (2015). IMF Country Report No. 15/186. *Greece: An Update of IMF Staff's Preliminary Public Debt Sustainability Analysis*, July 14, 2015, https://www.imf.org/external/pubs/ft/scr/2015/cr15186.pdf (accessed 21 September 2016).

Isakhan, B. and Slaughter, S. (2014). Crisis and Democracy in the Twenty-First Century. In B. Isakhan and S. Slaughter (Eds) *Democracy and Crisis: Democratizing Governance in the Twenty-First Century*. London: Palgrave Macmillan, pp. 1–22.

Iyengar, S. (1990). Framing Responsibility for Political Issues: The Case of Poverty, *Political Behavior*, 12(1): 19–40.

Iyengar, S. (1991). *Is Anyone Responsible? How Television Frames Political Issues*. Chicago: University of Chicago Press.

Kaplanoglou, G. and Rapanos, V. (2011). *The Greek Fiscal Crisis and the Role of Fiscal Governance.* GreeSE, 48. London, UK: Hellenic Observatory.

Kensicky, L. (2004). No Cure for What Ails Us: The Media Constructed Disconnect between Societal Problems and Possible Solutions, *Journalism & Mass Communication Quarterly*, 81: 53–73.

Knowles, S., Phillips, G. and Lidberg, J. (2015). Reporting the Global Financial Crisis, *Journalism Studies*, doi:10.1080/1461670X.2015.1058182

Ladi, S. (2014). Austerity Politics and Administrative Reform: The Eurozone Crisis and its Impact upon Greek Public Administration, *Comparative European Politics*, 12(2): 184–208.

Lyrintzis, C. (2011). *Greek Politics in the Eera of Economic Crisis: Reassessing Causes and Effects.* Hellenic Observatory papers on Greece and Southeast Europe, GreeSE paper no. 45. London, UK: The Hellenic Observatory, London School of Economics and Political Science.

Manning, P. (2013). Financial Journalism, News Sources and the Banking Crisis, *Journalism*, 14(2): 173–189.

Matsaganis, M. and Flevotomou, M. (2010). *Distributional Implications of Tax Evasion in Greece,* Hellenic Observatory Papers on Greece and Southeast Europe, GreeSE Paper No. 31. London: LSE.

Mazzoleni, G. and Schultz, W. (1999). Mediatization of Politics: A Challenge for Democracy?, *Political Communication*, 16(3): 247–261.

McChesney, R. (2002). *Our Media, Not Theirs: The Democratic Struggle Against Corporate Media*. New York: Seven Stories Press.

McChesney, R. and Nichols, J. (2010). *The Death and Life of American Journalism: The Media Revolution that Will Begin the World Again*. Philadelphia: Nation Books.

Mercille, J. (2013). The Role of the Media in Sustaining Ireland's Housing Bubble, *New Political Economy*, doi:10.1080/13563467.2013.779652

Milioni, D., Spyridou, L.-P. and Vradatsikas, K. (2015). Framing Immigration in Online Media and Television News in Crisis-stricken Cyprus, *The Cyprus Review*, 27(1): 155–185.

Monastiriotis, V. (2011). The Geographical Dimension of Austerity. In V. Monastiriotis (ed.) *The Greek Crisis in Focus: Austerity, Recession and Paths to Recovery*, Special Issue Hellenic Observatory Papers on Greece and Southeast Europe. London: LSE, pp. 45–71.

Monastiriotis, V. and Antoniades, A. (2009). *Reform That! Greece's Failing Reform Technology: Beyond 'Vested Interests' and 'Political Exchange'*, GreeSE Paper No 28. London: Hellenic Observatory Papers on Greece and Southeast Europe.

Mylonas, Y. (2012). Media and the Economic Crisis of the EU: The 'Culturalization' of a Systemic Crisis and *Bild-Zeitung*'s Framing of Greece, *tripleC*, 10(2): 646–671.

Norris, P. (2000). *A Virtuous Circle: Political Communications in Postindustrial Societies*. Cambridge: Cambridge University Press.

OECD. (2015). *Economic Policy Reforms 2015: Going for Growth*. Paris: OECD.

Papathanassopoulos, S. (2001). Media Commercialisation and Journalism in Greece, *European Journal of Communication*, 16(4): 505–521.

Papathanassopoulos, S. (2007). The Mediterranean or Polarized Pluralist Model Countries. In G. Terzis (ed.) *European Media Governance: National and Regional Dimensions*. Bristol: Intellect Book, pp. 191–200.

Pleios, G. (2013). *Η Κρίση και τα ΜΜΕ* [*The Crisis and the Media*]. Athens: Papazisis.

Poggioli, S. (2013). Greece's Economic Crisis Reveals Fault Lines in The Media, February 18, http://www.npr.org/2013/02/18/172313291/greeces-economic-crisis-reveals-fault-lines-in-the-media (accessed 11 September 2016).

Prasopoulou, E. (2011). In Quest for Accountability in Greek Public Administration: The Case of the Taxation Information System (TAXIS). GreeSE Papers, 53. London: London School of Economics and Political Science, Hellenic Observatory.

Quiring, O. and Weber, M. (2012). Between Usefulness and Legitimacy: Media Coverage of Governmental Intervention during the Financial Crisis and Selected Effects, *The International Journal of Press/Politics*, 17(3): 294–315.

Rafter, K. (2014). Voices in the Crisis: The Role of Media Elites in Interpreting Ireland's Banking Collapse, *European Journal of Communication*, 29(5): 598–607.

Reuters Institute Digital News Report. (2013). Tracking the Future of News, Edited by Nick Newman and David A. L. Levy, https://reutersinstitute.politics.ox.ac.uk/sites/default/files/Digital%20News%20Report%202013.pdf (accessed 21 September 2016).

Schechter, D. (2009). Credit Crisis: How Did We Miss It?, *British Journalism Review*, 20(1): 19–26.

Scheufele, D. (1999). Framing as a Theory of Media Effects, *Journal of Communication*, 49: 103–122.

Scheufele, D. and Tewksbury, D. (2007). Framing, Agenda Setting, and Priming: The Evolution of Three Media Effects Models, *Journal of Communication*, 57(1): 9–20.

Schifferes, S. and Coulter, S. (2012). Downloading Disaster: BBC News Online Coverage of the Global Financial Crisis, *Journalism*, 14(2): 228–252.

Schranz, M. and Eisenegger, M. (2011). The Media Construction of the Financial Crisis in a Comparative Perspective: An Analysis of Newspapers in the UK, USA and Switzerland between 2007 and 2009, *Schweizerische Zeitschrift für Soziologie*, 37(2): 241–258.

Schudson, M. (2003). *The Sociology of News*. New York: W. W. Norton.

Schulz, W. (2004). Reconstructing Mediatization as an Analytical Concept, *European Journal of Communication*, 19(1): 87–101.

Smyrnaios, N. (2013). *Manufacturing Consent and Legitimizing Austerity: The Greek Media Before and After the Crisis*, ESA 11th Conference, Crisis, Critique and Change, Turin, August 2013.

Spyridou, L.-P. (2015). Producing Protest News: Representations of Contentious Collective Actions in Mainstream Print Media, *The Cyprus Review*, 27(1): 71–105.

Spyridou, L.-P., Matsiola, M., Veglis, A., Kalliris, G. and Dimoulas, C. (2013). Journalism in a State of Flux: Journalists as Agents of Technology Innovation and Emerging News Practices, *The International Communication Gazette*, 75(1): 76–98.

Starkman, D. (2009). Power Problem. The Business Press Did Everything But Take on the Institutions that Brought Down the Financial System, *Columbia Journalism Review*, May 14, http://www.cjr.org/cover_story/power_problem.php?page=all (accessed 11 September 2016).

Stiglitz, J. (2011). The Media and the Crisis: An Information Theoretic Approach. In A. Schiffrin (ed.) *Bad News: How America's Business Press Missed the Story of the Century*. New York: The New Press, pp. 22–36.

Strömback, J. (2008). Four Phases of Mediatization: An Analysis of the Mediatization of Politics, *Press/Politics*, 13(3): 228–246.

Tambini, D. (2010). What are Financial Journalists For?, *Journalism Studies*, 11(2): 158–174.

Thompson, P. (2013). Invested Interests? Reflexivity, Representation and Reporting in Financial Markets, *Journalism*, 14(2): 208–227.

Tinios, P. (2010). *Vacillations around a Pension Reform Trajectory: Time for a Change*? GreeSE Paper 31. London: Hellenic Observatory, London School of Economics.

Titley, G. (2012). Budgetjam! A Communications Intervention in the Political-Economic Crisis in Ireland, *Journalism*, 14(2): 292–306.

Tracy, J. (2012). Covering "Financial Terrorism", *Journalism Practice*, 6(4): 513–529.

Tuchman, G. (1978). *Making News. A Study in the Construction of Reality*. New York: Free Press.

Usher, N. (2012). Ignored, Uninterested, and the Blame Game: How *The New York Times*, *Marketplace*, and *The Street* Distanced Themselves from Preventing the 2007–2009 Financial Crisis, *Journalism*, 14(2): 190–207.

Zeri, P. (2014). Political Blogosphere Meets Off-Line Public Sphere: Framing the Public Discourse on the Greek Crisis, *International Journal of Communication*, 8: 1579–1595.

14 Industrial competitiveness and the search for a sustainable path out of the crisis

Lessons from the Greek experience

Ioanna Kastelli and Stavros Zografakis

Introduction

The prevailing interpretations regarding the Greek but also the euro area crisis focus on macroeconomic issues and relate the crisis to macroeconomic imbalances. Following this approach, recovery was expected until now to result from consolidation, austerity and deregulation policies – briefly what is called the Washington consensus recipe. In the context of the (nationally driven or externally determined) austerity adjustment programmes that are being put in place in southern euro area countries, a main concern is changes in the regulation of labour market and reduction of wages, which aim to increase the flexibility and improve cost competitiveness of the overall economy.

However, the dramatic turmoil in the Greek economy is not due to a unique cause but derives from the interplay of macroeconomic imbalances and structural deficiencies. The main explanation why Greece in particular was severely hit by the crisis is the failure to transform and enhance its productive base over the last 30 years. The generalisation and implementation of austerity programmes accentuate productive and technological divergence from other economies in the euro zone as the crisis restricts the financial margins for enhancing productive and technological capabilities.

In this chapter we address the question of effectiveness of austerity measures implemented in Greece as an answer to the current crisis and the impact of internal devaluation, in terms of raising its competitiveness. We focus on the manufacturing sector as it is acknowledged for its important interdependencies and by this its direct and indirect effects within and across sectors. Our main argument is that in the Greek case significant parameters are neglected as the economy is facing problems in terms of capabilities, structural competitiveness, export orientation and policy implementation. With weaknesses related to specialisation pattern and export structure, weak research and innovative performance, feeble interactions among actors of the National System of Innovation (NSI), new entrepreneurial activities with low potential for contributing to growth, the persisting focus to changes in the regulation of labour and to the improvement in cost competitiveness risks the economy being trapped in low-wage production and competitiveness pattern.

The chapter is structured as follows. The first section gives a theoretical discussion of the determinants of competitiveness and the challenges for industrial development and industrial strategy at the national level. The second section presents the evolution of the Greek competitiveness of the manufacturing sector. The third section addresses the reasons for inadequacy of the policy implemented so far in order to exit the crisis. Policy propositions and concluding remarks are developed in the final section.

Theoretical considerations

The discussion regarding the determinant factors of competitiveness goes back to the 1970s, when, according to the neoclassical approach, prices, the cost of production factors (especially labour cost) and currency were the main determinants. However a number of studies (Kaldor, 1978, 1981; Kellman, 1983) have challenged the argument that reduction of the unit labour cost and export prices would improve international market shares. It then has been argued by many scholars (Fagerberg, 1996; Lall, 2001; Fagerberg et al., 2007; Decramer et al., 2014) that other non-price elements and structural characteristics were at the core of competitiveness.

According to Lall (2001) and UNIDO (2002), industrial competitiveness is defined as the capacity of countries to increase their presence in international markets whilst developing industrial sectors and activities with higher value-added and technological content. This implies that to increase industrial competitiveness we should not focus on cost advantages but on climbing up the technological ladder and value chain and/or deepening the capabilities within the same functions or in additional functions along the value chain. Thus competitiveness in industrial activities means developing relative efficiency along with sustainable growth – the capability of the industrial system to change its specialisation in response to competitive pressures.

Industrial competitiveness of any economic system depends on building productive and technological capabilities and the development of industrial skills through formal education and training (UNIDO, 2013; Nübler, 2014). Then firms' technological and organisational capabilities, which are micro-level characteristics, are affected by capabilities at the meso and macro level. Collective learning processes taking place not only at the firm level but also at the interorganisational level and the interplay between capabilities, incentives and institutions determine structural change and transformation potential of the productive system (Lall, 1992, 2001).

In this context, the role of the manufacturing sector was acknowledged as important because it boosts technologically driven productivity growth and has strong interdependencies with other high value-added sectors and especially services in the economy (Chang et al., 2013). According to the analysis of Park and Chan (1989), it was shown that the manufacturing sector has strong interdependencies and as a result direct and indirect effects not only at the intra-industry level bur also with services and especially with sophisticated and knowledge-intensive services in more advanced levels of industrialisation. In any case manufacturing is becoming 'weightless', incorporating knowledge-intensive activities of high value-added such as research, design, marketing, networking and developing interdependencies with other activities in the economy (Lall, 2003).

The recent economic crisis found many countries in the position of catching up and needing convergence, as far as industrial activities are concerned. As the complementarity of an innovation and export-led growth in northern Europe with a domestic demand-led configuration in the south sustained the divergence among national productive systems in the Eurozone (Boyer, 2014), during the crisis this divergence revealed the disproportionate effort required by southern European countries in order to achieve the turnaround of intensified de-industrialisation.

It is obvious then, that under increasing divergence, investment for countries lagging behind is of crucial importance. However during the crisis, although the EU recognised the importance of speeding up investments and facilitating deployment of EU funds for investment (European Recovery Programme), new instruments for intervention were focusing on fiscal consolidation and lowering indebtedness, as if this was enough for spontaneous growth. 'Budget cuts do not automatically create growth and growth does not automatically create more industrial production' (Kollatz-Ahnen and Bullmann, 2014). Policies aiming for structural changes concerning the state, public administration, technological and productive capabilities in industry and funding mechanisms for supporting industrial development should reverse the downward trend of de-industrialisation under conditions of additional investment.

The controversy of this approach with mainstream policy propositions is obvious. The focus of policies implemented under the memorandum agreements is fiscal consolidation and internal devaluation. In the Greek case, despite aiming to address macroeconomic imbalances, adopted policies concentrated to a large extent on wage cuts and liberalisation of the labour market. The rationale behind these measures is that improvement in cost competitiveness will improve export performance and attract foreign direct investment (FDI) and consequently will improve the country's capability to serve its debt.

However, this is contestable. As we have already pointed out, there are non-price and structural elements that determine competitiveness. The key policy tool of wage cuts and dismantlement of labour legislation for restoring competitiveness may prove to be inefficient and even create adverse effects on the economy. If the problem is related to the divergence between wage growth and productivity growth then an adjustment could be justified and efficient, *ceteris paribus*. If the structure of production and exports is less developed and there is a weak productive and technological base then a significant shift in production structure and the development of capabilities through knowledge creation and acquisition (including product and organisational innovations) are needed and could not occur without major investments. Implemented policies during the crisis undermine this path to industrial development and upgrading, because of a dramatic drop in income and production activity, uncertainty and ravaging of existing productive capabilities. Financial distress creates very negative conditions for investing in technological development and upgrading of productive structures. Integration into global value chains and international production networks that could create dynamic advantages for national actors is challenged by day-to-day survival issues.

The competitive position of the Greek manufacturing sector

Competitiveness of the Greek economy was lagging behind well before the economic crisis. After its integration into the European Monetary Union, Greece displayed increases in labour cost that counterbalanced productivity gains to a larger extent than in other European countries, with negative effects on competitiveness. However, it is a simplification to relate the weak competitive position of Greece solely to increases in unit labour cost. For the same period there has been an important and higher increase in inflation, due to other factors such as oligopolistic behaviour, public deficits and overconsumption (Giannitsis et al., 2009). In addition the technological content of exported goods was anaemic *vis-à-vis* other European countries long before the crisis occurred.

The economic crisis, although financial in its origins, has hit at the heart of the Greek production system in terms of macroeconomic imbalances related to productive inefficiencies and important lags in terms of structural competitiveness.

As we may observe in Figure 14.1, unit labour cost in total cost and wage cost in manufacturing has decreased sharply after 2008 falling well below the levels of 2005. At the same time prices have resisted and export prices have even increased until 2014. Thus although competitiveness in terms of cost has improved, it shows a resistance in terms of prices.

In addition, although Greek competitiveness has improved in terms of cost, it still lags substantially and persistently behind other countries, and especially in medium- to high-tech and high-tech products when measured with export measures (Figure 14.2).

This implies that there are a number of other elements of the Greek productive system that determine structural competitiveness and a difficulty of the productive system to capture and increase/expand international market shares. These elements determine as well the impact that the troika (EU, European

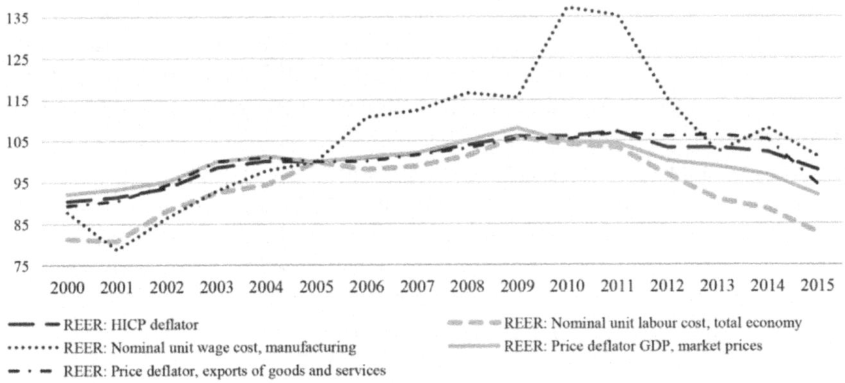

Figure 14.1 Greece: annual real effective exchange rates (REER) vs. IC37 (2005 = 100).
Source: EUROSTAT

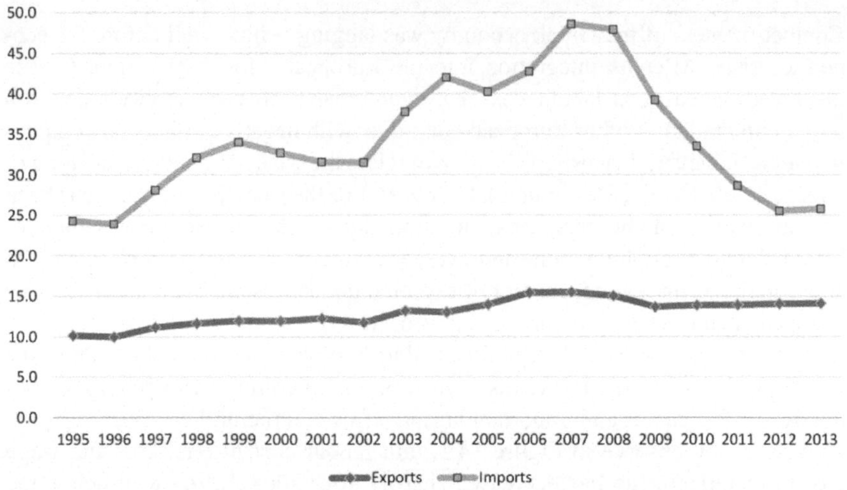

Figure 14.2 Greek imports and exports, tradable goods 1995–2013 (in billion € 2010 constant prices)

Source: OECD.Stat (http://stats.oecd.org/), International Trade and Balance of Payments

Central Bank, International Monetary Fund) policy toolkit focused on wage cuts and deregulation of labour market will have on export performance.

It should be noticed that to some extent wage reductions during the crisis adjusted for previous increases that outpaced productivity growth. However in manufacturing, employee compensation declined by 25.5% between 2010 and 2013, exceeding what could be justified and leading to contraction of domestic demand. In addition, the effect on exports was worthless, as shown in Figure 14.2.

Compared to Spain, Italy, Portugal and Turkey, Greek competitiveness is persistently lower. During the period 2001–2008, there was an underlying/implicit connection between fiscal deficits and trade balance deficits. Debt to some extent resulted in increased demand that was satisfied either from domestic firms or from imports.

Although industrial competitiveness measured with the Balassa index shows some improvement during the crisis (Figure 14.3), this is mainly due to the decrease in imports. As shown in Figure 14.2, imports have declined as there was a dramatic drop in investment and in production following the contraction of incomes. At the same time exports (excluding ships, oil and other non-classified products) and export performance have not displayed any important improvement on average and dropped to a lower level than 2008. Restrictive fiscal policies and changes in labour market regulations resulted in an improvement in cost competitiveness in terms of labour cost, but improvement in trade balance mainly reflects the decline of economic activity and not export strength.

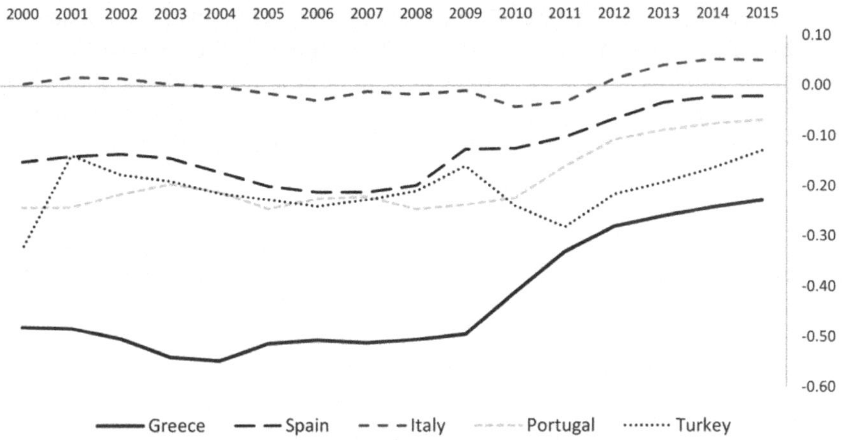

Figure 14.3 Balassa index $(X-M)/(X+M)$

Source: European Commission, Economic and Financial Affairs, AMECO database (http://ec.europa.eu/economy_finance/ameco/user/serie/SelectSerie.cfm)

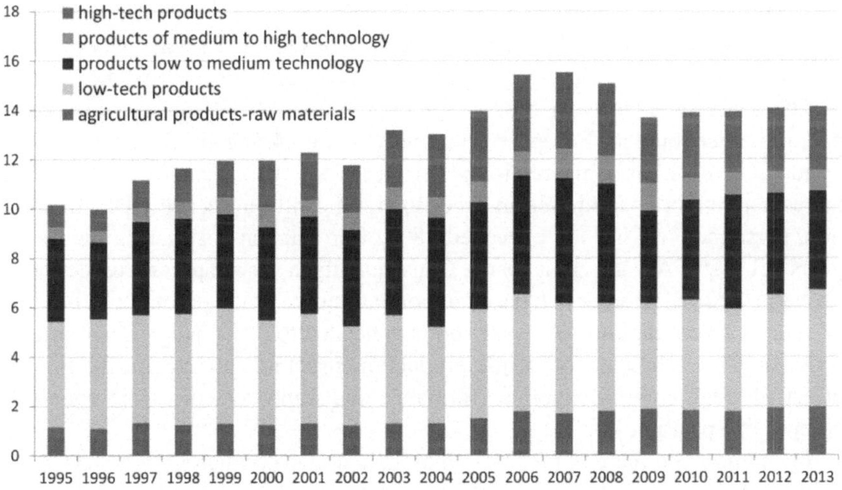

Figure 14.4 Exports by product category in billion euros (excluding ships and oil)

Source: OECD.Stat (http://stats.oecd.org/), International Trade and Balance of Payments

Some more insights into the evolution of exports are useful:

- During the period 1995–2013 the share of agricultural and low-tech products to total exports increased, whereas the share of all other categories decreased (Figure 14.4).

- As shown in Table 14.1, the share of exports directed to the Eurozone decreased, contrary to the share of exports directed to countries outside the EU. The losses of market shares in the Eurozone are counterbalanced by gains of market shares in countries from the rest of the EU and the rest of the world. This change of export destination was supported by the important presence of Greek firms and financial institutions to neighbour countries (Balkan countries).

According to the above highlights, internal devaluation efforts using wage cuts do not seem to have had the expected effects. On the one hand, exports reached a lower level compared to 2008. On the other had, Greek manufacturing lost market shares in traditional markets of the Eurozone with small gains in new markets such as China, Russia, the Balkans and Turkey. During the crisis, any slight increase in exports was mainly related to products of low technological intensity. This is an indication of lack of technological deepening and upgrading of the productive system.

Linking competitiveness to structural characteristics of the Greek productive system

Our main argument is that the issue of competitiveness of the Greek productive system is related to structural characteristics which should be set at the centre of a transformation process aiming at industrial and economic development.

The share of exports in gross domestic product (GDP) is very low compared to other southern European countries (Figure 14.5) and decreases over the period 2009–2013 as compared to the period 1995–2001. This means that a large increase in exports is required in order to significantly influence GDP. In addition, personnel cost has not exceeded 18% of production cost during the recent years (EUROSTAT, different years). Consequently, a very important reduction in wages is required in order to have an important impact on the production cost and, of course, a very high increase in exports is needed to make a significant impact on GDP. This characteristic of the production structure can explain the limited effect of wage cuts on export performance and improvement of the country's competitive position.

In addition, the share of medium- to high- and high-technology products in the value-added and exports is low and lower than all reference countries. The main contribution to exports comes from agricultural, low and medium to low products (Figure 14.5).

Table 14.2 shows the weak position of Greece in the euro zone *vis-à-vis* Italy, Portugal, Spain and Turkey in terms of exports. Greek market shares shrank while Spain, Portugal and Turkey performed better even during the period of economic crisis. Italy, although in a stronger competitive position, presented losses as well. Productive transformation towards higher added-value and technological intensity is very slow and with feeble improvement of competitiveness in dynamic categories of products.

Table 14.1 Percentage export structure based on products and regions

		Exports						*Exports*					
		Euro area	*Other EU countries*	*USA Japan*	*China Russia*	*Rest of the world*	*Total*	*Euro area*	*Other EU countries*	*USA Japan*	*China Russia*	*Rest of the world*	*Total*
1 Agricultural products – raw materials	95-01	51.7	13.9	8.7	1.6	24.1	100.0	12.6	6.9	17.0	5.3	10.8	10.9
	02-08	50.3	20.9	7.0	3.4	18.3	100.0	3	7.9	17.3	11.3	8.0	10.9
	09-13	47.8	22.9	4.0	4.6	20.7	100.0	17.9	10.9	14.5	16.3	9.9	13.5
2 Low-tech products	95-01	44.3	20.1	5.4	5.4	24.8	100.0	39.1	35.9	37.9	63.9	40.4	39.5
	02-08	35.3	24.1	5.2	6.4	29.1	100.0	28.1	25.5	35.8	60.0	35.7	30.6
	09-13	32.4	27.1	3.9	6.7	30.0	100.0	28.5	30.4	33.2	55.9	33.9	31.8
3 Products low to medium technology	95-01	51.9	21.1	5.4	1.1	20.4	100.0	37.7	31.0	31.5	10.5	27.4	32.5
	02-08	41.1	30.3	4.0	1.5	23.1	100.0	34.5	33.8	28.9	15.1	30.0	32.3
	09-13	36.7	29.4	3.0	2.2	28.7	100.0	30.0	30.7	23.9	16.7	30.2	29.5
4 Products of medium to high technology	95-01	25.1	26.1	7.1	9.3	32.3	100.0	3.0	6.2	6.7	14.7	7.0	5.3
	02-08	25.0	35.1	6.1	2.5	31.3	100.0	4.3	8.1	9.2	5.1	8.4	6.7
	09-13	23.8	28.2	8.8	1.1	38.1	100.0	4.3	6.5	15.5	1.8	8.8	6.5
5 High-tech products	95-01	28.4	37.4	3.2	1.6	29.4	100.0	7.5	20.0	6.8	5.6	14.4	11.9
	02-08	37.0	36.7	2.0	1.4	22.8	100.0	18.8	24.7	8.7	8.5	17.9	19.5
	09-13	37.4	32.4	2.6	1.9	25.7	100.0	19.4	21.4	13.0	9.3	17.1	18.7
Total	95-01	44.7	22.2	5.6	3.4	24.2	100.0	100.0	100.0	100.0	100.0	100.0	100.0
	02-08	38.5	28.9	4.4	3.3	24.9	100.0	100.0	100.0	100.0	100.0	100.0	100.0
	09-13	36.1	28.3	3.7	3.8	28.1	100.0	100.0	100.0	100.0	100.0	100.0	100.0

Source: OECD.Stat (http://stats.oecd.org/), International Trade and Balance of Payments

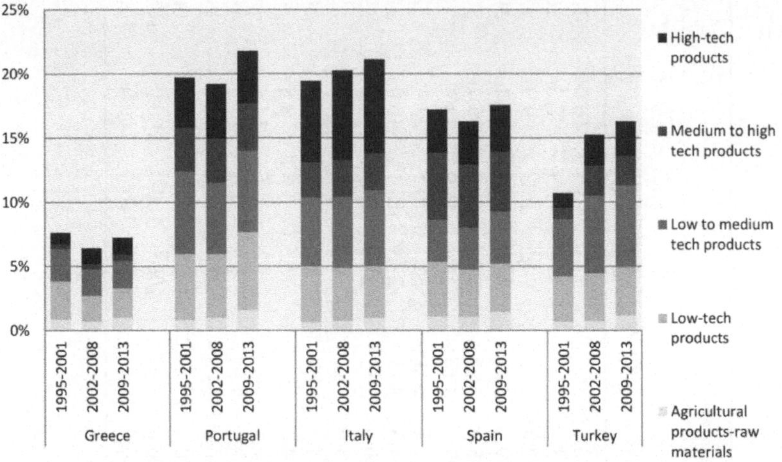

Figure 14.5 Total exports of goods as percentage of GDP (1995–2013) in Greece, Portugal, Italy, Spain and Turkey

Source: OECD.Stat (http://stats.oecd.org/), International Trade and Balance of Payments

Table 14.2 Exports of Greece, Italy, Spain, Portugal and Turkey in the euro area by product group (% of total exports)

		Greece	*Italy*	*Portugal*	*Spain*	*Turkey*	*Total*
1 Agricultural products – raw materials	95-01	5.4	41.8	6.7	41.6	4.6	100.0
	02-08	4.5	39.5	7.4	43.7	4.9	100.0
	09-13	4.7	39.3	8.3	43.2	4.5	100.0
2 Low-tech products	95-01	3.5	51.4	7.4	31.0	6.7	100.0
	02-08	2.4	45.6	8.2	35.1	8.6	100.0
	09-13	2.4	41.8	9.8	36.4	9.6	100.0
3 Products low to medium technology	95-01	3.1	57.7	9.4	20.9	8.9	100.0
	02-08	2.3	52.6	8.8	25.2	11.2	100.0
	09-13	2.0	49.2	9.5	27.5	11.8	100.0
4 Products of medium to high technology	95-01	0.3	39.3	7.3	51.2	2.0	100.0
	02-08	0.4	35.5	6.7	49.2	8.3	100.0
	09-13	0.4	33.5	7.3	48.7	10.1	100.0
5 High-tech products	95-01	0.7	67.0	6.3	23.3	2.8	100.0
	02-08	1.4	62.7	5.8	24.5	5.7	100.0
	09-13	1.5	60.2	5.6	25.7	6.9	100.0
Total	95-01	2.2	53.7	7.6	31.2	5.3	100.0
	02-08	1.8	49.0	7.4	33.4	8.3	100.0
	09-13	1.8	46.2	8.1	34.5	9.3	100.0

Source: OECD.Stat (http://stats.oecd.org/), International Trade and Balance of Payments

Table 14.3 Competitiveness indicators: Balassa index

		$X-M/X+M$					
		Euro area	*Other EU countries*	*USA Japan*	*China Russia*	*Rest of the world*	*Total*
1 Agricultural products – raw materials	95-01	–0.56	–0.39	0.02	–0.26	–0.36	–0.47
	02-08	–0.57	–0.27	0.37	–0.31	–0.47	–0.47
	09-13	–0.51	–0.25	0.36	0.11	–0.26	–0.38
2 Low-tech products	95-01	–0.28	–0.01	0.00	–0.14	–0.01	–0.16
	02-08	–0.47	–0.03	–0.04	–0.46	–0.09	–0.29
	09-13	–0.32	0.03	0.02	–0.31	0.07	–0.13
3 Products low to medium technology	95-01	–0.25	–0.06	0.34	–0.81	–0.20	–0.21
	02-08	–0.42	0.10	0.04	–0.88	–0.32	–0.33
	09-13	–0.34	0.12	0.15	–0.81	–0.11	–0.22
4 Products of medium to high technology	95-01	–0.91	–0.63	–0.91	–0.04	–0.60	–0.81
	02-08	–0.91	–0.50	–0.91	–0.63	–0.58	–0.80
	09-13	–0.85	–0.41	–0.65	–0.84	–0.31	–0.66
5 High-tech products	95-01	–0.86	–0.41	–0.89	–0.78	–0.43	–0.71
	02-08	–0.77	–0.27	–0.85	–0.88	–0.34	–0.63
	09-13	–0.70	–0.27	–0.64	–0.88	–0.21	–0.55
Total	95-01	–0.54	–0.24	–0.52	–0.44	–0.26	–0.44
	02-08	–0.63	–0.15	–0.58	–0.70	–0.31	–0.49
	09-13	–0.54	–0.11	–0.31	–0.63	–0.12	–0.36

Source: OECD.Stat (http://stats.oecd.org/), International Trade and Balance of Payments

As shown in Table 14.3 competitiveness is weak in all five product categories, although it improved slightly during the crisis. However, the revealed comparative advantage (Table 14.4), which focused on the positive side of specialisation, i.e. exports, shows a decline even in those categories where Greece presents a comparative advantage *vis-à-vis* the four reference countries. Therefore the slight improvement in competitiveness captured by the Balassa index is mainly due to the economic downturn and the subsequent decline in imports. Interestingly, a weak but positive improvement is apparent in medium- to high-tech and hight-tech products, a sign for further consideration.

The above elements point to a weak and not improving export quality and technological complexity *vis-à-vis* other southern European countries.

Another important structural characteristic is that dependence of exports on imported raw materials and intermediate products reached 30–50% of export value (Athanassiou and Tsouma, 2013), resulting in leakage from the manufactured export value.

A last mention should be made of the level of technological development of the Greek industrial system and manufacturing. The pattern of specialisation depends on national technological capabilities arising from the interplay between learning

Table 14.4 Revealed comparative advantage of Greece with Italy, Portugal, Spain and Turkey in individual markets by product category

		Italy						*Portugal*					
		Euro area	*Other EU countries*	*USA Japan*	*China Russia*	*Rest of the world*	*Total*	*Euro area*	*Other EU countries*	*USA Japan*	*China Russia*	*Rest of the world*	*Total*
1 Agricultural products – raw materials	95-01	3.23	2.31	6.56	2.18	3.68	3.26	2.87	5.03	4.94	0.57	2.03	2.72
	02-08	3.11	2.19	5.46	7.47	3.06	2.97	2.50	2.20	6.39	1.66	1.43	2.06
	09-13	3.00	2.12	3.73	6.61	3.12	2.91	2.49	2.06	3.34	1.12	1.18	1.86
2 Low-tech products	95-01	1.69	1.49	1.64	3.25	2.02	1.77	1.66	1.38	0.91	2.56	1.24	1.51
	02-08	1.41	1.14	1.62	3.15	1.95	1.53	1.18	1.01	0.98	2.18	1.19	1.20
	09-13	1.46	1.37	1.64	3.01	2.04	1.67	1.10	1.03	0.72	1.98	1.12	1.14
3 Products low to medium technology	95-01	1.34	1.23	0.97	0.49	1.06	1.18	1.16	0.73	1.34	0.22	1.08	1.00
	02-08	1.20	1.27	1.02	0.58	1.16	1.17	1.08	1.02	1.99	0.83	1.60	1.11
	09-13	1.02	1.11	1.01	0.71	1.09	1.06	0.93	1.22	1.52	1.13	1.25	1.01
4 Products of medium to high technology	95-01	0.20	0.44	0.45	2.58	0.56	0.37	0.15	0.46	0.94	4.12	0.52	0.31
	02-08	0.27	0.57	0.54	0.74	0.73	0.47	0.22	0.43	1.10	0.76	0.78	0.38
	09-13	0.28	0.49	0.89	0.20	0.76	0.48	0.23	0.40	1.21	0.07	0.86	0.39
5 High-tech products	95-01	0.25	0.60	0.25	0.11	0.37	0.36	0.38	1.19	0.28	0.39	0.62	0.59
	02-08	0.61	0.74	0.30	0.18	0.43	0.56	1.00	1.30	0.23	0.21	0.51	0.87
	09-13	0.65	0.68	0.37	0.20	0.42	0.54	1.22	0.90	0.62	0.62	0.64	0.98

			Spain						*Turkey*					
			Euro area	*Other EU countries*	*USA Japan*	*China Russia*	*Rest of the world*	*Total*	*Euro area*	*Other EU countries*	*USA Japan*	*China Russia*	*Rest of the world*	*Total*
1	Agricultural products – raw materials	95-01	1.89	2.04	1.79	0.37	1.86	1.72	2.89	1.50	3.19	0.58	1.12	1.70
		02-08	1.91	2.07	2.47	1.14	1.36	1.64	4.28	3.53	4.49	0.87	1.10	2.21
		09-13	2.04	1.35	1.72	1.26	1.49	1.63	5.27	4.09	3.24	0.67	1.08	1.86
2	Low-tech products	95-01	1.63	1.34	1.44	2.77	1.61	1.60	1.27	1.04	1.29	1.75	1.13	1.20
		02-08	1.25	1.12	1.57	2.88	1.73	1.38	1.27	1.21	1.37	1.68	1.49	1.31
		09-13	1.26	1.31	1.63	2.57	1.94	1.49	1.29	1.47	1.18	1.57	1.53	1.38
3	Products low to medium technology	95-01	2.15	1.91	1.11	0.59	1.28	1.74	0.85	0.75	0.62	0.26	0.78	0.78
		02-08	1.70	1.97	1.37	0.74	1.29	1.58	0.95	0.84	0.53	0.67	0.70	0.82
		09-13	1.36	1.45	1.19	0.70	1.15	1.29	0.86	0.80	0.70	0.99	0.67	0.76
4	Products of medium to high technology	95-01	0.09	0.19	0.37	1.31	0.31	0.17	0.37	1.11	0.80	2.37	0.86	0.69
		02-08	0.13	0.25	0.45	0.24	0.35	0.22	0.20	0.46	1.19	0.31	0.82	0.41
		09-13	0.15	0.25	0.88	0.11	0.39	0.25	0.19	0.38	0.74	0.17	1.16	0.46
5	High-tech products	95-01	0.43	0.94	0.38	0.17	0.57	0.60	0.61	1.43	1.12	0.68	1.29	1.04
		02-08	1.06	1.05	0.31	0.31	0.69	0.94	1.14	1.31	1.19	0.69	1.12	1.21
		09-13	1.13	0.98	0.39	0.38	0.64	0.89	1.14	1.02	1.04	0.77	1.09	1.13

Source: OECD.Stat (http://stats.oecd.org/), International Trade and Balance of Payments

processes, capability building processes, institutional set-up and incentives, as mentioned above.

In Greece there is a long-standing gap between different dimensions of the Greek Innovation System and other European Innovation Systems concerning the creation and exploitation of knowledge and technology.

This gap is reflected in weak research and innovative performance, feeble interactions among actors of the NSI and inadequate potential of new entrepreneurial ventures in contributing to growth.

As shown in Table 14.5, research and innovative performance are below the European average and, especially as far as the business sector is concerned, there is a reluctance to improve its competitive position through research and development and innovation. New ventures, according to the Global Entrepreneurship Monitor surveys, although reaching one of the highest percentage among innovating economies, display at the same time one of the highest rates of suspension of business activity every year. This, combined with the fact that new ventures are not creating high numbers of new jobs, is evidence of new entrepreneurial activities with low potential for contributing to growth. Surveys investigating entrepreneurial venturing of graduate engineers from the National Technical University of Athens, the oldest and biggest Greek Polytechnic University, show that even in a pool of highly educated and technologically skilled people, entrepreneurship keeps poor characteristics with weak potential (Papayannakis, 2007; NTUA, 2008, 2016).

During the crisis further constraints have impeded any redressing of exports:

Table 14.5 The Greek national system of innovation

	EE-28			*Greece*		
	2008	*2011*	*2013*	*2008*	*2011*	*2013*
GERD as % GDP	1.85	1.97	2.01	0.66	0.67	0.80
BERD as % GDP	1.17	1.24	1.28	0.18*	0.23	0.27
% GERD funded by business sector	54.80	55.00	55†	29.20	32.70	30.30
High-tech exports: % of total exports	15.40	15.40	15.30	5.00	4.10	2.60
Patent applications to the EPO per million inhabitants	113.37	112.73	112.6†	8.40	7.57	7.28
	2008	2011	2014	2008	2011	2014
Summary innovation index	0.519	0.545	0.555	0.374	0.38	0.365

*2007; †2012

GERD, gross expenditure on research and development, GDP, gross domestic product; BERD, business expenditure on research and development; EPO, European Patent Office.

Source: EUROSTAT

- A prolonged evaporation of market and funding liquidity combined with a credit tightening on Greek firms. From 2010 to 2015 it is estimated that 35 billion euros have been deprived from the market due to the repayment of bank loans and there has been almost a 20% decrease of outstanding amounts of credit from 2013 to 2015 (Bank of Greece).
- A persisting recession in manufacturing reflected in a 41% decrease in employment (2008–2014) and 20% decrease in production (2010–2014). Once generated, the crisis had strong implications for the productive capacity of the economy, the firm sector and employment. In particular, since 2009, the crisis has caused severe destructive effects on the production base and microstructures in Greece, leading to a shrinking of its real economy and affecting its future growth and perspectives. These effects undermine the participation of firms in global value chains, that is, the level of integration into the global economy (Karadeloglou and Benkovskis, 2015). In the long run a persistent withdrawal from global production chains normally occurs in those tasks where the country has its comparative advantages (Karadeloglou and Benkovskis, 2015).

In addition, consolidation measures and especially wage cuts chosen to improve firms' export performance could result in an adverse situation for the following reasons:

- They might generate disincentives for investing in all areas where Greek firms lag behind: investment in knowledge and knowledge-intensive activities, more efficient production techniques, innovation and transformation of the productive base. Although persistence in these measures could result in short-term benefits, they could not ensure quality and productivity improvement in the long run. In addition, in highly flexible labour markets firms tend to invest less in training, as part of this investment might prove beneficial for their competitors (Reati, 2014).
- They might result in a deterioration in the quality of production if followed by a reduction in hours worked and effort from the employees' side.
- Although wage cuts could result in a short-term improvement of competitiveness, there is always a risk of a low-wage specialisation trap. Hence, competing on the base of low wages may result in further wage cuts, except if the production system introduces new methods and new characteristics, generating higher added value.
- Last but not least, there are negative implications in terms of demand. Persistent shrinking of income may result in a vicious cycle of recession and disinvestment.

Thus, the combination of financial constraints with the reduction in manufacturing share in GDP risks having adverse effects on both research and innovative activity and the quality of exports. The persistence in these measures in combination with recession deviates the production system from the required long-term transformation process and any short-term benefits remain unsustainable.

Concluding remarks and emerging policy issues

In Greece there is a combination of macroeconomic imbalances and structural deficiencies that renders the necessity for structural policies. However, the focus of policies implemented under the memorandum agreements has been consolidation and internal devaluation. During the last 6 years, but especially after 2012, there has been an important reduction in wages and many measures for the liberalisation of the labour market have been put in place.

Although there was the need to face macroeconomic imbalances, it is clear that the nature and extent of these measures created an unprecedented contraction of domestic demand, resulting in a cumulative reduction of 27% for GDP over the period 2009–2014, high unemployment, shrinking in revenue from social security contributions, rise of capital cost and squeeze in liquidity. These effects counterbalanced any possible positive effects from wage cuts and labour liberalisation and in no case improved the Greek competitive position. It could even be argued that they undermined even the 'baseline' of industrial upgrading.

A critical issue for policy making is ahead.

In these exceptional conditions of crisis it is indispensable to move towards 'out-of-the-box' solutions.

It is important to preserve what has been built, transform patterns that are obsolete in the context of the global economy and find the resources to boost investment.

Competitiveness will improve considerably if productivity rises and if products and services acquire quality characteristics of high added value. To this end production transformation should aim to develop or maintain upstream components of the production and innovation cycle. The development of more complex activities in manufacturing could generate strong multiplicative effects and structural change within the sector but also across sectors, inducing the development of knowledge-intensive service activities. In addition, there is space for import substitution in a range of activities where there is accumulated experience and capabilities, in order to address domestic demand as a learning process in the direction of scaling up existing or new firms.

Technological capability building, improvement in production capabilities and capital accumulation appear to be the main challenges for the industrial system in order to boost growth (Giannitsis and Kastelli, 2014). The necessary investment cannot be expected to come solely and automatically from the private sector, especially in the context of financial tightening and an uncertain macroeconomic environment. With that given, one possibility for industrial policy is to stimulate other funding mechanisms such as venture and seed capital and to redistribute financial resources (e.g. from tax evasion) towards activities that will raise competitiveness. As far as EU resources are concerned, there is an issue of relevance of the different programmes initiated, in addressing the specificities of the Greek productive system, as there is a mismatch of requirements and real needs and a lack of learning from failures and inefficiencies of previous funding periods (Hellenic Foundation for European and Foreign Policy (ELIAMEP), 2012).

The main challenge today is to find the mix of policies that will address a twofold problem: On one hand macroimbalances call for fiscal consolidation but on the other hand the nature and the competitive disadvantages of the productive system call for a different agenda based on investment in upscaling and upgrading productive capacity and capabilities, human resources, research and innovation and capability building. Even if this investment is supposed to come from the private sector, it remains difficult to see how the private sector will find the financial resources (reduced revenue, lack of liquidity, reluctance of banks to lend) in a constrictive macroeconomic environment. With that given, following more long-term objectives, resources should be directed to activities that will raise competitiveness, targeting the transformation and modernisation of the productive base, the improvement of technological, organisational, managerial capabilities and extroversion, although in the short run liquidity is also an important challenge to face.

Continuing in the line of 'business as usual' will result in further social and political destabilisation and this is a message that also concerns other southern European countries facing similar challenges.

References

Athanassiou, E. and Tsouma, A. (2013), "The import component of consumption and exports in Greece: sector analysis and development perspectives through import substitution", *Centre of Planning and Economic Research, Greek Economic Outlook*, 20: 74–81, in Greek.

Bank of Greece. "Credit to domestic non financial corporations by domestic MFIs excluding the Bank of Greece, breakdown by branch of activity", http://www.bankofgreece.gr/Pages/el/Statistics/monetary/financing.aspx (accessed 11 September 2016).

Boyer, R. (2014), "The unsustainable divergence of national productive systems" in A. Teixeira, E. Silva and R. Paes Mamede (eds), *Structural Change, Competitiveness and Industrial Policy. Painful Lessons from the European Periphery*, London: Routledge.

Chang, H.-J., Andreoni, A. and Kuan, M.L. (2013), "International industrial policy experiences and the lessons for the UK", Policy Report for the UK Foresight Future of Manufacturing Project, London: UK Government Office of Science.

Decramer, S., Fuss, C. and Konings, J. (2014), "How do exporters react to changes in cost competitiveness?", Working Paper Series, No 1752, Frankfurt: ECB.

EUROSTAT. (different years), "Structural business statistics", European Commission.

Fagerberg, J. (1996), "Technology and competitiveness", *Oxford Review of Economic Policy*, 12(3): 39–51.

Fagerberg, J., Srholec, M. and Knell, M. (2007), "The competitiveness of nations: why some countries prosper while others fall behind?", *World Development*, 35: 1595–1620.

Giannitsis, T. and Kastelli, I. (2014), "Industrial policy in times of crisis: the case of Greece", in A.A.C. Teixeira, E. Silva and R. PaesMamede (eds), *Structural Change, Competitiveness and Industrial Policy: Painful Lessons from the European Periphery*, Abingdon: Routledge, pp. 221–240.

Giannitsis, T., Zografakis, St., Kastelli, I. and Mavri, D. (2009), *Competitiveness and Technology in Greece*, Athens: Papazissis, in Greek.

Global Entrepreneurship Monitor (different years), *Greek National Reports*, Athens: Foundation for Economic & Industrial Research (IOBE).

Hellenic Foundation for European and Foreign Policy – ELIAMEP. (2012), *Evaluation of the Effects of European Funded Policies to the Greek Economy*, Athens: ELIAMEP, in Greek.

Kaldor, N. (1978), "The effect of devaluations on trade in manufactures", in N. Kaldor (ed.), *Further Essays on Applied Economics*, London: Duckworth.

Kaldor, N. (1981), "The role of increasing returns, technical progress and cumulative causation in the theory of international trade and economic growth", *Economie Appliquée*, 34(4): 593–617.

Karadeloglou, P. and Benkovskis, K. (2015), "Compendium on the diagnostic toolkit for competitiveness", Occasional Paper Series no 163, Frankfurt: European Central Bank.

Kellman, M. (1983), "Relative prices and international competitiveness. An empirical investigation", *Empirical Economics*, 8(3–4): 125–138.

Kollatz-Ahnen, M. and Bullmann, U. (2014), "Industrial and investment policy – what a well-structured package can achieve", Foundation for European Progressive Studies.

Lall, S. (1992), "Technological capabilities and industrialisation", *World Development*, 20(2): 165–186.

Lall, S. (2001), *Competitiveness, Technology and Skills,* Cheltenham, UK: Edward Elgar.

Lall, S. (2003), "Reinventing industrial strategy: the role of government policy in building industrial competitiveness", QEH Working Paper Series – QEHWPS111. Oxford: Queen Elizabeth House, University of Oxford.

NTUA. (2008), *Entrepreneurship of Engineers Graduates from the National Technical University of Athens*, Report Summarising Survey Results, Athens: NTUA, in Greek.

NTUA. (2016), *Entrepreneurship of Young Graduates from the National Technical University of Athens,* Report Summarising Survey Results, Athens: NTUA, in Greek.

Nübler, I. (2014), "A theory of capabilities for productive transformation: learning to catch up", in J.M. Salazar-Xirinachs, I. Nübler and R. Kozul-Wright (eds), *Transforming Economies. Making Industrial Policy Work for Growth, Jobs and Development*, Geneva: International Labour Office, pp. 113–150.

Papayannakis, L. (2007), *National Technical University of Athens and the labour market*, Athens: NTUA, in Greek.

Park, S.-H. and Chan, K. (1989), "A cross-country input-output analysis of intersectoral relationships between manufacturing and services and their employment implications", *World Development*, 17(2): 199–212.

Reati, A. (2014), "Economic policy for structural change", *Review of Political Economy*, 26(1): 1–22.

UNIDO. (2002), *Competing Through Innovation and Learning*, Industrial Development Report 2002–3, Vienna: UNIDO.

UNIDO. (2013), *The Industrial Competitiveness of Nations. Looking Back, Forging Ahead,* Competitive Industrial Performance Report 2012/2013, Vienna: UNIDO.

Index